COLLINS
DIY
QUESTIONS &
ANSWERS

COLLINS

DIY

QUESTIONS &
ANSWERS

JACKSON · DAY

COLLINS

Published by William Collins Sons & Co. Ltd
8 Grafton Street,
London W1X 3LA

This book was created exclusively for
William Collins Sons & Co. Ltd by
Jackson Day Jennings Ltd trading as
Inklink.

Text
Albert Jackson
David Day

Text editor
Geraldine Christy

Illustrators
David Day
Robin Harris

First published in 1990

The text and illustrations in chapter 16,
What tools should I choose? and in the
Glossary of terms were previously published in
Collins Complete DIY Manual
All other text and illustrations are
original to this book.

Copyright © 1990
William Collins Sons & Co. Ltd

**A CIP catalogue record for this book
is available from the British Library.**

ISBN 0 00 412538 X

Printed in Great Britain
by William Collins Sons & Co. Ltd
Glasgow

INTRODUCTION. Do-it-yourself radio phone-ins are among the most popular of that type of programme. Nearly every local-radio station runs a regular feature on the subject or occasionally invites a guest writer or presenter to 'wax lyrical' and field phone-in queries from the listening public.

Twelve years ago we received our first invitation to answer DIY questions on a London-based radio station. We really did not know what to expect. Would anybody be interested enough to phone us or would there be long embarrassing breaks between callers? Would all the questions be so obscure that we would be unable to offer plausible solutions? We were relieved and delighted to discover that listener after listener was eager to discuss his or her DIY problem, and many others were pleased to offer suggestions that might help a previous caller. In all, it was a thoroughly enjoyable experience and an opportunity to swap notes with a great many genuine DIY enthusiasts.

Since that first appearance we have made regular tours of the local-radio network to talk on a range of practical subjects and discuss related problems. Over a period of time we realized that certain queries were cropping up time and again, and recognized the fact that specific subject areas were causing widespread concern. This book is a collection of some of those queries and is an attempt to cover those subjects that seem to us to be the most troublesome.

In so many cases the solution to a problem lies in knowing that a certain product exists, and although someone with considerable experience might be familiar with two or three brands of microporous paint or a range of timber preservatives, another reader might appreciate some help in finding commercially available products. Consequently, we have included in the reference section of this book a brand-name list of products of the type that are mentioned in each chapter. The inclusion of a product does not necessarily imply a recommendation on our part nor is it meant to suggest that one product is better than another that may not have been included. The list serves merely to help you identify the type of product that may resolve a particular problem●

Albert Jackson & David Day

ACKNOWLEDGMENTS

Inklink wish to thank the following individuals, organizations and companies for their help in the preparation of this book:

A. Bell & Co Ltd
Addis Safety Ltd
Ademco Products
Akzo Coatings plc
Anthony Green & Company
Aquaseal Ltd
Artex Ltd
Artur Fischer UK Ltd
Asbestos Information Centre
Bartol Ltd
Bituminous Roofing Council
Black & Decker
Borden (UK) Ltd
Bostik Ltd
British Gypsum Ltd
British Ivy Society
Cement and Concrete Association
Chubb Fire Security Ltd
Ciba-Geigy Plastics
Crown Decorative Products Ltd
Cuprinol Ltd
DDD Ltd
Delmar Ltd
Department of the Environment
Draught Proofing Advisory Association Ltd
DRG Sellotape Products
Dunlop Adhesives
E. Aldridge & Son Ltd
Edincare Ltd
European Industrial Services Ltd
Evode Ltd
External Wall Insulation Association
Fastnet Products Ltd
Frazer Ltd
Goddard's Ltd
Gyproc Insulation Ltd
Heating World Ltd
Homeguard UK Ltd
Imperial Chemical Industries Ltd
International Paint Ltd
James Jamieson's (Aberdeen) Ltd
John Myland Ltd
Langlow Products Ltd
Loctite U.K.
London Electricity Board
National Association of Loft Insulation Contractors
National Cavity Insulation Association
National Conservancy Council
National Supervisory Council for Intruder Alarms
Neve Industrial & Technical Services
Nitromors Ltd
Noel Dunne
Oracstar Ltd
Payless DIY Ltd
Picreator Enterprises Ltd
Pilkington Insulation
Polycell Products Ltd
Porcelain Newglaze Ltd
Reckitt Products Ltd
Rentokil Ltd
Renubath Services Ltd
Rockwool Ltd
Royal Institution of Chartered Surveyors
Rustins Ltd
Sainsbury's Homebase Ltd
Smiths Industries
Snocem PMC Ltd
Stapeley Water Gardens Ltd
Sterling Roncraft
Tetrosyl Ltd
The Art Veneer Co Ltd
The Fire Protection Association
The Syglas Company
Thoro London
3M Consumer Products
Tor Coatings Ltd
Transbyn Ltd
UniBond Ltd
Uni-Tube Ltd
Woodfit Ltd

CONTENTS

CHAPTER		PAGE
1	Getting Official Approval	9
2	Decorating	15
3	Curing Damp	29
4	Insulation and Ventilation	37
5	Plumbing and Central Heating	45
6	Electricity	55
7	Household Repairs	67
8	Home Security	87
9	Working Outdoors	95
10	Repairing China and Glass	109
11	Fixings and Fittings	117
12	Repairing Furniture and Woodwork	123
13	Cleaning Metalware	131
14	Repairing Books and Pictures	135
15	Removing Stains	139
16	What Tools Should I Choose?	143
	Reference Section	167
	Product Brand Names	168
	Glossary of Terms	182
	Index	186

GETTING OFFICIAL APPROVAL

Dealing with the bureaucrats at the Planning Department or Building Control Office is for some people a daunting prospect. In reality, most of the rules and regulations are for our own protection, while the planners and surveyors are content to be our servants not our masters.

Planning legislation and the Building Regulations are complex subjects that are regularly under review. The information in this chapter is intended as a guide to obtaining Planning Permission or Building-Regulations Approval and should not be regarded as an authoritative interpretation of the law. Always check with the relevant authority for confirmation or further clarification ●

What is the difference between Planning Permission and Building-Regulations Approval?

Before you undertake certain alterations or make additions to a house you are obliged to obtain permission from your local authority. The two main controls that exist are Planning Permission and Building-Regulations Approval.

Planning controls regulate the use and siting of buildings and other structures as well as their appearance to a certain extent. Building Regulations are concerned with the structural stability of new work and alterations. They also recommend suitable materials to provide adequate durability and the prevention of damp as well as fire and weather resistance. In addition, Building Regulations require adequate means of ventilation to be provided for habitable rooms.

Some work will require both Planning Permission and Building-Regulations Approval, and obtaining local-authority consent, for one does not necessarily imply consent for the other.

From whom do I get Planning Permission?

You can obtain the necessary application form from your local planning authority. Alternatively you can ask an architect or builder to apply on your behalf.

From whom do I get Building-Regulations Approval?

Apply to your local Building Control Officer (District Surveyor) for Building-Regulations Approval. You are required to fill in a form known as a Building Notice and return it along with the necessary information, plus a site plan for new structures, at least two days before work commences. In practice it is wise to give as much advance notice as possible so that you will have plenty of time to discuss any difficulties with the Building Control Officer.

My builder tells me that local authorities always withhold Planning Permission if they can. Is this true?

Planning Permission is always granted unless there are very sound reasons for refusal, in which case the local authority must give you a full and detailed explanation so that you can amend your plans and resubmit them for further consideration. As a last resort you can appeal against a decision to the Secretary of State for the Environment.

How long will it take to get Planning Permission?

You can expect to receive a decision from a local planning authority within eight weeks and, once granted, Planning Permission is valid for five years. If a local planning authority fails to reach a decision within eight weeks you may appeal to the Secretary of State for the Environment.

Why do I need Building-Regulations Approval when I am hiring a professional builder?

If every builder could be relied upon to act responsibly the Building-Regulations procedure would not be necessary. As part of the approval procedure, a surveyor must be allowed to inspect the building work at specific stages, and if it does not comply with the Regulations the work must be done again. This protects you and future householders against shoddy workmanship.

I live in a listed building. Does this mean I have to get special permission for any alterations?	Yes. Listed buildings are considered to be of architectural or historical importance, and as such are protected by statute for the benefit of the community as a whole. Listed-Building Consent must be obtained from the local planning authority before demolition or alterations are carried out. It is also essential that you obtain Conservation-Area Consent prior to any proposal to demolish even an unlisted building located within a conservation area. A conservation area is a specific part of a town or village that has been designated by the local authority as being worthy of conservation and restoration. You should bear in mind that it is a criminal offence not to obtain consent before carrying out such works. If you are in any doubt about your rights and responsibilities, contact your local planning authority and ask to speak to the Conservation Officer for advice.
Do I need to get local-authority approval to paint the outside of my home?	You do not have to apply for consent of any kind before proceeding with exterior decorations unless the building in question happens to be listed.
Do I need Planning Permission in order to make structural alterations inside my house?	Not normally, provided the use of the building is unchanged. You will, however, need to obtain Building-Regulations Approval.
Do I need Planning Permission for new doors and windows?	Not unless they will project beyond the wall facing a highway. However, check with your Building Control Officer to see if your plans require Building-Regulations Approval. Listed-Building Consent must be obtained before replacing doors or windows in a listed building. Similarly, approval should be obtained if the building in question is located within a conservation area.
Do I need Planning Permission to convert my loft into a bedroom?	No, provided the volume of the house remains unchanged and the highest part of the roof is not raised. However, the Building Regulations will apply.
Can I demolish part of my house without permission?	Yes, provided the house is not listed or in a conservation area. You will need Building-Regulations Approval to ensure that the remaining part of the house is safe and the structural stability of any adjoining buildings is not adversely affected by the demolition. You do not need Building-Regulations Approval to completely demolish a detached house. You must, however, give prior notice to the local authority of any intention to demolish a house because they are entitled to make certain requirements controlling the demolition and site operations.

Do I need Planning Permission to build an extension?

Planning controls for extensions differ depending to some extent on the type of house you live in.

You must apply for Planning Permission if a new extension will result in an increase in volume of the original house by whichever is the greater of the following:

Terraced houses – 50cu m (65.5cu yd)
         or – 10 per cent up to a maximum of 115cu m (150.4cu yd)
Other houses   – 70cu m (91.5cu yd)
         or – 15 per cent up to a maximum of 115cu m (150.4cu yd)
In Scotland   – 50cu m (65.5cu yd)
         or – 20 per cent

You will also need Planning Permission if any part of an extension is higher than the highest part of the house roof; any part projects beyond the foremost wall of the house facing a highway; any part within 2m (6ft 6in) of a boundary is more than 4m (13ft) high; if the area of the extension will cover more than half the original area of the garden; or if the extension is to be an independent dwelling.

Will I need Planning Permission before I can erect a conservatory?

For planning purposes you should consider a conservatory attached to the house as if it were an extension.

Can I convert my home into a number of 'bedsitters' without applying for Planning Permission?

No. Converting a house into bedsitters or flats constitutes a 'change of use' and as such requires Planning Permission.

Do I need Planning Permission before I erect a TV aerial?

There is no need to apply for Planning Permission in order to erect a straightforward TV aerial, but you are obliged to get permission before you erect a satellite TV dish that is greater than 900mm (3ft) in diameter. No satellite dish must be higher than the highest part of the roof on which it is installed and you must seek the appropriate consent if you plan to erect a satellite dish on a listed building or within a conservation area.

Can I build a new garden wall without Planning Permission?

You must apply for permission to build a boundary wall that will be higher than 1m (3ft 3in) if it adjoins a highway. Planning Permission is required for any new wall that is to be more than 2m (6ft 6in) high.

Do I need Planning Permission for a new driveway?

In most cases you will have to get Planning Permission, but it does depend on the type of road that is accessed by the driveway. You may also need permission to cross a public footpath or verge. Contact your local planning authority for advice.

Is Planning Permission required for a hardstanding for my car?

No, provided the hardstanding is within your boundary and is not used for a commercial vehicle.

Do I need permission to cut down a tree in my garden?

Not unless the tree is protected or you live in a conservation area. Even under these circumstances, a local authority may give permission to lop or fell a tree that is in a dangerous condition or causing damage to buildings. However, mature trees in particular are a valuable resource and it would be a pity to cut down or drastically prune any tree without first considering all the other options. Expert advice will be available from your local planning authority.

Do I need to get a neighbour's permission to carry out improvements?

Not necessarily, but your neighbours can make official objections to your application for Planning Permission. However, the authority will consider objections concerning planning matters only and will disregard personal squabbles or disagreements. Even so, as a matter of courtesy, it is always worth discussing your plans with a neighbour to avoid future problems and unpleasantness.

What is understood by the term 'ancient light'?

Ancient light is the right to access of natural light through a window. This is recognized by law if the privilege has been enjoyed for a minimum of 20 years without interruption.

I think I need an architect to help me design an extension. Would an architect even consider that type of work?

Not only will the majority of architects be willing to design an extension and prepare the necessary drawings, but he or she will give you expert advice on the need for Planning Permission and apply on your behalf. Similarly, an architect can obtain Building-Regulations Approval, recommend a reputable builder, negotiate building costs and inspect the work at specific stages.

How do I find an architect?

You can write to The Client's Advisory Service of the Royal Institute of British Architects at their headquarters in 66 Portland Place, London W1N 4AD, or contact the RIBA Regional Office nearest to you. You will be supplied with names and addresses of professionals practising in your area. Make appointments to visit several architects to discuss your requirements and their fees.

Do I need a full structural survey before buying a house?

A full structural survey is carried out by a chartered surveyor who will furnish you with a detailed report on the present condition of the house in question, and recommend any repairs he or she thinks are necessary. Any house can be surveyed in this way, but it is particularly advisable if the house is old or very large. Alternatively, you can instruct a surveyor to make out a more concise House Buyer's Report that will at least give you a professional opinion on whether the house in its present condition is worth the 'asking price'. The surveyor will inspect the main structure of the house and its services, including the wiring, and will recommend a test by a specialist if he or she suspects there may be a problem.

If you are buying a flat, ask for a Flat Buyer's Report and Valuation that will, in addition to the normal survey, comment on shared services and common areas.

How can I contact a qualified chartered surveyor?

You can write to either the Royal Institution of Chartered Surveyors at 12 Great George Street, Parliament Square, London SW1P 3AD or the Incorporated Association of Architects and Surveyors, Jubilee House, Billing Brook Road, Weston Favell, Northampton NN3 4NW.

How can I be sure that a builder is reliable?

Choose a builder who is a member of the Federation of Master Builders, 33 John Street, London WC1N 2BB. A builder must be reliable and supply bank and insurance references before he or she can be a member of this federation.

How do I know if a builder's quotation is reasonable?

Always ask two or preferably three builders to quote for a job so that you can compare prices. If the prices vary considerably, don't automatically agree to the cheapest – that builder may be inexperienced and might have to cut corners at a later stage to compensate for an unrealistically cheap price. Similarly, don't assume that one builder is better than another just because his or her charges are higher. A busy builder will sometimes submit a high price rather than appear to be turning work away. Always be prepared to discuss how a price was calculated and then, if it seems reasonable, you can proceed with confidence. Before you finally agree to a price, check whether it is VAT inclusive.

Should I pay a builder in advance?

You should never pay for the whole job in advance. Agree to a series of stage payments and pay promptly once you are satisfied with the work up to that point. Retain approximately 10 per cent of the total fee until the work is finished.

DECORATING

Decorating is probably the most popular of all DIY pursuits. Even those DIY enthusiasts who are eager to take on each and every aspect of house maintenance and construction still seem to get the most pleasure and satisfaction from painting and papering. It comes as no surprise to discover there's an equally fervent desire to find out exactly what to use and where to use it, especially when things go wrong ●

How can I remove a textured coating from my ceiling?

This is a perennial problem, and one for which there is no simple solution. First, you must determine whether you are dealing with one of the plaster-based textured coatings or a vinyl/acrylic resin-bonded textured paint. Use a pocketknife to pick a small sample of the material from the ceiling and drop it into warm water. If your sample does not dissolve after a few minutes it is almost certainly a paint that can be stripped with a proprietary textured-paint remover.

A genuine textured coating is water soluble and warm water containing a mild detergent will soften the material so that it can be scraped from the ceiling. This is an extremely time-consuming, dirty job which is why textured-coating manufacturers usually recommend you apply a fresh skim coat of the material over the existing ceiling to leave a flat surface ready for decorating.

Many frustrated householders resort to the time-honoured method of hacking off textured coating with a bolster, but as some older coatings contain asbestos, creating any form of dust can be dangerous. For the same reason you should never attempt to flatten this sort of textured material with a power sander.

How can I strip painted wallpaper?

Use a lightweight steam stripper

Undoubtedly the best way to remove any wallpaper that has been painted is to soften it first with a steam-generating wallpaper stripper. Rather heavy, cumbersome strippers with separate reservoirs for water are available from tool-hire companies, but you can also buy a lightweight electrically powered tool with its own built-in reservoir. Holding the stripper against a wall or ceiling loosens ordinary paper in moments so that it can be lifted easily from the surface with an ordinary decorator's scraper. To puncture the impervious surface of a painted or washable wallpaper, it is necessary to run a toothed perforating tool over an area of paper before applying the stripper to it. This tool is normally supplied with the stripper.

The joints in my plasterboard ceiling are showing. Can I fill and paint them or will they crack again?

Differential movement between sheets of plasterboard, whether it is caused by shrinkage or flexing, will often result in cracks appearing along the joints unless they have been reinforced with a paper or scrim tape. This is normally applied by the plasterer when the ceiling or wall is being constructed. You can probably fill and paint hairline cracks in the normal way, but it is best to apply a self-adhesive wall-repair tape, especially over wider cracks. This is a 50mm (2in) wide open-mesh tape that you can cut to length with scissors. Having centred the tape over the crack, spread ordinary decorator's cellulose filler along it with a filling knife, feathering off the filler on both sides. You should be able to buy wall-repair tape at any good builders' merchant.

I have a badly stained plaster ceiling. How can I make sure that the stains will not show when I have emulsioned it?

If the ceiling is stained overall with nicotine or smoke, prime it with an aluminium-based sealer or use an alkali-resistant primer. It's cheaper to seal an isolated stain with white eggshell oil-based paint, leaving it to dry thoroughly before you apply emulsion.

My wall is covered with a white furry deposit. How do I get rid of it?

The deposit is the result of soluble salts within building materials being brought to the surface by water evaporating where they form white crystals known as efflorescence. These crystals can form on new plaster while it is drying, and they can also occur on old brick-work, stone or plaster if the wall becomes damp. The crystals themselves are harmless, but you must locate the cause of the damp and cure it. Let the wall dry, then remove efflorescence with a piece of coarse sacking or a stiff-bristle brush. Don't wash the wall or the salts will be reabsorbed only to appear later.

Keep brushing the wall until no more crystals appear, then seal the surface with alkali-resistant primer before applying an oil-based paint. You can emulsion the wall without priming first.

I have green mould growing on an outside brick wall. How can I remove it and prevent it recurring?

First, you must locate the source of the damp conditions that is providing the mould with the moisture it needs in order to flourish.

If the mould is growing in the vicinity of downpipes or guttering it is likely that the plumbing is corroded or possibly blocked, allowing water to spill out onto the brickwork. Check that all pipework and guttering joints are sound.

If the damp appears to be close to ground level, make sure the damp-proof course is in working order and has not been bridged by piled earth or debris.

Perhaps the affected wall permanently faces away from the sun, in which case there is little you can do except increase ventilation by cutting back overhanging foliage in the vicinity.

When you have eradicated the cause of the damp, use a stiff-bristle brush to clean the mould from the wall. This is a dirty job and it is worth wearing goggles and a gauze face mask. Finally, treat the wall with a proprietary fungicide to kill remaining spores.

Can I decorate new plaster?

Wait until the plaster dries out – even when it is touch-dry, moisture may still be working its way to the surface. If you are in a hurry, and you really cannot wait any longer, paint the walls and ceiling with emulsion only. This type of paint is porous and will allow trapped moisture to escape harmlessly. You will probably have to thin the first coat with water because new plaster will be very absorbent.

If you want to use an oil-based paint you must wait until the plaster is thoroughly dry, then seal the walls and ceiling with an alkali-resistant primer.

Don't hang a wallcovering until you are sure the

plaster is dry, then seal the wall with a proprietary size or with a heavy-duty wallpaper paste. To hang paper on an unsized wall will almost certainly result in poor adhesion.

My old painted ceiling is flaking. What should I do before painting it?

You can strip the whole ceiling with an appropriate paint remover, but before you go to all that trouble and expense scrape off all loose material, then feather the edges of sound material with wet-and-dry paper. Apply a general-purpose primer. If you can still detect the edges of old paintwork, prime those areas again and rub down lightly before you paint the ceiling.

I suspect my ceiling has been distempered in the past. Will I have to wash it off before painting with emulsion?

Distemper is an outdated wall and ceiling finish composed of powdered chalk or whiting mixed with glue size and water. As it can be redissolved with water it forms a poor base upon which to apply paint or wallpaper.

Try washing a small area with warm water, and if the finish starts to coat the cloth or sponge you are using, wash the rest of the ceiling to remove the distemper, then apply a stabilizing primer to bind any remaining traces to the plaster before painting or papering.

A rusting gutter has stained the painted wall below it. What can I do about it?

Make sure you repair or replace the gutter, then prime the stained area with an aluminium spirit-based sealer before redecorating the wall.

Can I paint ceramic tiles?

You can paint ceramic tiles with oil-based paint provided the tiles are washed down first with sugar soap to remove all grease and dirt.

Should I seal knots before painting?

Resinous knots in new timber should always be sealed to prevent them staining subsequent coats of paint. First, pick off any hardened resin from the surface of the wood, then paint the knots with shellac knotting. Even old knotty timber can be activated by a chemical stripper, so treat stripped wood in the same way.

There are several holes in the plasterwork along one side of my hall and staircase. In some cases the laths are intact and in others they are broken. What is the best way to patch them?

To patch a hole with intact laths, use a plant spray to dampen the wood and surrounding plaster, then fill the hole flush with fresh plaster, smoothing it with a trowel or float.

When the laths are broken, dip a ball of newspaper in wet plaster and pack it into the hole before you fill it flush as described above. This method is appropriate for holes under 75mm (3in) wide.

Provide a backing for larger holes using a piece of fine expanded-metal mesh that you can buy from builders' merchants and some DIY stores. Cut the mesh patch to shape with tinsnips so that it is slightly larger than the hole, then bend it until you can tuck its edges into the sound plaster around the hole. Tap the mesh flat against the broken laths and fix it with a staple to any solid studs or noggings. Apply a thin coat of plaster to fill the mesh, then let it set before filling the hole flush.

Tuck expanded metal into the hole

I want to patch some small holes in a plasterboard wall. How can I prevent the filler falling into the wall cavity?

Cover small holes with a self-adhesive wall-repair tape. Cut this 50mm (2in) wide open-mesh tape into short lengths and stick them over the hole in a star shape. Spread decorator's cellulose filler across the tape, feathering it off on all sides with a filling knife. When the filler has set hard, rub it down gently with medium-grade abrasive paper, taking care not to break through to the wall-repair tape.

Alternatively, cut a patch of plasterboard that is slightly wider than the hole but narrow enough from top to bottom to be 'posted' through it. Bore a hole in the centre of the patch and thread a length of string through it. Tie the string to a nail behind the patch, then butter the ends of the patch with filler and feed the plasterboard into the hole. Pull on the string and manoeuvre the patch until it bridges the hole, then spread more filler around the edges of the hole to hold the patch in place. When the filler has set hard, cut off the string and fill the hole flush with wet plaster.

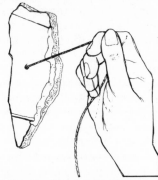
Pull on the string to hold patch

What can I use to seal creosoted wood before I paint it?

Seal creosoted fences, gates and other garden woodwork with aluminium wood primer before you paint them.

What is the best way to clean a dowdy marble fire surround?

Use a soft paintbrush to remove loose dust from crevices and mouldings, then wash a marble surround with hot soapy water containing a little ammonia. Wear protective gloves and wash upwards from the bottom to avoid leaving dirty streaks that might stain the marble. Rinse with clean water and dry the marble thoroughly with a soft cloth. If the surface is still looking lifeless, try a proprietary marble polish.

It is worth noting that what appears to be marble could be painted softwood. Skilled craftsworkers can imitate marble so successfully that it can be difficult to detect even with close inspection. The temperature of the material is one clue. Genuine marble is cool to the touch whereas a painted fire surround would feel no colder than the skirting board next to it. If you suspect that the surface is faked do not apply abrasive polishes. You can wash the surface gently with warm soapy water, but check first on the underside of the mantle shelf that the paint is not water soluble.

What can I do to prevent metal railings rusting?

If the railings are already rusty, brush them with a wire brush or use a wire wheel or cup brush in a power drill. Always wear protective goggles when cleaning rusty metal. Wash off greasy deposits and dust with white spirit, and when the metal is thoroughly dry, protect it with a rust-inhibitive calcium-plumbate or zinc-phosphate primer.

What should I use to repair a cracked concrete drive?

Use sand and cement mortar, but prime the cracks first with PVA bonding agent. Press the mortar into them once the primed surfaces become tacky.

Does basically sound paintwork require any preparation before applying a fresh top coat?

You can wash it down with sugar soap, or for even better adhesion between coats, wipe over the old paintwork with a liquid sander that chemically keys the surface. These chemicals are supplied in liquid form or as an impregnated pad.

Is there a simple way to clean old brickwork?

Many householders are resorting to professional sand-blasting to clean the outside walls of their homes. The end result is often crude and garish. Preserve the mellow colour of your old brickwork by scrubbing it with a stiff-bristle brush while gently playing water onto the wall with a hose. Wash heavy deposits with half a cup of ammonia in a bucket of water. Wear protective gloves and goggles.

My window frames are now so overpainted I would like to strip off the old paint and start again. What would be the best method?

Many professionals still prefer to use a blow lamp or gas torch to burn off old paintwork, but using an electric hot-air stripper is both safer and easier for the amateur. There is far less risk of fire with this type of tool and it avoids any serious scorching of the wood. This could be important if you are planning to apply a clear varnish instead of a paint.

Hold the nozzle of a hot-air stripper about 50mm (2in) from the surface of the paint and slowly move the tool from side to side. As soon as the paint blisters, scrape it from the woodwork with a flat scraper or shavehook. A shaped shavehook is ideal for stripping mouldings and glazing bars.

To avoid cracking window glazing, clip a metal shield (they are supplied with most tools) to the stripper's nozzle to deflect the heat from the glass.

Although this method strips painted woodwork very efficiently, old primer is often left deep in the pores or grain of the wood. This acts as an ideal grain filler if you are repainting, and all you need to do is sand the surface lightly with a medium-grade abrasive paper. However, if you apply a transparent varnish, the old primer will show as white flecks and the finish will be patchy. To avoid this, rub the bare wood with balls of very fine wire wool dipped in a chemical stripper, then wash the surface with white spirit.

I want to varnish all the doors that open onto my hall and landing, but I can't face stripping them all by hand. Should I have them stripped professionally?

Stripping one door by hand is a relatively simple and satisfying task, but it becomes extremely tedious by the time you get to number three or four. Professional stripping is a very attractive option, but there are risks involved. Most stripping companies immerse a whole door in a tank of hot caustic-soda solution which must be washed out of the wood by hosing it with water. This harsh treatment is very efficient, but it raises the grain, leaving a rough surface that will require sanding before you can varnish it. Worse still, the door may warp, its joints may shrink, leaving unsightly gaps, and in severe cases the door panels may split.

You can avoid most problems by searching out a

company that offers a cold-chemical stripping service. You might have to sand the surface lightly, but you are unlikely to have to deal with anything serious. Unfortunately, cold-chemical dipping is likely to cost you almost twice as much as the hot-caustic method.

There are so many chemical paint strippers on the market. How can I decide which one to use?

The easiest way to decide which paint stripper is the most appropriate is to consider the type of paint and the nature of the surface you intend to strip rather than attempt to compare the chemical composition of the strippers themselves.

There are thick gel-like strippers that cling to doors and other large vertical surfaces. They are perfect for all general household joinery, but they are neutralized by washing the stripped woodwork with water. Water raises the grain, so for good-quality furniture, especially if it is veneered, use a thinner paint stripper that is neutralized with white spirit. The thinner consistency is also ideal for delicately carved work. Both strippers will remove ordinary household oil-based paint, but as polyurethane varnishes are difficult to remove, there are specially formulated strippers designed to remove modern as well as traditional copal varnishes. There is also an all-purpose stripper that will remove varnish, emulsion and oil-based paint, and unlike other chemical strippers, it will not burn your skin and is fume free. However, removing paint is a relatively slow process with this somewhat 'milder' stripper. It can be cleaned off the wood with water or white spirit.

You can use thick textured-paint removers to strip vinyl and acrylic resin-bonded paints from walls and ceilings, but scraping and picking the softened paint from deep plaster mouldings is very time consuming. To strip moulded cornices and ceiling roses, apply a paste stripper that is covered with a special blanket and left in place for up to 48 hours. When you peel off the blanket it takes with it up to 30 coats of emulsion, distemper or oil-based paint. Similar poultice strippers are also available for carved or turned woodwork.

Chemical strippers must be handled with care. In most cases you should wear protective gloves and goggles, especially when working on a surface above your head, and always follow the safety measures recommended by stripper manufacturers.

How do I strip paint from a fire surround?

It depends on what the fire surround is made of. Use a pocketknife to scrape a small section of paint from an inconspicuous part of the fire surround to see what material is revealed.

Cast-iron surrounds are very common. There is no point attempting to remove paint from cast-iron with an electric hot-air stripper – the metal simply dissipates the heat. Use a chemical stripper if the surround is still in place or, if it has been removed from the fireplace, you can take it to be sand blasted by a professional.

However, sand blasting will occasionally expose sub-surface defects in the cast iron which will have to be filled before you repaint or polish the surround.

Use a chemical paint remover to strip a painted marble surround, but clean off the softened paint with a wooden spatula and wash the surface as soon as possible to avoid the risk of staining the marble.

If test scraping reveals wood grain you have a choice of hot-air or chemical stripping, but before you launch into the job, carefully scrape what appear to be carved or moulded details to check that they are not made from fibrous plaster or gesso. This type of material is easily damaged by paint stripper, especially when you have to use a sharp tool to remove it. Unless the surround is very overpainted it's best to leave well alone. You can use a paste-like poultice stripper, but as timing is critical you would be advised to hire an experienced professional.

Can I strip painted brickwork or should I repaint it?

Paint is notoriously difficult to strip from brickwork. Not only is it a very laborious process but most strippers cannot cope with a deeply textured surface and traces of paint are always left in the deeper crevices. However, there are paste-and-poultice textured-paint removers that are left to dry on the wall, and when the coating is peeled from the surface it strips all the paint with it. Check the instructions on the container to ensure the stripper you choose is suitable for brickwork, and follow the manufacturer's recommendations implicitly.

What is the best time of year for painting outside?

Ideally you should decorate outside during late summer or early autumn so that the previous warm weather has dried out the structure of the house. Don't try to paint when it is likely to rain and, if possible, avoid painting in direct sunlight – both conditions can spoil your paint-work. Warm but overcast days are best for decorating. Windy weather is a nuisance because airborne dust is sure to be deposited on your fresh paintwork.

A painted brick wall is flaking badly. What should I do before repainting it?

It depends on what is causing the paint to flake. If the wall is damp, the cause of the problem must be eradicated or any subsequent coating will be similarly affected. If the flaking was caused by poor preparation, remove all loose material with a paint scraper and a stiff-bristle brush. Feather the edges of sound patches of paint with coarse abrasive paper, then bind the whole surface with a coat of stabilizing primer.

How many coats of paint should I apply to new woodwork?

This depends on what type of paint you are using. The standard method using familiar oil-based paints is to sand the bare timber and seal it with a wood primer. Available in pink or white, wood primer prevents subsequent coats of paint soaking into the timber.

Heavily pigmented undercoats are designed to obliterate the colour of the primer and to build up a protective body of paint. Choose a white undercoat for pale-coloured paintwork and a grey one for dark colours. Apply one or possibly two undercoats, rubbing down between coats with wet-and-dry paper to achieve a perfect finish.

Finally, apply one decorative top coat that provides a wipe-clean attractive surface.

There are also finishes described as one-coat paints that are applied directly to primed wood. Certain exterior microporous (breathing) paints will cover timber successfully with one coat even without having to apply a primer first.

Is there some way to stop paint forming a skin in a half-used can?

Wipe the rim clean before you replace the lid securely, then store the can upside down.

Can I use emulsion as an undercoat?

Most people who use emulsion as an undercoat do so because they hate the smell of oil-based paints. You will get better results, however, if you use a purpose-made low-odour undercoat that can be washed from the brush with water.

How do I estimate how much paint to buy?

It is impossible to estimate precisely how much emulsion you will require for painting walls and ceilings because the absorbency of the surfaces affects the calculation. However, to get a rough estimate, calculate the area of your walls and ceilings, then allow one litre of emulsion for every 10 to 13sq m (108 to 140sq ft). Double your estimate to allow for a second coat.

Estimating how much oil-based paint you will require for woodwork is even more difficult, but one litre should be enough for one coat on doors, windows and skirtings in an average-size room.

Is lead still being used in the manufacture of paint?

Lead is added to certain industrial paints to give them specific properties. These paints must be labelled appropriately if they contain more than one per cent of soluble lead. For example, lead is added to some metal primers, but they are available to the trade only.

Lead used to be added to decorative paints to act as a drier, but that is no longer a common practice, and many paints will be labelled 'No added lead'. A tiny amount of lead may still be found in a paint, however, because it occurs naturally as part of one of the ingredients or simply because it is present in the environment.

Paints that are labelled as being safe for use on toys must conform to the stringent Toy (Safety) Regulations SI 1367. Their manufacture is strictly controlled and batches of paint are analysed to ensure that it does not contain lethal doses of lead and other highly toxic heavy metals.

What are the advantages of microporous paints?

Microporous or 'breathing' paints are designed to be used outside where they have several advantages over ordinary paints. All exterior woodwork, including joinery, has a relatively high moisture content. The microporous nature of these paints allows the moisture to escape from the wood without damaging the finish yet provides a weather-resistant finish. As a result there is less chance of paint blistering, peeling or cracking. Microporous paints are described as one-coat finishes that do not need to be preceded by a primer and undercoat. There are also translucent microporous wood stains if you want the grain to show.

What should I use to paint galvanized window frames?

If possible, check with the window manufacturers to determine whether the frames have been treated chemically ready for painting. If in doubt, use a galvanized-metal and aluminium paint based on special resins that requires no primer or undercoat. However, you must clean the metal first with a degreaser supplied with the paint. This paint is made in a limited range of colours so you may want to use ordinary oil-based paints; in which case, wash the metal with white spirit and paint it with a calcium-plumbate primer.

Can I paint asbestos?

Asbestos-cement sheeting was often used to construct sheds and garages, and although one would use an asbestos-free material nowadays, these earlier structures are still standing and may need to be redecorated. It is asbestos dust that is so harmful, so provided you do not intend to cut or sand asbestos you should not be in any immediate danger. If the old sheeting is beginning to break or crumble, take professional advice about safe disposal of asbestos.

Before you apply an oil-based paint, prime the surface with an alkali-resistant primer. Try to treat both sides and edges of a sheet to prevent water absorption. Before you fill any exposed nailheads or screws, paint them with a metal primer. There is no need to prime asbestos sheeting if you are planning to use exterior-grade emulsion.

Can I repaint a gloss-painted wall with emulsion?

Yes. If the paintwork is in good condition, wash it with sugar soap to remove dirt and grease, and lightly key the surface with medium-grade wet-and-dry paper.

The smell of fresh paintwork makes me feel ill. Are there any alternatives?

The vast majority of solvent-based (oil) paints have a rather strong and distinctive odour that some people find unpleasant. However, there are one-coat gloss paints made with low-odour solvents or you could use one of the water-based gloss paints.

How can I avoid smearing paint on the glass when I'm painting a window?

Ideally, when painting glazing bars you should overlap the glass by almost 2mm ($\frac{1}{16}$in). This stops rain or condensation seeping between the glass and frame where rot can start.

The best method on ordinary flat glass is to run masking tape around the edge of the window pane, leaving a slight gap between tape and glazing bars. When the paint is touch dry, peel off the tape to leave a neat edge.

Masking tape can't be used on the textured side of patterned glass. To paint around this type of glazing, use a plastic or metal shield to protect the glass.

If all else fails you can scrape dried paint from window glass with a sharp blade clipped into one of the special handles that are sold in most DIY stores.

What paint should I use to paint a radiator?

If you intend to paint a factory-finished radiator you can use most paints, including emulsion. This is especially convenient when matching room colour schemes. There is also a special heat-stoving acrylic paint usually referred to as radiator enamel. Running the heating for two hours bakes the enamel onto the radiator and after another six to eight hours you can apply a second coat.

Radiator enamel will not affect old paintwork under normal circumstances, but if you must rub the paintwork down prime it afterwards with a special compatible primer. Use the same primer to cover new gloss paint and factory-applied primer before you use radiator enamel.

My neighbour tells me he is painting the outside of his house with emulsion. Is that type of paint suitable for exterior use?

Yes, provided it is exterior-grade emulsion. It dries to a smooth matt finish just like ordinary interior emulsion and it is also thinned with water. However, exterior-grade emulsion is weatherproof and contains an additive to prevent mould growth.

Very fine aggregates such as powdered mica are added to some exterior emulsions. These 'reinforced' emulsions dry to an attractive textured finish and are recommended for use in coastal districts and industrial areas where the highly protective nature of these paints is an advantage.

What is cement paint?

Cement paint is one of the cheaper finishes suitable for decorating exterior masonry. It is made with white cement plus other pigments to provide a range of colours. It is supplied as a dry powder packed in drums for you to mix with water to a thin creamy consistency. Two coats should be sufficient for a flat even coverage, but dampen the walls first with a water spray before the first coat if you are painting porous masonry.

Cement paint is not as weatherproof as certain other exterior-grade paints, but its protective qualities can be improved by adding a fine clean sand, preferably silver sand. The recommended proportions are one part sand to four of cement-paint powder. If you find that the addition of sand changes the colour of the paint, use it to reinforce the first coat only, then apply a top coat of pure cement paint.

I have never tried creating decorative-texture paint effects. What would be the easiest to start with?

A sponge makes a speckled texture

A rag creates a bolder effect

A complete beginner would have to practise for months, perhaps years, to master painting techniques such as marbling or graining, but you can achieve a very attractive mottled effect on your walls or ceilings without any previous experience. Select two emulsion paints with contrasting tones or colours and paint your walls or ceiling with two coats of the paler tone. Once this flat basecoat is dry, pour a tablespoon of the darker paint into a roller tray. Take a damp natural sponge (not the synthetic variety) and dip it in the paint. Dab excess paint onto scrap paper until the sponge is leaving a pleasant mottled texture, then apply the sponge lightly to the wall. Stipple the surface leaving closely grouped spots of paint to form an even speckled texture. Pressing too hard leaves an unsightly patch of solid colour, but don't attempt to correct mistakes at this stage – just leave them to dry naturally. Replenish your sponge at regular intervals until you have stippled the entire wall or ceiling. Stand back to view your work and touch in any areas that appear too light or open. Those areas that are too dense or smeared can be modified by stippling them with the lighter basecoat once the first stippled coat is dry.

If you want a bolder stippled effect, use a ball of crumpled cotton rag to apply the paint. Keep turning and refolding the rag to present the most creased parts of the fabric to the wall – this creates interesting and varied textures.

If I decide to hang one of the patterned relief wallcoverings, should I use ordinary wallpaper paste?

Use heavy-duty wallpaper paste to hang modern pressed-paper or blown-vinyl relief wallcoverings. Traditional Lincrusta (a solid film of linseed oil and fillers on a paper backing) is hung with a special ready-mixed adhesive. You can spread Lincrusta adhesive with a wallpaper scraper or scrub it onto the wallcovering with a stiff-bristle nail brush.

Should I hang strips of ceiling paper towards the windows or parallel with them?

Hang ceiling paper parallel with the window wall and work away from the light.

How do I estimate how much wallpaper I will need?

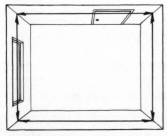

Unless paper is expensive, ignore windows and doors when estimating

Most wallpaper manufacturers supply printed charts to help you estimate the amount of paper you will need for a particular room. These charts are based on standard-size rolls of wallpaper that measure 530mm (1ft 9in) wide and 10.05m (33ft) long. If you want to hang a non-standard wallcovering (or you want to check a manufacturer's chart), first measure the height of the walls from skirting to ceiling. Divide the length of the roll by this figure to see how many 'lengths' you can cut from one roll. Measure around the room to see how many roll widths fit into the combined lengths of the walls. Divide this total by the number of paper lengths you can cut from one roll to find how many rolls you will need. Normally you can ignore windows and doors, treating all walls as if they were solid, but if the wallpaper is very expensive or the windows are particularly large, calculate for solid sections of wall and make a separate allowance for short lengths of wall above doors and below windows.

Do I really need to line the walls before I hang wallpaper?

It isn't absolutely necessary, but professional decorators line the walls with cheap off-white paper before hanging expensive wallcoverings or heavy embossed papers. Lining paper helps to prevent shrinkage and masks uneven or imperfect walls that might show through a thin wallcovering. Lining paper is hung horizontally so that the butt joints cannot align with those in the top wallcovering which is always hung vertically.

I recently hung lining paper on my ceiling and it keeps peeling off. What am I doing wrong?

It may be that the ceiling was painted with distemper, in which case you should have washed it off or bound it to the plaster with a stabilizing solution. A kitchen ceiling can be very greasy and must be washed thoroughly with sugar soap before paper will adhere to it. It is also possible that the plaster is very absorbent and needs to be sized before the paper will stick firmly.

I've been told that hand-printed wallpaper is difficult to hang. Is this true?

You do need to take extra care when hanging hand-printed wallcoverings, especially as they are always relatively expensive. The inks used to print the patterns can sometimes be smeared by traces of wallpaper paste and you may have to trim the rolls to width yourself.

What paste should I use to hang vinyl wallpaper?

Because vinyl wallcoverings are impervious to water it is essential to use a heavy-duty wallpaper paste that contains a fungicide to prevent mould growth.

How can I strip vinyl wallpaper?

A vinyl wallcovering comprises a thin surface layer of plastic fused to a paper (sometimes cotton) backing. Soaking the impervious vinyl surface has no effect on the paste holding it to the wall. To strip a length of this type of wallcovering, lift both bottom corners of the vinyl surface, then pull firmly and evenly to peel it off the wall, leaving the paper backing in place. You can leave this backing to act as a lining paper for another wallcovering or soak the paper and scrape it off the wall.

How can I clean old floor tiles?

If normal household cleaners have no effect on old tiles you should try one of the many industrial preparations available to professional cleaning and maintenance companies. Suppliers of industrial tile-cleaning materials are listed in the *Yellow Pages* directory. Describe the material and condition of the tiles to the supplier who will be able to suggest an appropriate cleaner. Old encaustic tiles can be especially difficult to clean as even industrial cleaners may not loosen ingrained dirt and grease. Having washed the floor once, scrub particularly stubborn patches of dirt with a soap-filled wire-wool pad before washing the whole floor again.

I have one cracked ceramic tile in the centre of an otherwise perfect wall. How can I replace that one tile?

If you have a spare tile left over from the original job or you can find a suitable alternative, replacing a single tile is not a difficult task. Scrape the old grout from around the damaged tile. Then, to avoid dislodging neighbouring tiles, drill several holes with a masonry bit to remove the centre of the damaged one. Wearing protective goggles, tap the cutting edge of a small cold chisel behind the remaining tile fragments to prise them off the wall.

Scrape the recess clean and butter the back of the replacement tile with fresh adhesive. Press the tile in place making sure it is flush with those surrounding it. Wipe off excess adhesive with a damp sponge and leave it to set before renewing the grouting.

Can I tile over old ceramic tiles?

Yes, providing they are clean and stuck firmly to the wall. Tap each tile to locate any loose ones and chop them out with a cold chisel, or use the tip of an old screwdriver to scrape out the surrounding grout and lever the loose tiles away from the wall. Remember to wear goggles to protect your eyes from flying fragments. Replace sound tiles using fresh adhesive or fill the recesses flush with mortar. Wash the tiled surface thoroughly with sugar soap to remove grease and dirt.

Can I lay ceramic tiles over floorboards?

Provided your joists are rigid you can level the floor for tiling by screwing 12mm ($\frac{1}{2}$in) plywood over the boards. Place the screws no more than 300mm (1ft) apart.

How do I go about removing an old tiled shower surround?

Wearing protective goggles, chop out one of the tiles with a narrow cold chisel, then drive a bolster behind the rest to prise them off the surface. Use the bolster again to clean old adhesive from the wall.

How can I cut ceramic tiles to fit around pipework?

Undoubtedly the easiest way to cut ceramic tiles is to use a saw file. This tool comprises a narrow steel rod coated with tungsten-carbide particles and held under tension in a hacksaw-like frame. As the file can cut in any direction you can cut curves and make tight turns with ease.

How can I drill into ceramic tiles?

Use a masonry bit in a power drill set at its lowest speed. To prevent the bit slipping on the glazed surface, stick a patch of adhesive tape over the position of the hole.

What drill bit can I use to bore a hole in glass?

Have a professional glazier drill large holes in glass, but for holes up to 13mm ($\frac{1}{2}$in) in diameter use a diamond spear-point glass drill. Set your drill to its slowest speed and use turpentine, oil or paraffin as a lubricant. Build a small reservoir with putty to contain the lubricant. Make sure you wear protective gloves and goggles.

Run a glass drill in a lubricant

3

CURING
DAMP

Like the weather itself, curing damp
seems to be a peculiarly British pre-
occupation. It hardly seems to matter
whether we live in a Victorian mansion or
a modern semi-detatched, we all appear to
suffer to some extent from the effects of
condensation, rising damp, leaking roofs
or perhaps broken gutters. And just when
we think we've thoroughly weatherproofed
our homes, the next winter brings with it
some other unexpected problem ●

Is penetrating damp the same thing as rising damp?

No, definitely not. Penetrating damp is the result of water soaking through the structure of the building from outside. The symptoms occur during wet weather only, although they frequently leave stains behind.

Rising damp occurs at ground-floor level only. Most houses are protected from rising damp by a waterproof barrier built into the walls and concrete floors to prevent moisture permeating beyond a certain level. If this damp-proof course in the walls or membrane in the floor breaks down, water can seep into the structure of the house. Some older houses may suffer from rising damp because a damp-proof course was not installed at the time it was built.

I have a damp patch on the wall just below my bedroom ceiling. What could be causing it?

Assuming your roof is sound, check the condition of the rainwater guttering. You may find that the gutter is blocked with silt or leaves so that rainwater can overflow, soaking the wall immediately below.

Similar symptoms occur if the guttering is corroded or one of its joints is broken or dislocated.

Although this type of penetrating damp can only occur during wet weather, the symptoms may last for some time while the saturated wall dries out.

I have a damp patch in one corner of the room, halfway up the wall. What can I do about it?

There is almost certainly a downpipe (drainpipe) mounted near the corner of the house where the damp is penetrating. Feel behind the pipe with your fingertips to see if it has corroded, causing splits or holes. Mould growth behind the pipe will often lead you directly to the leak. Don't be misled into thinking plastic downpipes cannot corrode. After perhaps 10 to 15 years of exposure to ultra-violet light, the plastic can become dry and crumbly. Patch any leaks temporarily with self-adhesive flashing tape, but replace the downpipe as soon as practicable.

Clear out any leaves that have become trapped behind the downpipe because they too can eventually lead to penetrating damp at that point.

How do I treat a damp chimney breast?

Check the condition of the chimney stack. Broken mortar flaunching around the chimney pots, cracked brickwork or loose pointing can all allow rainwater to enter and soak the chimney breast below. Repoint or fill cracked masonry with mortar mixed with a little PVA bonding agent.

Inspect the flashing – the flexible-metal or mortar seal found at the base of the stack where it meets the roof. If the flashing is in very poor condition have it replaced by a professional, otherwise paint it with a liquid-rubber compound or patch it with self-adhesive flashing tape. If a mortar fillet has shrunk away from the chimney stack, inject a flexible caulking compound into the gap.

Ever since I blocked off an unused fireplace the chimney breast is damp. I have checked the chimney stack and everything appears to be in good condition. Where is the rainwater getting in?

It isn't rainwater that's soaking your chimney breast. Damp air trapped inside the unused flue is condensing on the brickwork and the moisture is finding its way to the interior of the house. Ventilate the flue by installing a small grille at a low level in the blocked-up fireplace.

Is the damp patch along the underside of my living-room window caused by rising damp?

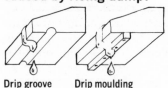

Drip groove   Drip moulding

If the damp patch was caused by rising damp, the wall would be affected from the skirting board up to window level. It is most probably caused by rainwater running back on the underside of the window sill and soaking the wall behind it. Exterior sills should be grooved longitudinally on the underside so that the water drops to the ground at that point. Check that this drip groove in your sill has not become filled with moss or paint. If the groove has been omitted, nail and glue a small hardwood strip to the sill, about 35mm (1½in) from the front edge.

What are the causes of rising damp?

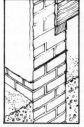 

Render bridge   Earth over DPC

Rising damp normally occurs when the protective damp-proof course or membrane deteriorates so that it no longer provides a barrier against water permeating from the ground. However, it is also possible for a damp-proof course to be bridged, allowing water to bypass it into the wall above. This can occur, for example, if exterior rendering is taken below the level of the DPC, or earth is piled against the wall.

A DPC should be at least 150mm (6in) above the level of the ground outside. If a path or patio has been built against the wall, splashing rain can soak the wall above the damp-proof course.

Can I install a new DPC myself?

Certain methods for installing a damp-proof course should be left to professionals, but it is possible to hire the necessary materials and equipment to inject a wall with a silicone-based chemical that forms a continuous waterproof barrier. However, doing the work yourself may not be cost effective in the long run. Rising damp can lead to expensive repairs unless it is eradicated completely, so hiring a reputable company may be a wise investment, especially as future house purchasers might want to see a professional guarantee. Ask the company you hire for a detailed specification (Agrément certificate) to ensure the work will be carried out to approved standards. Check that any guarantee that is offered is covered by insurance in case the company goes out of business.

How can I cure a musty wardrobe?

Provided your house is not affected by rising or penetrating damp, the musty smell in your wardrobe is almost certainly caused by condensation. One simple solution is to place a container of absorbent crystals in the wardrobe to extract moisture from the surrounding air. They are available from leading DIY stores.

What causes condensation?

Air holds water vapour in the same way that a sponge can absorb water. As the air in our homes becomes heated it can absorb still more water vapour generated by cooking, baths, showers and even breathing, until it finally becomes saturated. When saturated air comes in contact with a surface that is colder than itself it is cooled until it can no longer hold the water vapour it has absorbed and deposits it in liquid form onto the surface.

There are four ways to prevent condensation: take the moisture out of the air with a dehumidifier before it becomes saturated; replace the moist air by ventilation; heat the air so that it can absorb more moisture before becoming saturated; insulate cold surfaces so that they will not cool water-laden air.

How can I prevent water vapour running down my walls?

If you plan to paper the room you can line the walls first with thin sheets of expanded polystyrene. This material is supplied in rolls and hung like wallpaper. After 72 hours, cover the lining with wallpaper of your choice.

Alternatively, use an insulating paint that contains hollow glass beads that act as thermal insulators. Insulating paint, which contains a fungicide to prevent mould growth, can be overpainted with emulsion.

How can heating a room with an oil heater be responsible for condensation?

An oil heater produces as much water vapour as the paraffin it burns. Changing to another form of heating will reduce condensation considerably.

Mould growth is covering my bedroom ceiling. What can I do to prevent it?

If the mould growth is distributed evenly across the ceiling the moisture upon which it thrives is almost certainly caused by condensation. You might also notice the lines of ceiling joists standing out as pale strips where mould grows less well along these relatively warm and drier areas. The solution is to increase the insulation in the loft above the bedroom, or if that is impossible, line the ceiling with mineral-fibre tiles.

I have been told the black specks on my wall are the result of mould growth. How should I treat it?

Before you do anything else cure the cause of the damp that is responsible for mould growth. Then make up a sterilizing solution of 1 part household bleach to 16 parts of water, and brush it onto the affected walls. Four hours later scrape off the mould and wipe it onto old newspaper. Wash the wall again with bleach solution and leave it to dry out thoroughly.

If mould is growing on wallpaper, soak it in bleach solution before you strip it in the normal way, then wash off paste residue with fresh solution.

Before you redecorate, paint the wall with a proprietary stabilizing primer.

My loft is damp and yet the roof seems perfectly sound. Where is the rain getting in?

It's probably not rainwater at all. Once a loft is insulated to reduce heat loss from the dwelling below it becomes much colder and moist air will readily condense on the roof timbers, slates or tiles. Ventilation is the answer.

Make sure the insulant is not restricting airways built along the eaves on both sides of the pitched roof. If soffit boards are blocking these airways, fit plastic soffit vents that plug into holes cut in the boards.

A damp strip runs right across my ceiling. What could be causing it?

It sounds as if there is an unlagged cold-water pipe in the loft above. A cold pipe will attract condensation that drips from the lowest points along its run. Check first that there are no actual leaks, then insulate the pipe with a foam-plastic tube that you can obtain from any good DIY store or plumbers' merchant.

What is a dehumidifier?

A dehumidifier is an appliance designed to remove moisture from ambient air. A fan draws air over cold coils upon which water vapour condenses and drips into a reservoir. The dry air is warmed and blown back into the room. When a dehumidifier is placed in a damp room it extracts moisture from fabrics and furnishings, then stabilizes the moisture content of the air.

What is causing the damp patch across the top of my window?

It sounds as if the concrete lintel above the window is forming a 'cold bridge', allowing condensation to form on the inside of the wall at that point. This will often occur when a cavity wall is filled with insulation, leaving the solid lintel unaffected. Line the walls and window reveal with thin expanded-polystyrene sheet or paint them with insulating paint.

How can I prevent damp patches that surround my windows?

These symptoms suggest that the mortar pointing surrounding the window frame on the outside has cracked or fallen out, leaving a gap where rainwater can enter. Replace missing pointing and seal the gaps with a flexible mastic, or use a strip sealant – a putty-like material sold as rolls – that you can press in place with your fingers.

I keep finding a damp patch on the floor by my front door. What can I do about it?

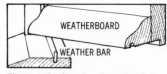

Fit a weatherboard and weather bar

Rainwater dripping from the door is being blown back into the house. Try fitting a weatherboard moulding across the bottom of the door to shed rainwater clear of the threshold. Form a weatherproof seal between the weatherboard and the door by painting primer onto the back of the moulding and screw it into place while the paint is wet.

In an exposed windy location you might also have to set a plastic or metal weather bar in a groove cut across the threshold.

After a heavy downpour a single damp patch appears in the middle of my wall. The pointing and bricks seem to be in perfect condition. What am I to do?

An isolated damp patch of this kind is usually caused by something bridging the gap between the two skins of a cavity wall. Mortar or some other building debris might have been dropped during construction, building up on one of the wall ties that link the two skins of masonry. This debris forms a bridge across which moisture can travel. One solution is to remove a brick from the outside wall and clear the debris with a probe. However, try a simpler solution first – paint the damp area of the wall with an internal damp proofer that will prevent penetrating damp spoiling internal decorations.

Is a waterproofing liquid effective in stopping damp coming through a brick wall?

Brickwork in good condition should be weatherproof, but old soft bricks become porous and the whole wall can become saturated through to the internal face. Painting an external waterproofing liquid onto the bricks inhibits penetration while allowing the moisture trapped within the wall to escape. There are also beneficial side effects: it helps prevent flaking brickwork caused by the expansion of freezing water; it improves the insulation of the wall. Waterproofing liquid can be brushed or sprayed onto the masonry, and although one coat is usually enough, very absorbent surfaces may need a second application as soon as the first has soaked in.

The concrete floor in my cellar is permanently damp. Is there a simple solution?

Seal a damp concrete floor with a heavy-duty moisture-curing polyurethane. It can be applied directly to a damp surface, but penetration is better if you force-dry the cellar first with a heater.

Make sure the floor is clean and grease-free, then prime any cracks with one coat of urethane and one hour later fill them with a mortar made from 1 part cement to 6 parts of sand plus enough urethane to produce a relatively stiff mix.

Brush on the first coat of urethane with a broom and two or three hours later apply a second one. Three or four coats in all will produce a water-resistant seal.

Water is seeping into my coal cellar through a crack in the wall. What can I use to seal the crack?

Patch any active leaks with a quick-drying hydraulic cement. Supplied as a powder for mixing with clean water, the cement expands as it hardens, sealing out running water.

Undercut the crack with a cold chisel. Hold a ball of the mixed cement in your hand until it is warm, then push it into the crack, holding it in place with a trowel for three to five minutes until it hardens.

I would like to replaster my cellar walls, but how can I ensure that penetrating damp will not ruin the new work?

Seriously damp cellars should be treated by a professional, but average dampness can be eradicated by painting the walls with bitumen latex emulsion. Hack off the old plaster, then apply a skim coat of mortar to smooth the surface. Paint the walls with two coats of bitumen latex emulsion, and before the second coat dries, throw clean dry sand onto it to form a key for the new plaster.

How can I recognize wet rot?

Wet rot frequently attacks the frames of windows and doors which have been neglected so that the wood has become exposed to rainwater or penetrating damp. Peeling or discoloured paintwork is often the first sign, and underneath, the wood will be spongy when wet but dark brown and crumbly when dry. As a test, press a key into the suspected area – decayed wood feels soft.

I suspect I have discovered dry rot in my house. How can I be sure?

Dry rot exhibits different characteristics depending on its state of development. It always starts in damp un-ventilated spaces, sending out fine grey tubules in all directions, even through masonry, to seek out other timber to infect. Once tubules reach dry wood, moisture is pumped through them from the damp area to provide ideal conditions for further growth. White cotton-wool-like mycelium grows on the damp wood, and once the rot is fully established, wrinkled pancake-shaped fruiting bodies develop rust-red spores that are expelled to cover surrounding surfaces. Infected timber becomes brown and brittle, finally breaking into cube-like pieces. Dry rot is always accompanied by a strong musty smell. If you're still not sure you are dealing with dry rot, have the site inspected by an expert.

How should I treat wet rot?

Assuming the woodwork is not seriously affected, dig out the softened timber until you reach reasonably sound wood. Leave it to dry out thoroughly (loosely tape plastic sheet over the frame to keep rainwater out but provide ventilation).

Paint the rotted areas with a wood hardener to bind and reinforce the fibres of the wood. Use a wood filler to rebuild the damaged areas and repaint the frame.

Badly rotted timber will have to be cut away and re-placed with new wood. Treat all the timber with three applications of a clear wood preservative.

Can I treat dry rot myself?

Dry rot requires urgent and drastic treatment to ensure that a potentially serious condition does not develop further. Unless the outbreak is minor and self-contained it should be treated by a specialist contractor who will guarantee results.

The source of the damp conditions must be cured, and infected timbers and plaster must be cut away and discarded. All replacement timbers plus surrounding masonry and woodwork within 1.5m (5 ft) of the infected area must be sprayed with three coats of preservative to kill remaining spores.

How can I protect my house against rot?

Regularly decorate and maintain window and door frames to prevent the ingress of water.

Provide adequate ventilation in roof spaces and under floors, making sure the airbricks around the perimeter of the house have not been covered or blocked with leaves or paint.

Eradicate plumbing leaks, and rising and penetrating damp as soon as possible – they lead to the conditions that encourage dry and wet rot to develop.

When it becomes practicable, protect sound struct-ural timbers by painting them with a general-purpose wood preservative.

Can I apply preservative to wood before painting it?

Yes, but leave the preservative to dry out for three to five days depending on the drying conditions.

What wood preservative should I use in my greenhouse?

There are several chemical preservatives that are harmless to plants. This type of preservative is often green in colour, but check the instructions on the container to be certain.

I have heard that immersing wood in chemical preservative is the best form of protection. How should I go about it?

Prolonged immersion is the ideal preservative treatment for wood, especially for those timbers that have to be in contact with the ground. Make a shallow tank from loose bricks and line it with thick polyethylene. Place the pieces of wood in the tank and weigh them down with bricks. Pour in chemical preservative to cover the wood and leave it to soak for a minimum of one hour. To empty the tank, bury a bucket near one end and remove some bricks to allow the preservative to pour out.

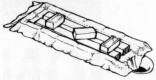

Drain the tank into a bucket

Are chemical preservatives safe to use?

Yes, provided you wear protective gloves when applying them and wear a facemask when you are using them indoors. Ensure there is good ventilation while preservatives are drying and do not sleep in a freshly treated room for at least two nights. Preservatives are flammable so extinguish naked lights and do not smoke while working with them.

INSULATION AND VENTILATION

No matter what fuel you are using, the cost of heating a house has risen steadily over recent years – and there's no reason to suppose the trend won't continue. Even if the expense of heating was not an important factor, the improved comfort that results from efficient insulation and draughtproofing more than justifies the effort.

Ventilation is the other side of the coin. Modern standards of insulation are such that there is a tendency to seal our homes almost too thoroughly, cutting off the supply of fresh air. Unless we provide the means to replenish the air we merely substitute one set of problems for another ●

I want to insulate my home, but on a limited budget I cannot afford to do it all at once. What should I choose to do first?

An unlagged hot-water cylinder squanders a surprising amount of expensive energy. Wrapping it in a close-fitting jacket will constitute a considerable saving in a few months. At the same time, slip foam-plastic tubes over exposed hot-water pipes that run through unheated areas of the house. Pipe-lagging materials and cylinder jackets can be obtained from leading DIY stockists and plumbers' merchants. Sealing all the major draughts from doors and windows is also very cost effective and easy to achieve.

As up to 25 per cent of the radiant heat from a radiator is lost to the wall behind it, the second stage of your insulation programme should be to stick metallic foil behind all radiators on outside walls to reclaim much of this wasted energy for a modest outlay. Foil-faced expanded-polystyrene lining is manufactured specifically for the purpose.

An estimated 25 per cent of your home's heat is lost through the roof, so insulate your loft as soon as you can afford it, especially as you may be eligible for a local-authority grant.

Draughts seem to be blowing from beneath my skirting boards. Is that possible?

Depending on prevailing winds it is quite possible for draughts to be generated in the spaces below your suspended floors via perforated airbricks placed at regular intervals around the house. When a skirting board shrinks it leaves a gap at floorboard level through which these draughts can enter your home.

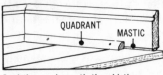

QUADRANT   MASTIC

Seal the gap beneath the skirting

Never block the airbricks – they are necessary to prevent rot developing under the floor. Instead, inject a flexible mastic into the gap under the skirting, then pin a quadrant moulding over the gap for a neat finish.

What is the best way to draughtproof a sash window?

There are several strips and seals that will draughtproof a sash window, but for perfect results you can fill all gaps with a clear flexible sealant squeezed from a tube. The sealant is practically invisible when set. At the end of the cold season you can peel off the sealant without harming the paintwork.

I want to insulate a loft myself. What material will be the easiest to use?

Provided you lay them between the ceiling joists you have a choice of materials, all of which are easy to use.

Perhaps the simplest of all are the glass-fibre, mineral- or rock-fibre blankets, made to fit snugly between the joists. They are normally sold as continuous rolls, but they are also available in relatively short strips known as batts. Rolls and batts are made in various widths to suit typical joist spacings, and both types are cut to length using large scissors or a sharp knife.

Alternatively, you can use loose-fill insulation in pellet or granular form. Exfoliated vermiculite is the most commonly used material, but mineral wool, expanded polystyrene and cork are also available. Loose-fill insulation is poured from sacks to fill the space between joists and raked level to the recommended depth.

What is the recommended thickness for loft insulation?

Blanket insulation should be at least 100mm (4in), but preferably 150mm (6in), thick. Loose-fill insulant should be laid to a depth of at least 130mm (5in), so check the ceiling joists are deep enough before you decide to use this type of insulant.

My neighbour was told that loose-fill insulation was unsuitable for where we live. How could that be?

If your house is built on an exposed windy site, loose-fill insulation can be blown about in a draughty loft. This can cause drifting, leaving areas of the loft with insufficient insulation. Under these conditions it is advisable to lay blanket insulant.

When I insulate my loft can I lay the insulant over electric wiring?

Wiring covered by insulation has a slightly higher chance of heating up, although this is normally only associated with circuits to cookers, storage heaters or showers. On balance it is best to lay all wiring on top of loft insulation and do not pack any type of insulant around recessed light fittings.

How can I insulate a loft that I want to use for storage?

You can lay insulation at ceiling level and lay floorboards or sheets of flooring chipboard over the top. Make sure the roofspace is adequately ventilated to prevent condensation.

If you want the storage space to be insulated also, you will have to install insulation between the sloping rafters. Blanket insulation is made with a foil backing that forms side flanges that can be stapled to the underside of the rafters. Alternatively, buy rigid mineral-fibre sheets and cut them to make a tight fit between rafters. Staple polyethylene sheeting over rigid insulant. Whatever type of insulant you choose, make sure there is a ventilated airspace of at least 50mm (2in) between the back of the insulation and the roof tiles or slates.

For a finished appearance, nail a plasterboard lining across the rafters.

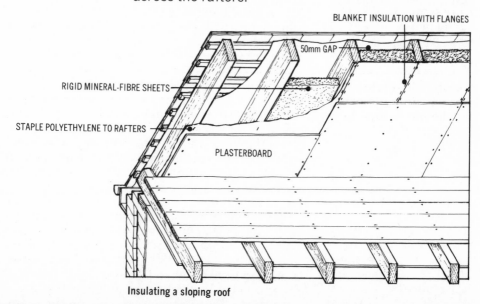

BLANKET INSULATION WITH FLANGES

50mm GAP

RIGID MINERAL-FIBRE SHEETS

STAPLE POLYETHYLENE TO RAFTERS

PLASTERBOARD

Insulating a sloping roof

How can I insulate a flat roof?

A flat roof can be insulated from above by laying on it rigid insulating sheets weighed down with paving slabs or a layer of pebbles. Have the roof surveyed by a professional to ensure it can take the additional weight.

Can I insulate a flat roof by fixing an insulant on the inside?

The best way to insulate a flat roof from below is to dismantle the old plaster ceiling and install rigid insulation between the rafters, then staple polyethylene to them before fitting a new plasterboard ceiling. You must ensure there is a ventilated void of at least 50mm (2in) deep above the insulant.

An easier method is to glue insulated plasterboard directly to the ceiling, using a special adhesive. This is standard plasterboard backed by expanded polystyrene, and incorporates a plastic vapour barrier to prevent condensation in the void above. The only possible disadvantage is having to reconstruct window architraves to allow for the extra thickness on the ceiling.

What does cavity insulation do for a house?

The two masonry skins of a cavity wall are separated by a 50mm (2in) gap. Filling the gap with an insulant prevents air circulation and greatly improves the thermal insulation of the building – cavity insulation cuts heat loss from an average house by up to 55 per cent. In addition, the house will be cooler in summer.

Can cavity insulation be installed in an old house?

Not if your house was built before 1920 because the walls would probably have been built of solid masonry. Professional contractors can inject a foam, fibre or granular insulant into the cavity walls of later buildings through holes drilled in the outer skin. When filled with mortar at the end of the job it should be practically impossible to detect the holes.

How can I be sure a contractor installing cavity insulation knows what he is doing?

Make sure the contractor is approved by the Agrément Board, is registered with the British Standards Institution or is a member of the National Cavity Insulation Association.

How cost effective is cavity insulation?

Cavity insulation should pay for itself in terms of fuel savings within four years.

Will cavity insulation cause penetrating damp?

In theory certain insulants could bridge the gap in a cavity wall and cause penetrating damp, but not if they are installed properly and any structural faults in the building are detected and repaired by the contractor beforehand. A reputable company will provide a written guarantee to cure, free of charge, any damp resulting from faulty materials or installation.

Does the expanded polystyrene sheeting sold in rolls have any effect on heat loss when it is applied to a wall?

This type of insulation is too thin to have any measurable effect on the heat lost through a masonry wall. It does, however, provide a warm surface to discourage condensation at that point.

What is the cheapest form of double glazing?

Cheap but effective double glazing can be achieved by stretching a flexible film of plastic across the window frame. Once the film is fixed with double-sided tape it is shrunk to form a taut wrinkle-free membrane by warming it with a hair dryer. At the end of the cold season the film is removed to gain access to the window.

There seem to be several clear plastics I could use for secondary double glazing. Which is the best?

Plastics are very popular for secondary double-glazing systems because they are lighter than glass, virtually unbreakable and they are easy to cut or plane to size. However, the cheaper plastics are likely to deteriorate with age, losing their clarity, and they are prone to static. Plastics are scratched relatively easily and have to be washed with a liquid-soap solution rather than cleaned with an abrasive polish.

Polyester film is used for inexpensive disposable double glazing that is renewed every season. It is tough and clear.

PVC is sold as a semi-rigid sheet that provides inexpensive double glazing where a high degree of clarity is not required – such as in bedrooms.

Polystyrene is also relatively cheap, but clearer than PVC. It will, however, deteriorate in strong sunlight and should not be installed in a south-facing window. It has an estimated life of three to five years.

Acrylic is a good-quality plastic made in rigid sheets with the clarity of glass. It will cost about 50 per cent more than polystyrene, but has an estimated working life of at least 10 years.

Polycarbonate is about twice the price of acrylic, but it provides lightweight vandal-proof double glazing with a high level of clarity and an estimated working life of 10 to 15 years.

In the event of fire, are double-glazed windows a safety risk?

There are no risks with factory-made double-glazed sealed units because they are designed to be opened like other windows and therefore provide an escape route in the event of fire. However, there are risks associated with secondary glazing, fitted to the inside of existing windows, when it comprises one single sheet of unbreakable plastic. Fire-prevention officers and safety campaigners recommend that if secondary glazing is fitted make sure there is at least one window in every occupied room that can be opened easily.

I am blocking off an unwanted fireplace. Why do I need to ventilate it?

Ventilating an unused fireplace provides a flow of air that prevents condensation and helps dry out penetrating damp. Ideally you should install an airbrick on the outside of the flue, but that would be impossible in a terraced house. An easier method is to fit a small plastic grille over a hole cut in the plasterboard or masonry you use to block off the fireplace, and leave the chimney uncapped.

Is there any reason why I cannot replace the airbricks around my house with ordinary bricks to prevent draughts coming through my floorboards?

Airbricks are built into the external walls to ventilate the spaces below suspended wooden floors. Without ventilation there is every possibility that dry rot will develop. Not only should you never replace them with solid bricks but you should inspect airbricks regularly to ensure they have not become blocked with leaves, earth or paint.

What is trickle ventilation?

Trickle ventilation provides a low-level but constant flow of air to prevent condensation, particularly in steamy bathrooms and kitchens. It is achieved by fitting a narrow adjustable grille in the window or door frame. Some factory-made windows are supplied with integral trickle ventilators.

I want to put an extractor fan in my kitchen. Where is the best place to install it?

Place the fan as high as possible and near to the cooker (but not directly over it), so that steam and cooking smells are extracted quickly without drawing them across the room.

What size of extractor fan will I need?

The size, or capacity, of extractor fan you need depends on the type of room in which it is to be installed and the volume of air it is required to move. An extractor in a kitchen, for example, must be capable of changing the air completely ten to fifteen times per hour. A bathroom requires six to eight changes per hour, and a separate toilet, ten to fifteen. If you want to fit a fan in a living room, it needs to change the air four to six times per hour only, but fit a slightly larger fan if there are heavy smokers in the family.

To calculate the required capacity of the fan in square metres (or square feet) per hour, find the volume of the room and multiply it by the recommended number of air changes per hour. Select a fan that matches the result or is capable of a slightly higher rate of extraction.

Is it just as easy to fit an extractor fan to a wall as it is in a window?

There's really not a great deal of difference. Although you can cut a large-diameter hole in existing window glazing, sometimes stresses within the glass will cause it to crack. And there is always a slight security risk while the glass is removed, especially if you take it to be cut by a glazier. It is better to have a new pane supplied with a hole cut for the fan.

To fit an exterior fan on a wall you must cut a hole for the plastic duct that leads to the outside. You need a long-reach masonry drill to bore a series of holes inside the edge of the planned ducting hole before cutting out the plaster and brick in the centre with a cold chisel. Work from both sides of a cavity wall having first marked the position of the hole by drilling centrally right through both skins of masonry.

What type of extractor fan should I install in a bathroom with no windows?

It must be capable of changing the air six to eight times per hour and it should be wired in conjunction with the bathroom light so that it is operated automatically as soon as someone enters. Choose a fan with a built-in timer that will keep the fan turning for up to twenty minutes after you have left the room.

Is a filtered recirculation cooker hood as effective as one that is vented to the outside?

Recirculation cooker hoods are fitted with filters that remove grease and moisture from the air before returning it to the kitchen. These filters have to be cleaned and changed regularly if they are to work efficiently, and even then, recirculation hoods are not as effective as those that dump stale air out through a duct in the wall.

Isn't ventilating my heated kitchen and bathroom costing me a lot of money?

Conventional extractor fans are very efficient at removing cooking smells and steam, but it is true to say that they waste a great deal of heat at the same time. You can reclaim most of this wasted energy by installing a heat-exchanging ventilator. On its way out, the warm contaminated air is passed through fine vents sandwiched between other vents containing cool fresh air being drawn from outside. Most of the heat is transferred to the fresh air before it is blown into the room.

How can I get an open fire to draw?

Efficient draughtproofing can sometimes cause problems with open fires by starving them of a fresh supply of oxygen. The ideal solution is to fit a controllable grille in the floor beside the fireplace to draw air from the space below.

What is the best material to use for lagging a cold-water tank in my loft?

Surround a rectangular tank with sheets of 25mm (1in) thick expanded polystyrene held together at the corners with sharpened wooden pegs so that you can dismantle the insulation at will. Make a lid from the same material and fit a plastic funnel into it to catch drips from the hot-water vent pipe.

Wrap a circular tank in glass-fibre blanket insulation. Cut a lid from man-made board and cover it with insulant. Wrap the insulated lid with plastic sheet to make sure the glass fibre does not contaminate the water.

Do not place insulation under the tank – the heat rising from the house keeps the water above freezing point.

My neighbours are very noisy. How can I sound-proof our dividing wall?

Fill any cracks in the plaster and make sure the plasterwork continues to the floor behind the skirting board. As an additional measure, try lining the party wall with well-filled bookshelves.

In exceptional circumstances build an independent wall at least 125mm (5in) from the party wall. Hang 25mm (1in) thick blanket insulant on the existing wall, then construct a stud partition without any point of contact with the party wall. Line the studs with polyethylene, then two layers of 12mm ($\frac{1}{2}$in) plasterboard.

Does double glazing really help reduce traffic noise from outside?

Yes, if the gap between the glass or plastic panes is 100 to 200mm (4 to 8in) wide. This can only be achieved by fitting secondary glazing in the window reveal. A combination of a factory-made sealed unit plus secondary glazing (triple glazing) is even more effective.

How do I soundproof the ceiling between my flat and the one above?

Try to get your upstairs neighbour to help you with reducing the level of noise transmitted to your flat, even if it means paying for the improvements yourself. Have all loose floorboards nailed firmly to the joists and lay a decent underlay beneath carpets. Place a piece of carpet or cork tiling beneath kitchen appliances such as washing machines and dishwashers to reduce the effects of vibration.

If you cannot get your neighbour to cooperate you can construct a false ceiling 250mm (10in) below the existing one. Line it with polyethylene and plasterboard, having laid 50mm (2in) thick blanket insulation in the cavity between the two ceilings.

5

PLUMBING AND CENTRAL HEATING

Plumbing, including the installation and maintenance of central heating, is no longer the prerogative of the professional. The DIY market has responded eagerly to the amateur's demands for products and materials that are easier to install and maintain. The DIY plumber can choose between plastic or metal pipework with modern push-fit or traditional soldered fittings, and there's a wide range of well-designed appliances as well as specialized tools and equipment to get you out of trouble ●

How can I cure an airlock in my plumbing?

Air trapped in a plumbing system can cause a tap to splutter or run dry. Force the air out using mains water pressure. Connect one end of a length of hosepipe to the affected tap and the other end to the cold tap in the kitchen – the tap that delivers drinking water under mains pressure. Open both taps and leave the water running for a few minutes, then try the airlocked tap again, and if necessary, repeat the procedure until water runs freely from the tap. A long hose will contain a lot of water so drain it into the kitchen sink before you remove it.

I've driven a nail through a pipe. What should I do?

Don't remove the nail until you have turned off the water and drained that section of pipe. As a temporary measure, patch the leak with a short length of hosepipe split lengthwise and clamped around the pipe with hose clips.

I've never tried plumbing myself. Is there some way to repair a hole in a pipe permanently without having to replace a section of pipe?

You can patch the hole with a plumber's two-part epoxy putty. Drain the pipe, then use wire wool to clean all round the pipe for 25mm (1in) on each side of the hole. Mix the putty and wrap it around the pipe, kneading it to seal the hole. Build up a 3 to 6mm ($\frac{1}{8}$ to $\frac{1}{4}$in) layer of putty, smoothing it to an even contour, then wrap it with self-adhesive tape before reinstating the water supply. Twenty-four hours later you can remove the tape.

What should I use to seal the gap between a bath and a tiled wall?

Don't use ordinary grout or adhesive to seal the gaps around baths, shower trays or even wash basins. These fittings can flex or distort in use and the slight movements can crack a rigid seal, allowing water to penetrate. Use instead a flexible silicone-rubber sealant sold in a tube or pressurized container with a pointed nozzle for accurate application. Flexible sealants are made in a range of colours to match most bathroom fittings or you can buy a clear variety. There is also a strip sealant, sold as a roll, that you can press in place with your fingers.

Can I re-enamel my old bath successfully?

You can repaint an old enamel bath yourself using a special two-part epoxy coating. Alternatively, you can hire a professional to respray the bath *in situ* and repair any chipped enamel at the same time.

Why is my toilet cistern overflowing?

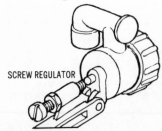

SCREW REGULATOR

Adjust screw to regulate water level

The level of the water in a toilet cistern is controlled by a float that lifts one end of a metal or plastic arm. The other end of the float closes an inlet valve, shutting off the supply of water to the cistern. If the valve is not closed at the right moment the water level continues to rise until it runs out through the cistern's overflow pipe. Bend a metal arm downwards slightly to reduce the level of water, or adjust a screw regulator on a plastic arm until the surface of the water is 25mm (1in) below the outlet to the overflow pipe.

If adjustment fails to correct the problem, change the washer or diaphragm in the inlet valve.

Why is my cold-water storage tank overflowing?

The cold-water tank in your loft is fitted with a float valve like those installed in toilet cisterns, and the water level is controlled in similar ways. However, the water flows into the tank under mains pressure, and if a low-pressure valve has been fitted in error it will never fully close. Dismantle the valve and replace the nozzle or, if necessary, change the whole valve for one matched to mains pressure.

My toilet cistern fills very noisily. How can I silence it?

A noisy cistern is caused by water splashing from the float-valve outlet. Fit a valve that has an outlet with a long flexible tube – a silencer tube – that hangs below the water level.

I have to replace my water-storage cistern, but I will not be able to pass a similar tank through my loft hatch. What am I to do?

The existing cistern was probably installed as the house was being built and never had to be passed through the relatively small loft hatch. Buy a circular plastic cistern of a similar capacity to your old tank and bind string around it to fold it into a shape that will pass through the hatch. Don't even attempt to remove the old cistern from the attic. Simply disconnect it and pull it to one side.

Can plastic pipework be used for hot water?

Flexible polybutylene pipes can be used for both hot-water and cold-water supplies – even central heating. The pipe, supplied in standard lengths or continuous coils, is connected with easy-to-use push-fit joints.

Is it possible to connect plastic pipework to existing copper plumbing?

Special connectors are used to join the majority of plastic plumbing to existing copper pipes. Polybutylene pipes can be joined to copper plumbing with push-fit connectors or standard brass compression joints.

Will I have to hire a plumber to join new copper pipework to my old lead rising main?

It is worth hiring a professional to make the traditional 'wiped' solder joint between copper and lead pipework, but you can buy a special compression joint to connect a lead rising main to new copper or plastic plumbing.

How can I thaw a frozen pipe in my attic?

Run an electric extension lead to your attic and warm a copper pipe with a hair dryer. If that does not work use a hot-air stripper, but place a flame-proof material behind the pipe and don't overheat the metal so that soldered joints are melted.

Wrap a hot towel round a plastic pipe.

Avoid freezing pipes in the future by wrapping them with foam-plastic lagging.

How can I improve the water pressure of my shower?

Water pressure in a conventional shower is determined by the height of the cold-water storage cistern in the loft. Ideally the bottom of the cistern should be 1.5m (5ft) or more above the shower head. If there is room in the loft you can raise the cistern on a well-braced frame, but that will involve lengthening all the pipework.

Alternatively, fit an electric booster pump to increase the pressure on the hot-water and cold-water supply pipes to the shower. Pumps can be hidden, possibly in an airing cupboard, or you can mount a specially designed pump in the shower cubicle or above the bath. If you are planning to replace the existing shower, buy a shower unit with an integral pump.

Why does my shower suddenly run cold?

A shower normally runs cold when the pressure on the hot-water supply is reduced by someone drawing hot water from a tap or with an appliance elsewhere in the house. A simple solution is to fit a thermostatic shower unit that compensates for a slight drop in water pressure on the hot or cold supply by balancing the pressure on the other.

Why does the water pressure suddenly drop while I'm showering?

Pressure drops when someone draws water from the same system. Ideally a shower should have an independent 15mm ($\frac{1}{2}$in) cold supply from the attic storage cistern and a 15mm ($\frac{1}{2}$in) hot supply running directly from the vent pipe above the hot-water cylinder.

Why is a syphonic toilet quieter than the more common washdown pan?

The heavy fall of water required to cleanse the standard WC pan is responsible for noisy flushing. The flow of water is restricted from a syphonic pan, creating a vacuum in the trap so that water and waste is expelled quietly by atmospheric pressure.

Is there any way I can install a second toilet in my basement?

The siting of a WC is normally dictated by the need to provide sufficient fall to discharge the waste to a soil pipe. As a basement is below ground level it is impossible to install a WC that operates using the conventional gravity-fed system. However, you can install a WC connected to an electrically driven pump and shredder that will discharge waste through a relatively small-bore pipe that can rise vertically from a basement to the soil pipe above ground.

I've tried unblocking a sink with a rubber plunger, but to no avail. What should I try next?

Buy or hire a force pump. With the rubber mouth of the tool over the sink outlet, water is forced along the wastepipe by pumping a handle at the other end.

If that doesn't work hire a 'snake' or wastepipe auger and pass it along the pipe, cranking its handle to help it round bends. If it is difficult to get the auger to negotiate the tight bends in the trap below the sink, dismantle the trap and probe the branch pipe behind it.

My toilet is blocked. Do I need to call a plumber?

There are solutions to try before calling out a plumber. Hire a manually operated toilet force pump that will drive water along the toilet wastepipe. If the trouble persists, pass a toilet auger into the wastepipe, cranking the handle to dislodge the blockage.

When I turn off a tap my plumbing thumps noisily for several seconds. How can I prevent it happening?

This rhythmic thumping, known as water hammer, is probably caused by the float arm oscillating as it tries to close the storage-cistern inlet valve against mains water pressure. Replace the existing float valve with an equilibrium valve that is designed to equalize water pressure on both sides of its diaphragm or piston so that the valve can close smoothly and silently. At the same time, make sure your plumbing is clipped securely at regular intervals to cut down vibration in the pipework.

How does an overflow safety valve work?

An overflow safety valve is a device designed to prevent a flood in the event of a mechanical breakdown or split hose in an appliance such as a washing machine or dishwasher. Connected to the water-supply inlet, the valve measures the amount of water flowing into the machine. If the volume of water exceeds the amount set to match the capacity of the appliance, the valve closes, preventing an uncontrolled discharge of water.

Are there any special problems with installing a garden tap?

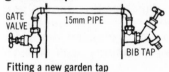

Fitting a new garden tap

To install a garden tap, simply connect a new 15mm ($\frac{1}{2}$in) pipe to the existing rising main and run it through the wall to the outside location. At that point connect the pipe to a bib tap made with a threaded spout to take a hose connector. It is worth fitting a gate valve to the new pipework inside the house so that you can isolate and drain the garden-tap supply pipe during the winter months to prevent it freezing.

What are the advantages of installing a water softener?

If you live in a naturally hard-water area your domestic supply will contain a high concentration of minerals dissolved from the ground. These minerals are not visible in tap water, but salts in the form of hard limescale are deposited in pipework, cisterns and particularly on the inside of hot-water cylinders and electric kettles, eventually reducing their efficiency by up to 70 per cent. Limescale also blocks shower heads and stains baths, sinks and wash basins. A water softener absorbs mineral salts before the water flows through the domestic plumbing system and therefore eliminates the usual effects of hard water.

How can I filter my drinking water?

The local-authority water-treatment process should reduce chemical pollution and sediment particles to an acceptable level, but as a precaution, it is possible to filter drinking water for a second time in your own home.

A jug filter that you fill from the tap and allow to stand before you drink the water is perhaps the simplest method, but it is not really practical for a large family. On-tap filters are connected by a flexible hose to the existing cold-water kitchen tap. They can be wall-mounted next to the sink or stand on a convenient worktop or drainer. In-line filters are connected to the pipe beneath the sink that feeds your cold-water tap. You can, if you prefer, connect the filter to a new branch pipe run from the rising main to a separate tap on the sink. This gives you the option to use unfiltered water for domestic cleaning purposes, reserving filtered water for drinking only.

How do I drain my cold taps and pipes?

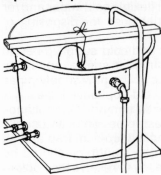

Tie float-valve arm to a batten

Close the stopcock (valve) on the rising main, then open the kitchen-sink tap and garden tap to drain the pipes.

Bathroom taps and toilet cisterns are fed by a pipe connected to the attic storage cistern near its base. If this pipe is fitted with a valve, close it and open all taps and flush the toilets on that section to drain the pipes. This leaves the storage cistern full so that it can still supply the hot-water cylinder. If there is no valve on the cold-water pipe you will have to drain the whole cistern using the bathroom taps.

If you want to drain the bathroom plumbing while providing drinking water in the kitchen, leave the mains stopcock open but place a stout wooden batten across the top of the attic storage cistern and tie the float-valve arm to it to cut off mains supply to the cistern.

How do I drain my hot-water pipes?

Turn off your boiler or immersion heater. Locate the cold feed pipe to the hot-water cylinder from the attic storage cistern. If this pipe is fitted with a valve, close it and drain the hot-water pipes by opening all hot taps. Even when water stops flowing, the hot-water cylinder itself will still be full.

If you cannot isolate the hot-water system with a valve, first tie up the float-valve arm to cut off mains supply, then empty the attic storage cistern by running bathroom cold-water taps. When the taps run dry, open hot taps to drain the hot-water pipes. If you run the hot water before emptying the attic cistern, all the hot water in the cylinder will be flushed out and wasted. In an emergency run all the taps together to empty the system as quickly as possible.

How do I drain a WC cistern?

To empty the cistern only, tie up its float-valve arm to cut off the supply of water, then flush the toilet.

There is very little room around my bath. Is there a simple way to run pipes to the taps?

The simplest way is to use proprietary flexible copper pipes that are made with a tap connector at one end and a compression or capillary joint at the other for attaching to the supply pipes.

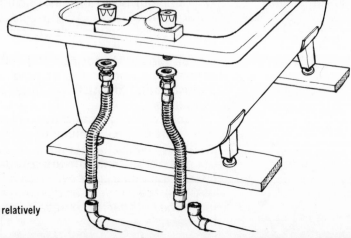

Flexible copper pipes make it relatively easy to fit bath taps

Do I need to hire a plumber to install a washing machine or dishwasher?

Not if you are familiar with the rudiments of joining plumbing fittings. Automatic washing machines and dishwashers are supplied with flexible cold-water and/or hot-water hoses, plus an outlet hose for disposing of dirty water.

Connect 15mm ($\frac{1}{2}$mm) hot and cold supply pipes to those already servicing the sink. Fit special appliance valves (small taps) to the ends of the new supply pipes for connecting to the hot and cold appliance hoses.

Construct a standpipe directly behind the appliance using 43mm ($1\frac{1}{2}$in) plastic wastepipe. You can usually buy a standpipe kit comprising a deep-seal trap and all the fittings. The open end of the standpipe should be 600mm (2ft) above the floor ready to receive the hooked end of the machine's outlet hose. Take the other end of the standpipe through the wall to the gulley (drain) or drainpipe hopper outside the house.

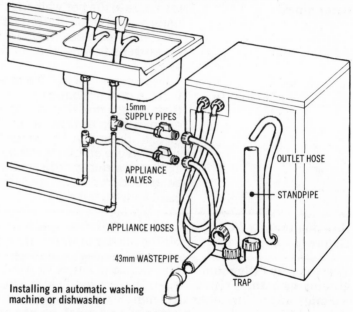

15mm SUPPLY PIPES

APPLIANCE VALVES

OUTLET HOSE

STANDPIPE

APPLIANCE HOSES

43mm WASTEPIPE

TRAP

Installing an automatic washing machine or dishwasher

I want to replace my hot-water cylinder. How do I empty the old one first?

Turn off your boiler or immersion heater and allow the water to cool. Cut off the cold-water supply to the cylinder, draining the attic cistern if necessary. Run off hot water from the taps.

Look for a draincock on the cold feed pipe where it enters the cylinder near its base. Attach a hose to the draincock and empty the cylinder into a drain or sink at a lower level.

If your water is heated by your central-heating boiler there will be a heat exchanger still full of water inside the cylinder. The exchanger can only be drained along with the rest of the central-heating system from a draincock next to the boiler.

As a last resort you can disconnect the vent pipe at the top of the cylinder, insert a garden hosepipe and syphon the water.

What is the difference between a cesspool and a septic tank?

Sewage from houses that are not connected to a public sewer is drained into a cesspool or a septic tank. A cesspool is simply a collecting point for sewage until it can be removed by the local authority. A septic tank, on the other hand, is a complete waste-disposal system in which the sewage is treated before water is discharged underground or into a local waterway.

Is it possible to descale my central-heating system?

To descale a corroded central-heating system, first drain and flush the system, then add a chemical descaler/corrosion inhibitor. Leave it for about eight weeks to break down limescale, then flush again.

How can I protect my new central-heating system from corrosion?

To protect a new central-heating system, drain off enough water to empty the feed and expansion cistern – about 20 litres (4 gallons) of water – then pour a chemical corrosion inhibitor into the cistern and refill with water. Check the manufacturer's recommendations for the amount of inhibitor to add to the system. Switch on the circulation pump to distribute the inhibitor around the system.

Can I remove a radiator to decorate behind it?

Unscrew cap-nuts to remove radiator

To remove a radiator for decorating, close the valve at each end, then unscrew the cap-nut that holds one of the valves to the radiator. Hold an old jug or similar container under the valve and slowly release the bleed valve at one top corner of the radiator to allow the water to flow. As the jug becomes full, transfer the water to a bowl until no more can be drained. Release the cap-nut at the other end of the radiator and lift it off its wall brackets. Carefully tip the radiator to drain any remaining water into the bowl.

Can I increase the temperature in my bathroom by fitting a thermostatic valve to my radiator?

A thermostatic valve is designed to control the temperature of a radiator, but when it is set at 'maximum' it is equivalent to an ordinary valve being fully open. The purpose of a thermostatic valve is to reduce the heat in a kitchen, for example, while the rest of the central heating might be running at a higher temperature.

What is causing the banging in my central-heating system when the boiler heats up?

The system is overheating for some reason. Check there is enough water in the system by inspecting the small feed and expansion cistern in the attic. If it is dry or the water level is very low, check the float valve to see why it is not permitting water to flow from the mains, and make sure there's not a frozen pipe somewhere.

If there seems to be plenty of water, have the boiler thermostat tested by a professional and have the system descaled.

Why are my radiators cold even though the boiler seems to be working normally?

The circulation pump may be faulty. Check the pump is working by feeling for vibration, then open its bleed valve to make sure it isn't airlocked. As a last resort, switch off the system, allow it to cool, then remove the pump and flush it to clean out a possible blockage.

My boiler's not working this morning. What could be the problem?

Check that the roomstat and the boiler thermostat have not been set too low. Ensure that the timer or programmer is switched on and set correctly. Make sure the boiler pilot light has not blown out. Try relighting the boiler according to the manufacturer's instructions, usually found inside the boiler's front panel. If the pilot fails to ignite have the boiler inspected by a professional.

I want to have my domestic hot water heated by my central-heating system, but does that mean I have to run the heating during the summer?

Heated water from the boiler passes through a coiled heat exchanger inside the hot-water cylinder. Heat is transferred to the stored water until it reaches the required temperature determined by a thermostat on the cylinder. During the summer months you could close the valves on all your radiators and programme the system to switch on for a short period simply to heat the water. Ideally, you should supplement the heat exchanger with an electric immersion heater so that you can turn off the central heating during warm weather.

Do I have to place a central-heating boiler against an outside wall?

Not necessarily, as modern central-heating boilers are relatively easy to accommodate. There are gas, oil or solid-fuel boilers with conventional flues that are designed to be connected to a chimney. A balanced-flue boiler, on the other hand, does not need a chimney. It is convenient to have this type of boiler against an outside wall because it draws fresh air and dumps flue gases into short ducts that pass through the wall.

You could choose a back boiler that fits into a fireplace behind a radiant fire or room heater.

Alternatively, there are electrically heated boilers that can be fitted anywhere that is convenient since they do not emit flue gases.

Are skirting-mounted convectors as efficient as conventional radiators?

Hot water passing through a convector heats thin metal fins that in turn warm the air that surrounds them. The rising warm air draws cooler air into the convector causing heat to circulate around the room. Because a convector does not emit radiant heat it does not feel as warm to the touch as a conventional radiator. However, it will eventually heat up the room to the required temperature.

Should a radiator be placed under a window?

A radiator was habitually placed beneath the window in a room because the rising column of warm air prevented condensation and reduced the effect of draughts. In addition, as tall furniture would not be placed in front of a window, the radiator did not take up valuable wall space in a small bedroom. However, with the widespread use of double glazing, heating engineers now place a radiator in whatever position is most convenient, particularly if it leads to economical pipe runs.

In terms of central heating, what is zone control?

We rarely use all the rooms in our homes simultaneously. During the day, for example, the bedrooms are likely to be unoccupied, and heating them is wasteful. Consequently, a central-heating system can be divided into zones with separate controls so that one area can be warm while the heating is dormant in another part of the house. Motorized valves, linked to a timer or programmer, isolate a circuit of pipes until, at a pre-determined time, the valves are opened automatically to direct heated water into that zone.

Why do I need a roomstat when there is a thermostat on my boiler?

A boiler thermostat measures the temperature of the circulating water whereas a roomstat measures the ambient temperature (temperature of the air surrounding it). Using a roomstat is the more accurate way to regulate a consistently comfortable environment.

I keep increasing the setting on my roomstat but the house never seems to warm up. Do I need a new roomstat?

The roomstat may be faulty, but try turning up the boiler thermostat. The boiler may be switching off before the ambient temperature reaches the roomstat setting.

How often should I have my boiler serviced?

The high efficiency of modern gas-fired or oil-fired boilers depends largely on their being serviced regularly, usually annually. It is advisable to take out a service contract with the fuel supplier or possibly with the central-heating installer.

Should I have my boiler serviced professionally or can I do it myself?

You can clean a solid-fuel boiler and sweep its flue yourself, but have an oil-fired or gas-fired boiler serviced by a professional.

How should I bleed air from a radiator?

Air leaking into a central-heating system collects in the radiators, forming pockets that prevent complete circulation of the water. As a result an affected radiator feels cooler at the top than at the bottom.

Release valve to bleed a radiator

Each radiator has an air-bleed valve at one of its top corners, identifiable by a small square shank in the centre of a round blanking plug. Obtain a special key that will operate the valve from a DIY shop or plumbers' merchant.

Give the bleed valve a quarter turn with the key and you will hear the hiss of escaping air. As soon as the hissing stops and the first dribble of water leaks from the valve, turn the key to close the valve firmly. As a precaution, have an empty jar or cup to hand to catch escaping water.

Why is it that when I bleed a radiator in the usual way I cannot exhaust all the air?

Suction created by the action of the circulation pump prevents the water in the radiator forcing the air out of the bleed valve. Switch off the pump and try bleeding the radiator again.

6

ELECTRICITY

It cannot be emphasized too strongly that one needs constantly to be aware of the potential hazards when working on electrical installations. Always turn off the power before you start work, avoid interruptions that would break your concentration, follow the recommendations in the Wiring Regulations and double-check your work before turning the power on again. If at any time you are unsure of your competence to complete a job safely, do not hesitate to ask a professional electrician for help or advice ●

How can I be sure that an electrician is fully qualified?

Check that he or she is registered with the NICEIC (National Inspection Council for Electrical Installation Contracting) or the Electrical Contractors' Association. In order to be a member of these organizations an electrician must have an in-depth knowledge of, and must comply with, a code of practice known as the Regulations for Electrical Installations (Wiring Regulations).

What are the Wiring Regulations?

The Wiring Regulations are a detailed set of rules for the safe wiring of electrical installations compiled by the Institution of Electrical Engineers. You can buy a copy of the Regulations from many good bookshops or directly from the IEE. The book is very technical and difficult to follow, but there is also a simplified illustrated guide to help interpret the regulations correctly.

Should I have a new electrical circuit tested?

Any significant rewiring, especially newly installed circuits, must be tested by a competent electrician and a certificate stating that the wiring complies with the Wiring Regulations must be submitted to the Electricity Board to apply for connection to the mains supply. The Board will undertake to test DIY wiring at the time of connection for a fee. You should never be tempted to make connections to the meter or the consumer's earth terminal yourself. If you are in doubt about whether an installation will require testing, contact your local Board for advice.

What are watts, amps and volts?

$$\frac{Watts}{Volts} = Amps$$

$$Amps \times Volts = Watts$$

Watts measure the amount of power used by an appliance when it is working.

Amps measure the flow of electricity necessary to produce the required wattage for an appliance.

Volts measure the 'pressure' provided by the Electricity Board's generators to drive the current along the conductors. Mains voltage is a constant 240V, and if you know one of the other factors you can determine the third by using simple formulae.

What does it mean when I read that an electrical appliance is double insulated?

Double-insulation symbol

A double-insulated appliance has a non-conductive plastic casing that insulates the user from any metal component that could become live. For this reason, double-insulated appliances do not have to be earthed with a third wire. The officially recognized symbol for double insulation is a square within a square and can be found printed or moulded on an appropriate appliance.

My son keeps leaving a light turned on overnight. Is that very wasteful?

Not really – light fittings are relatively cheap to run. A 100W bulb, for example, will give you 10 hours of illumination for 1 unit of electricity.

There's a strong smell of fish in my bedroom. What on earth is it?

The smell is almost certainly caused by the overheating of a plastic component in an electrical appliance or fitting. Check your table lamps and light fittings to ensure you have not inadvertently used a light bulb with a higher wattage than that recommended by the manufacturer of the fitting. This is a common problem with enclosed light fittings.

Check your sockets and switches by holding your hand against their faceplates to see if they feel warm to the touch. If you find a suspect fitting, turn off the power at the consumer unit and use a screwdriver to tighten the terminals holding the conductors in the socket or switch. Check your plugs in a similar way, tightening the terminals and using wire wool to clean the cartridge-fuse caps and the three square pins. If the symptom persists, call in an electrician because there is a risk that over-heating could start a fire.

Where do I turn off the supply of electricity?

In an emergency you can switch off the electricity supply to the whole house by operating the main switch on your consumer unit. The consumer unit is a box containing the fuses or miniature circuit breakers that protect the house circuits, and it is usually situated near the meter.

Once you have turned off the main switch you can remove an individual circuit's fuse holder or switch off its miniature circuit breaker, cutting the power to that particular circuit. That circuit will be safe to work on even when you restore power to the rest of the house by turning on the main switch. When you are working on the house circuitry, leave a note on the consumer unit to say that the power has been turned off intentionally or keep the relevant fuse holder in your pocket.

What is the purpose of a fuse?

A fuse is designed to protect a circuit or appliance from overloading. In its simplest form a fuse is a wire calculated to melt at a given temperature when a circuit is overloaded, breaking contact and isolating the circuit or appliance automatically. Fuse wire is made in different thicknesses to suit the various circuits.

There are also cartridge fuses. This type of fuse comprises a ceramic tube packed with sand, with a metal cap at each end. A fuse wire running through the centre links the caps. Cartridge fuses are found in some consumer-units and in appliance plugs.

What is a miniature circuit breaker?

Miniature circuit breakers (MCBs) are used in modern consumer units in place of fuses. Each circuit breaker is made with a switch or button that is used to isolate the circuit it is protecting. In the event of an overload on that circuit, the switch moves automatically to the 'off' position or the button pops out.

What are the advantages of miniature circuit breakers over conventional fuses?

A miniature circuit breaker reacts to a small overload in a fraction of the time it takes for a fuse to melt. It is simple to use: operating a switch or pushing a button is all that is required to isolate a circuit or restore the power. When using fuses there is always a risk that you will run out of the correctly rated fuse when one of them blows (melts). There is nothing to replace with an MCB.

How can I tell which consumer-unit fuse has blown?

Everything on a particular circuit will have stopped working because that circuit is no longer receiving a supply of electricity. Having turned off the consumer-unit main switch, open the unit and look for the appropriately marked fuseholder – lighting circuit upstairs, power circuit downstairs and so on. Pull out the suspect fuseholder and inspect the fuse itself. If there is naked fuse wire stretched between two terminals a visual check will usually detect a break in the wire, often accompanied by scorch marks. If in doubt pull gently on each end of the wire with the tip of a screwdriver.

The simplest way to check a cartridge fuse is to replace it with a new one. However, you can test a cartridge fuse, including one from a three-pin plug, with a metal-cased torch. Remove the bottom cap from the torch and touch one end of the fuse against the base of the battery and rest the other end of the fuse against the torch casing. If the torch bulb lights up when you switch on, the fuse is sound.

Should I always use a 13amp fuse in a 13amp plug?

Although most square-pin plugs are supplied with 13amp fuses only, you should substitute a 3amp (red) cartridge fuse for use with appliances rated up to 720W. These appliances are likely to be table lamps, radios, tape recorders and so on. Use a 13amp (brown) fuse for appliances rated between 720 and 3000W (3kW), including kettles, dishwashers and toasters. The wattage is marked on every appliance.

There are so many different designs for 13amp plugs. What is the best type?

You can use any design of plug you wish provided it carries the British Standards number BS 1363 that signifies it is made to an acceptable quality and will be safe to use.

What size of fuse should I use for the various domestic circuits?

Use the chart below as a guide to the size of fuses to use in domestic circuits. Bare fuse wire comes wrapped around a clearly labelled card. Cartridge fuses are colour-coded and marked with their amp rating.

FUSE RATINGS		
Circuit	**Fuse**	**Colour coding**
Doorbell	5amp	White
Lighting	5amp	White
Immersion heater	15 or 20amp	Blue or yellow
Storage heater	20amp	Yellow
Radial circuits 20m²	20amp	Yellow
50m²	30amp	Red
Ring circuits	30amp	Red
Shower unit	45amp	Green
Cooker: up to 12kW	30amp	Red
over 12kW	45amp	Green

What is the difference between a ring circuit and a radial circuit?	A ring circuit is the most common form of power circuit for feeding socket outlets. A continuous cable runs from the consumer unit to every socket outlet before returning to the consumer unit to be connected to the same terminals from which it started. A radial circuit feeds a number of socket outlets, but its cable terminates at the last socket and does not return to the consumer unit.
Is a ring circuit and a ring main one and the same thing?	Yes, a ring main is an unofficial term for a ring circuit.
How many sockets can I have on a ring circuit?	There is no limit to the number of socket outlets you can have on a ring circuit, provided the circuit does not serve a floor area greater than 100sq m (120 sq yd). In practice most two-storey houses are wired with two ring circuits, one for the upper floor and the other for downstairs.
How many sockets can I have on a radial circuit?	Any number of socket outlets can be connected to a radial circuit, but this type of circuit can only serve a maximum floor area of 50sq m (60sq yd), and only then by using $4mm^2$ cable protected by a 30amp cartridge fuse or MCB (a rewirable fuse using bare wire is not permitted). A smaller radial circuit for a floor area of up to 20sq m (24sq yd) can be run in $2.5mm^2$ cable protected by a 20amp fuse of any type or a miniature circuit breaker.
What is the difference between flex and cable?	Cables with relatively heavy-weight metal conductors (wires) are used for the permanent wiring of a building. Most cables have three conductors – live (also known as line or phase), neutral and earth. There is also cable with four conductors for wiring two-way lighting that is controlled from separate switches. Flex (flexible cord) has conductors made up of many fine wires bunched together and is used to connect relatively small, often portable, appliances and light fittings to the permanent wiring system, usually by means of a three-pin plug.
When replacing a socket I noticed that the copper wire attached to the earth terminal wasn't insulated like the other two wires. Is this normal?	It is quite normal for this type of cable to have PVC-insulated live (line) and neutral conductors with a bare earth conductor lying between them. All three conductors are covered with an outer sheathing of PVC. However, when the earth conductor is exposed for connecting to a socket (or any other fitting) the bare wire should be covered with a yellow and green plastic sleeve that is available from any electrical supplier.
My cables are colour-coded red and black, but hasn't electrical colour-coding been changed?	The colour-coding of conductor insulation was changed for flexible cord with brown denoting live (line), blue for neutral and green/yellow for earth. Colour-coding for cable remained unchanged with red for live (line) and black for neutral. The earth conductor is uninsulated, but once exposed for connection must be protected with

green/yellow sleeving.

The only exception is the cable for two-way lighting which is colour-coded red, blue and yellow plus the usual uninsulated earth conductor.

How do I recognize out-of-date cable?

Old electrical cable was insulated and sheathed in rubber that made it more flexible than the modern white or grey PVC-sheathed cable. Rubber sheathing is normally matt black. Lead was also used to sheath some old cables.

Over the years, rubber insulation deteriorates and is often dry and crumbly. All old cable should be replaced as soon as possible.

What size cable should I use for domestic circuits?

The size of electrical cable is always specified in square millimetres. The chart below gives the recommended sizes for the major domestic circuits.

CIRCUIT CABLE SIZES		
Circuit	Size	Type
Lighting	1·0mm^2	Two-core and earth
Bell or chime transformer	1·0mm^2	Two-core and earth
Immersion heater	2·5mm^2	Two-core and earth
Storage heater	2·5mm^2	Two-core and earth
Ring circuit	2·5mm^2	Two-core and earth
Spurs	2.5mm^2	Two-core and earth
Radial — 20 amp	2·5mm^2	Two-core and earth
Radial — 30 amp	4·0mm^2	Two-core and earth
Shower unit	10·0mm^2	Two-core and earth
Cooker up to 12 kW	6·0mm^2	Two-core and earth
Cooker over 12 kW	10·0mm^2	Two-core and earth
Consumer earth cable	6.0mm^2	Single core
Meter leads	16·0mm^2	Single core
	All cable sizes in square millimetres	

What size flex should I choose for lighting and appliances?

Flex is rated in square millimetres according to the area of the cross section of its conductors and that is determined by the flow of current, measured in amps, that it can handle safely. The chart below shows the recommended sizes of flex that are matched to the power (wattage) of appliances and light fittings.

Conductor	Current rating	Appliance
0.5 mm^2	3 amps	Light fittings up to 720W
0.75 mm^2	6 amps	Light fittings and appliances up to 1440W
1.0 mm^2	10 amps	Appliances up to 2400W
1.25 mm^2	13 amps	Appliances up to 3120W
1.5 mm^2	15 amps	Appliances up to 3600W
2.5 mm^2	20 amps	Appliances up to 4800W
4.0 mm^2	25 amps	Appliances up to 6000W

What type of flex should I use for table lamps and appliances?

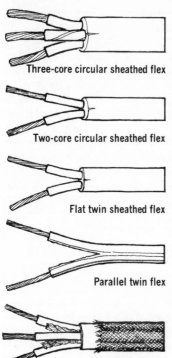

Three-core circular sheathed flex

Two-core circular sheathed flex

Flat twin sheathed flex

Parallel twin flex

Unkinkable braided flex

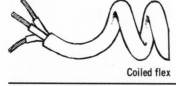

Coiled flex

A three-core (three conductors) circular sheathed flexible cord is the most commonly used for all types of appliance. It has colour-coded live (line), neutral and earth conductors insulated in PVC.

Double-insulated appliances are wired with two-core circular sheathed flex (without an earth conductor) because this type of appliance does not need to be earthed. The same flex is ideal for plastic pendant light fittings. (A metal lampholder must be wired with three-core flex.)

Table lamps and small double-insulated appliances are often wired with a flat twin sheathed flex with two colour-coded conductors insulated in PVC.

Hi-fi speakers are wired to an amplifier with a light-weight parallel twin flexible cord. The two conductors run side by side and both are insulated in PVC. The insulation is joined between the conductors by a thin web of plastic that can be pulled apart to separate the conductors ready for connection. This type of flex is not colour coded, but one conductor is identified with a stripe.

Appliances like kettles and irons are often wired with unkinkable braided flex. It has three colour-coded rubber-insulated conductors in a rubber sheathing that is bound on the outside with braided material.

Coiled flex, sold in standard lengths, stretches and retracts. It is ideal for portable lamps or appliances.

I want to extend the flex on a table lamp. Is it safe to tape a new length of flex to the one attached to the lamp?

Using insulating tape to join lengths of flexible cord is a dangerous practice. Instead, use a plastic flex connector made with metal terminals for the flex conductors. Alternatively, replace the short flex with a new continuous length of a similar type.

When I lifted my floorboards I noticed that the electric cables were simply lying loose on the ceiling below. Is this safe?

It is perfectly safe for cables to lie loose under floorboards provided they are secured to a joist with plastic cable clips or metal buckle clips near to the ceiling roses, junction boxes or sockets they are feeding.

How should I run cable across the line of joists between the floor and the ceiling below?

To run cable at right angles to the line of the joists, drill a series of 12mm ($\frac{1}{2}$in) holes, one through each joist along the line of the cable run. Each hole should be at least 50mm (2in) below the top of the joist so that floorboard nails will not penetrate the cable.

If I drill a hole for a cable in the joist next to the wall I can't get the cable up behind the skirting. What do I do?

If the joist is too close to the wall for you to be able to pass the cable up behind the skirting board to a socket outlet, cut a notch across the top of the joist, and once the cable is in place, screw a thick protective metal plate over it.

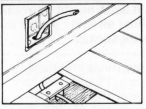

Screw a metal plate over a cable

How can I run a cable up behind a skirting board?

Cut a channel in the plaster behind a skirting board by drilling with a long masonry bit held at a shallow angle to the wall. If the skirting board is very deep you may have to extend the hole with a slim cold chisel. Use the same tool to rake out the debris from below and behind the skirting board.

Pass a length of stiff wire with a hook formed at one end behind the skirting. Attach the cable to the wire and pull it through while feeding the cable from below with your other hand.

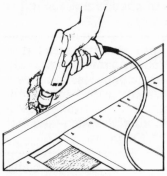

Drill at an angle behind a skirting

Is it safe to use a plug adaptor to run more than one appliance from a socket?

It's safe to use multi-outlet plug-in adaptors to run more than one small appliance from single sockets, but don't overload a circuit by plugging one adaptor into another. Nevertheless, having to use an adaptor indicates that you do not have sufficient sockets to meet your needs. You should consider swapping your single sockets for double ones, adding spurs to install additional sockets or extending the ring circuit itself.

Can I simply fit a double socket in place of a single one?

You can replace any single socket with a double: the wiring is identical. However, if you want a flush-mounted socket, you will have to chop a recess in the wall with a bolster chisel to fit the larger metal mounting box.

Can I convert a single socket into a triple?

Yes. There are very slim surface-mounted plastic pattresses that are mounted directly over an existing flush-mounted metal box. No additional wall fixings are required as the pattress is screwed directly to the mounting box itself. The existing wiring is connected to a three-gang fused socket.

Similar two-gang sockets and pattresses are available.

I still have a few round-pin sockets in my house. Is it safe to use them?

Provided the house has been rewired with modern cable and the socket outlets are in good condition, there is no immediate danger except that round-pin plugs are not fused. As soon as you can, have the wiring checked and install square-pin sockets.

Can I have a socket outlet in my bathroom?

No socket outlets should be fitted in a bathroom except approved shaver sockets that conform to BS 3052.

At what height above the floor should I install a new socket?

The optimum height for a socket outlet is 225 to 300mm (9in to 1ft) above the floor.

Are flush-mounted sockets and switches safer than surface-mounted ones?

A flush-mounted socket projects from the wall by no more than the thickness of its faceplate which is about 9mm ($\frac{5}{16}$in). A surface-mounted plastic box (pattress) plus the socket faceplate projects something like 45mm ($1\frac{3}{4}$in) and consequently there is a slightly greater risk that the fitting could become broken by being struck by a vacuum cleaner, perambulator or child's tricycle. In all other respects the method of mounting sockets or switches does not affect their safety.

What is a fused connection unit?

A fused connection unit is used instead of a socket to connect a fixed appliance to a power circuit. The circuit-cable conductors and the appliance flex (sometimes a cable) are connected to terminals at the back of the unit. Each connection unit contains a small cartridge fuse.

Some connection units are made with switches so that you can isolate appliances from the mains.

How many sockets should I install in my kitchen?

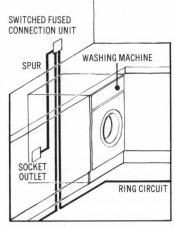

SWITCHED FUSED CONNECTION UNIT

SPUR

WASHING MACHINE

SOCKET OUTLET

RING CIRCUIT

Wiring a socket for a machine

This depends, of course, on the size of the kitchen and the number of work stations within it, but you should fit a minimum of four double sockets mounted 150mm (6in) above the worktops. Fit more sockets if you have a lot of small appliances, or you could fit a proprietary ready-wired socket track that incorporates several outlets along a moulded-plastic strip. Connecting one end of the track to the ring circuit provides power to all the outlets.

You can plug large appliances like a fridge, dishwasher or washing machine into a standard socket outlet. However, with these appliances fitting snugly under worktops it is difficult to reach sockets mounted directly behind them. The best method is to mount a switched fused connection unit above the worktop and wire it into the ring circuit, then run a spur to a socket outlet behind the appliance. You will be able to switch the appliance on and off conveniently using the connection unit.

Why can't I plug an electric cooker into a normal socket?

Apart from a microwave oven, electric cookers should not be connected to a ring circuit. These appliances need their own individual radial circuits running from separate fuseways in the consumer unit. A circuit for a cooker with a loading of up to 12,000W (12kW) must be protected with a 30amp fuse and should be wired in 6mm^2 cable. A cooker with a loading greater than 12kW requires a 45amp circuit fuse and must be fed with 10mm^2 cable.

What is a spur?

A spur is a branch cable connected to a ring or radial circuit in order to feed a socket or fused connection unit. The spur cable can be run from the back of a socket or a junction box on the circuit (non-fused spur) or it can be connected to the circuit by means of a fused connection unit (fused spur). Don't connect a spur to a socket or fused connection unit that is already feeding a spur or is itself fed by a spur cable.

How many spurs can I connect to a circuit?

You can have an unlimited number of fused spurs, but the number of non-fused spurs must not exceed the number of socket outlets and items of stationary equipment already connected to the circuit. Each double socket counts as two sockets for this calculation.

How many sockets can I have on a spur?

To comply with the Wiring Regulations, each spur can feed one single or one double-socket outlet.

How should I wire a waste-disposal unit to avoid accidents?

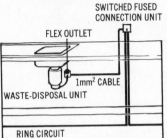

Wiring for a waste-disposal unit

The waste-disposal unit itself is housed in the kitchen-sink base cupboard, and is connected to the sink waste outlet. To wire it safely, and reduce the risk of it being operated accidentally, mount a switched fused connection unit 150mm (6in) above a worktop, conveniently close to the sink but out of reach of someone using it. Label the unit 'Disposal'.

From the unit run a 1mm² cable to a flex outlet (a fitting with terminals for joining appliance flex to circuit wiring) mounted next to the waste-disposal unit. Connect the waste-disposal unit flex to the flex outlet.

Does it matter which way up a light switch is mounted?

A standard one-way switch will work just as well upside down, but switch faceplates are conventionally mounted so that their rockers are depressed at the top when the light is off. The backs of faceplates are marked 'top' to ensure that switches are not mounted upside down.

What is an RCCB?

The term residual-current device (RCD) is often used to describe an RCCB.

A residual-current circuit breaker (RCCB) is a device that protects a circuit by switching off the power immediately it detects an imbalance of current in the live (line) and neutral conductors caused by an earth leakage. RCCBs are built into some consumer units to protect whole-house circuitry, as separate devices for mounting near existing consumer units, as part of a socket outlet and even as a plug-in adaptor or three-pin plug to protect an individual appliance or power tool.

What is supplementary bonding?

All non-electrical metallic components such as pipes, baths, radiators and so on could become dangerous if they were to come into contact with a live (line) conductor. For this reason these components must be connected one to another by an earth conductor which itself is connected to the earthing block in the consumer unit. This is known as supplementary bonding. A qualified electrician can test whether the supplementary bonding in your house conforms with the Wiring Regulations.

What is PME?

Protective multiple earthing (PME) is a system of protection employed by the Electricity Board in some areas whereby earth-leakage current is fed back to the substation by means of the neutral return wire, and so to earth. If you live in a house with PME you should employ an electrician to undertake all but the most minor type of electrical work.

What can I do if there are no spare fuseways in my consumer unit for new electrical circuits?

Individual radial circuits for cookers or showers, for example, can be run back to a double-pole switchfuse unit – a small box that has a single fuseway (or MCB) plus its own isolating switch. The unit is mounted near the existing consumer unit for the Electricity Board to connect to their meter and the consumer's earth terminal.

If you plan to install several new circuits – for a storage-heater system, for example – then it's worth installing a second consumer unit.

Is an electric-powered shower safe to use?

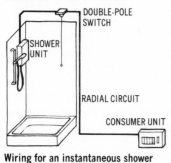

DOUBLE-POLE SWITCH

SHOWER UNIT

RADIAL CIRCUIT

CONSUMER UNIT

Wiring for an instantaneous shower

An electric-powered instantaneous shower is perfectly safe provided it is installed correctly. It must be fed by a separate radial circuit, using $10mm^2$ cable and protected by a 45amp circuit fuse. Although a shower has its own built-in on/off switch, there must be a separate isolating switch in the circuit. The switch must be out of reach of anyone using the shower. The most practical way of conforming with this regulation is to install a ceiling-mounted switch.

Choose a 45amp double-pole switch with a contact gap of at least 3mm and preferably with a neon 'on' indicator. The shower unit, metallic pipes and fittings must be 'supplementary' bonded to earth.

Can I put lighting in the garden myself?

You should hire an electrician to wire mains-powered outdoor lighting, but you can install low-voltage lighting yourself. Outdoor-lighting kits are available comprising a transformer that reduces mains voltage to 12 volts, lengths of flex, plus a number of light fittings.

Unless the manufacturer's instructions state otherwise, you can run the flex across the ground without further protection, but don't let it trail over stone steps or other sharp edges that could damage the flex insulation. Don't bury the flex with earth or grass in case someone accidentally severs it with garden tools. If you need to extend the flex use a waterproof cable connector, available from any electrical supplier.

Install the transformer indoors close to a socket outlet. Connect the outdoor-lighting flex to the 12 volt transformer terminals.

How can I run the flex from my garden-pool pump to the transformer indoors?

Electric pumps for fountains and waterfalls are placed underwater on the bottom of the pond. To run the pump flex to the house, first take it through a short length of plastic pipe or garden hose laid underneath the paving stones forming the edge of the pond. In order to be able

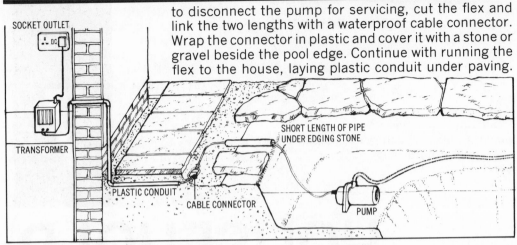

SOCKET OUTLET

TRANSFORMER

SHORT LENGTH OF PIPE
UNDER EDGING STONE

PLASTIC CONDUIT

CABLE CONNECTOR

PUMP

to disconnect the pump for servicing, cut the flex and link the two lengths with a waterproof cable connector. Wrap the connector in plastic and cover it with a stone or gravel beside the pool edge. Continue with running the flex to the house, laying plastic conduit under paving.

Running flex to a garden-pool pump

Can I run electrical cable underground from my house to the garage?

Any cable that is to be buried must be sheathed in PVC.

Special armoured cable and mineral-insulated copper-sheathed (MICS) cable can be run underground without further protection, but they should be buried at least 500mm (1ft 8in) below the surface, even deeper under areas such as vegetable plots where there is likely to be digging. It is best to avoid these areas altogether, but you can provide extra protection by laying a row of housebricks on each side of the cable to support protective paving slabs. Bury the cable itself in sand before covering the slabs with earth.

Ordinary PVC-insulated and sheathed cable can be run underground provided it is protected by impact-resistant plastic conduit. Bury and protect it carefully as described above.

To avoid having to dig up a concreted area, how can I safely run electric cable overhead from my house to a workshop?

Ordinary PVC-insulated and sheathed cable can be run overhead from one building to another provided it is at least 3.5m (12ft) above the ground and it is supported at each end so that there is no strain on the conductors or a likelihood of the plastic sheathing being chafed. If the cable is run through rigid steel conduit the height it is suspended above the ground can be reduced to 3m (10ft). Metal conduit must be earthed. If the cable is to be suspended over a driveway accessible to vehicles, it must be at least 5.2m (17ft) above the ground whether it runs through conduit or not.

If the distance between the buildings is no more than 3m (10ft) the cable can be slung unsupported or through a steel conduit. Over greater spans the cable must be supported by a catenary wire stretched taut between buildings, and to which the cable can be clipped or hung from slings. The catenary wire must be earthed.

If PVC-insulated and sheathed cable has to run up the outside of the house it must be protected by a conduit.

Can I run electric cable along a garden fence?

No, a fence is too flimsy, but you can run it along a garden wall.

HOUSEHOLD REPAIRS

This chapter deals with repairs to the fabric of the house – the walls, ceilings, roof, doors and windows – those jobs that many people prefer to leave to a builder. Even so, it pays to be well informed so that you can brief your builder with confidence, or simply to be reassured that certain things are as they should be. Then there are some repairs that are so simple that it would be a pity to have to hire professional help when you could easily do them yourself. Whatever you decide, do make sure that urgent repairs are not neglected for too long – eventually they will lead to even more trouble and expense ●

What are loadbearing walls?	Loadbearing walls are structural walls that transmit the weight of the roof, floors and other internal loads to the foundations. Loadbearing walls are usually made of brick or loadbearing concrete blocks, but in some cases they are timber framed. A wall may also be considered to be loadbearing where it is adding to the stability of the structure by stiffening an adjacent wall even though it might not be supporting a vertical load itself. Consult a builder or surveyor before you make any alterations to loadbearing walls.
What is a cavity wall?	A cavity wall is a relatively modern form of external-wall construction that is more efficient in preventing moisture penetration and heat loss than most solid walls. It is made with two 100mm (4in) thick walls or 'leaves' separated by a 50mm (2in) gap. Bricks, concrete blocks, clay blocks, timber framing or a combination of these materials may be used in its construction. Metal ties placed at regular intervals are used to join the two leaves together.
What are partitions?	Partitions are internal dividing walls that can be loadbearing or non-loadbearing. Bricks, concrete blocks, clay blocks or timber framing may be used in their construction and they are usually finished with a plaster coating or with sheets of plasterboard on both sides.
What is a lath-and-plaster wall?	A lath-and-plaster wall is a traditional timber-framed partition wall that uses wooden laths nailed to the studs as a backing for a plaster rendering.
What are party walls?	Party walls are those which separate houses built side by side as in a terrace. They are usually of solid construction designed primarily to prevent the spread of fire and reduce the transmission of sound.
What is a nogging?	A nogging is a short length of wood nailed horizontally between wall studs or floor joists to stiffen them and provide a fixing for plasterboard or chipboard flooring.
Can I remove a wooden stud partition myself?	If the wall is non-loadbearing you can dismantle it yourself. It is a messy job, so fit a dust sheet over the room door and leave the window open while you are working. First, disconnect or reroute any electrical fittings and cables that will be affected by the demolition. Prise off the skirting and any other mouldings such as a picture rail. Hack off the lath and plaster or plasterboard covering, putting the debris in plastic bags. Knock out the noggings and studs, and remove all the surrounding framework. Repair the holes left in the ceiling and walls, and if necessary, fill the gap between the floorboards.

How do I work out the size of the rolled steel joist I need?

Rolled steel joists, or RSJs as they are commonly known, are stiff I-section beams that are often used as load-bearing lintels to support the wall above when two rooms are knocked into one.

The joist should be wide enough to support the width of the wall above it and it must be deep enough to carry the load without bending. When calculating the depth of an RSJ builders will often use a rule-of-thumb method whereby they will allow 25mm (1in) on the depth for every 300mm (1ft) that the joist must span. The next largest standard size would be used.

Always have the size of an RSJ checked by your Building Control Officer and consult an architect or structural engineer for a more accurate specification.

How do I locate the positions of joists or wall studs?

With standard floorboards, look for the line of the fixing nails to locate the position of floor joists. However, with 'secret-nailed' tongued and grooved floorboards it is not so straightforward. The joists will run at right angles to the boards and you can approximate their positions by measurement. Joists are typically 400mm (1ft 4in) apart to their centres. Assuming the first joist is 50mm (2in) from the wall, roughly mark out their positions. A series of small drill holes along a joint between boards will pinpoint a joist.

A simple way to locate plaster-covered ceiling joists or wall studs is to tap the surface listening for the change in tone – the deeper tone indicates a space behind the plaster while a higher tone indicates the position of solid wood. A series of small drill holes will help locate it precisely.

You can also use a battery-powered metal detector, available from DIY stores, to locate studs by seeking the fixing nails that are usually placed down their centres.

What sort of plaster can I use on my wall?

It will depend on what you are plastering. If you are patch-repairing the surface of a plastered wall you could use a cellulose filler. For larger repairs that may expose structural parts of the wall you could use a one-coat plaster. Manufacturers claim that this can be applied up to 50mm (2in) thick in one coat.

If you are intending to plaster a new wall of brick or concrete blocks, then you could use an undercoat plaster followed by a finishing plaster. The most common undercoat plasters are pre-mixed lightweight-aggregate gypsum plasters known as 'browning' and 'bonding'. Each is formulated to suit backgrounds with different suction values. Browning plaster is used for normal-suction brick and block walls while bonding plaster is for low-suction materials such as dense bricks or blocks. A compatible finishing plaster can be applied to either type of undercoat plaster once it has set.

Plasterboard can be used to dry-line walls, and if it is applied grey face outwards, it can be given a coat of board-finish plaster.

I want to plaster a block-work wall. How can I ensure the plaster is of even thickness?

Level the plaster with a rule

Divide the area into manageable panels by nailing 10mm (⅜in) thick planed softwood battens known as 'screeds' to the wall. Place them about 600mm (2ft) apart and plumb them with a spirit level. Pack out any hollows as required.

Using a plasterer's trowel, apply an undercoat plaster between two of the screeds starting with the top right-hand corner of the panel. Build up the thickness of plaster, then level it with a straight piece of wood called a 'rule', scraping it up the faces of the screeds with a zig-zag motion. Fill any hollows in the plaster and level it again. Finally, scratch the surface lightly to provide a key for the top coat. Work across the wall, panel by panel, then let the plaster set. Remove the screeds and fill the gaps flush.

Apply a thin coat of finishing plaster, starting at the top left-hand corner of the wall. Screeds are not used for this stage of the work as it is relatively easy to judge the thickness of finishing plaster over the flat undercoat. You can use the rule to scrape the new surface level, but take care not to drag the wet plaster off the wall.

If you are using a one-coat plaster, fill out to the faces of the screeds, and after levelling, smooth the plaster with a trowel and leave it to set. Remove the screeds and fill the gaps.

Can I plaster over tiles or must I remove them?

It is not necessary to remove old tiles provided they are soundly fixed to the wall, but you must provide a key for the new plaster. Mix a slurry of 1 part cement to 2 parts sharp sand with a mixture of equal parts water and bonding agent until it has a thin creamy consistency. Stipple the slurry on the tiles with a stiff-bristle brush and allow it to dry for a day before applying an undercoat bonding plaster.

What is the best way to store bags of plaster?

Try to buy only as much plaster as you are going to need. Some DIY plasters are sold in non-porous plastic bags, but plaster used by professionals is invariably sold in paper sacks that absorb moisture over a period of time. Store paper sacks in dry conditions and keep them off concrete or earthen floors by placing them on wooden boards or plastic sheeting. If the atmosphere is damp, cover them with another sheet of plastic. Once a sack has been opened, store it in a plastic bag sealed with adhesive tape.

Is it still possible to obtain plaster overdoors?

You will often discover that decorative plaster overdoors have been removed from old houses in a misguided attempt to modernize a house. You can still buy reproduction plaster mouldings in various styles and sizes to reinstate the decorative detail once found over many an interior doorway. Overdoors are fitted in a similar way to reproduction ceiling roses.

Look in *Yellow Pages* or interior-design magazines for the names of suppliers.

How can I replace a plaster ceiling rose?

Assuming the original ceiling centre or 'rose' has been removed at some time in the past you must first buy a replacement. There is a wide range of plaster reproductions to choose from. If you are unable to determine the size and style of the old rose from marks on the ceiling, an example in another room or a neighbour's house, look through different manufacturers' catalogues to select a suitable example. Choose a plain or decorative version to suit the scale of the room and the style of any cornice moulding.

If no light fitting is present locate the centre of the room by snapping a taut chalked string held from corner to corner across the diagonals of the room. Where they cross marks the centre. If you plan to install a light fitting, move the centre mark over the nearest ceiling joist. Always switch off the electricity at the consumer unit before removing or installing a light fitting.

Hold the rose in position and mark around its edge with a pencil. Scratch the ceiling plaster within the marked area and locate the position of ceiling joists. Make screw-fixing holes through the timber-reinforced sections of the rose to coincide with the positions of the joists. Also make a central hole for the electric cable.

Dampen the back of the rose and the ceiling, then spread tile adhesive about 3mm ($\frac{1}{8}$in) thick on the back of the moulding. Press it into position and fix it with brass screws. Use a wooden prop with a foam-covered crossmember nailed to it to help support the rose if you are working alone. Use a filling knife to scrape away excess adhesive squeezed out around the edges of the rose. Cover the screw fixings with cellulose filler shaped to follow the contour of the moulding. Leave the filler and adhesive to set before painting the rose with thinned emulsion followed by a full-strength coat after the first coat has dried.

Connect your light fitting to the cables passed through the hole in the rose, then switch on the power.

Is it possible to replace ornate plaster cornices?

Yes. Plain and decorative fibrous-plaster cornices are still produced, often from the original moulds.

A cornice should complement the room in which it is to be installed. A simple moulding would suit a small bedroom, for example, while an elaborate cornice would look better in a lounge. Suppliers of fibrous-plaster mouldings would be pleased to give you advice and provide fixing instructions.

A small section of plaster ceiling is sagging. Can I replace it?

Rather than replace your sagging ceiling you could refix it. Prop up the sagging section and secure it with galvanized or plated washers held with plated countersunk screws driven into the ceiling joists. The washers should be at least 25mm (1in) in diameter and placed about 300mm (1ft) apart. The washers should embed themselves into the plaster so that you can apply a filler to conceal them.

What exactly is a vapour barrier and why do I need one?

When insulating materials are installed, the parts of the house outside the insulation are colder than those inside it. As a result condensation is likely to occur if moisture-laden air is allowed to contact the colder surfaces. The condensed moisture can reduce the efficiency of the insulation and may lead to dry rot breaking out on woodwork in unventilated areas of the house. A vapour barrier is designed to prevent water vapour passing through thermal insulation.

The vapour barrier itself is usually a thin plastic sheet or layer of metal foil which may be supplied as part of the insulant. A layer of impervious paint can also provide a barrier on a wall or ceiling. Any vapour barrier must be placed on the inside or 'warm' side of the insulation and it should be continuous if its efficiency is not to be impaired.

A builder has quoted a fortune for pointing my house. Can I do it myself?

Press mortar into the joints

Yes, but be prepared for a lot of hard work preparing the mortar joints between the bricks for the new pointing. Pointing can make or mar the appearance of brickwork so try not to smear the mortar over the bricks. Rake out the old mortar or use a special plugging chisel and heavy hammer to remove extra-hard sections of mortar. Recess the joints to not more than 25mm (1in) in depth and brush out the loose material. Wet the walls and mix a stiff mortar of 1 part cement to 1 part lime and 6 parts builder's sand.

Place the mortar on a 'hawk' (flat board) and pick up a strip of it on the back of a small trowel blade. Press this mortar into the vertical joints followed by the horizontal ones, working on a small area of wall at a time. Shape the mortar joints to recreate the style of the original pointing.

How do I make weather-struck pointing for my brick wall?

Trim excess mortar from the joints

Older houses are usually pointed with weatherstruck joints, sloped to shed rainwater from the wall.

After preparing the wall and applying mortar to the joints, use a small trowel to form a shallow slope in the vertical joints. Slope the joints to the left or right, but be consistent across the whole wall. Work a similar slope along the horizontal joints. The bottom edge of the mortar will be somewhat ragged and must be trimmed to a neat edge. Make a wooden straightedge that has packing pieces nailed to it to keep it about 6mm ($\frac{1}{4}$in) from the surface of the wall. Hold the straightedge level with the bottom of each joint and run a trowel along it to trim off excess mortar.

My brick walls seem to be flaking. What is the cause and what should I do about it?

Flaking brickwork, known as spalling, is the result of frost damage causing porous bricks to disintegrate. Rainwater will eventually penetrate spalled brickwork, causing damp patches on the inside of the house.

Provided the condition of the wall isn't serious, brush down the surface and paint it with a clear water repellent. If spalling is extensive and the natural appearance

of the brickwork is unimportant you can apply a stabilizing solution to bind the surface, then paint it with textured paint.

Quite often it is only individual inferior-quality bricks
that are prone to spalling. In these cases it is simple
enough to remove the affected bricks and replace them
with matching ones. Using a plugging chisel and club
hammer, cut out the mortar from around each brick and
prise it out. If the mortar is too hard to remove make a
series of holes in the brick with a drill and chop it out.

Dampen the hole and apply mortar to the bottom and
one end of it. Spread mortar onto the top and opposite
end of the dampened brick. Push the brick into place
and shape the joints to match the pointing of the surrounding brickwork.

How do I estimate how many bricks I will need?

First calculate the area of the proposed brickwork in
square metres or square yards, then allow about 58
bricks per square metre or 48 bricks per square yard
for a wall of one-brick thickness. Add about five per cent
to allow for breakages.

For a 225mm (9in) thick wall or a cavity wall with bricks
on both sides, double the amount calculated for a single-
skin wall.

Should I use second-hand bricks to build an extension?

If an extension is to look like an integral part of the building to which it is attached it is best to use second-hand
bricks to match as closely as possible the weathered
colouring of the original brickwork. You may have to pay
extra for second-hand bricks as they are likely to be in
short supply.

You can buy cleaned second-hand bricks from some
builders' merchants. If you buy them from elsewhere
make sure they are properly cleaned. Lumps of old
mortar make accurate bricklaying even more difficult
than usual and plaster can react with new mortar.

As an alternative to genuine old bricks you could look
for new multi-coloured or mottled brindled bricks which
closely resemble the originals.

What is the best way to finish off the top of our new garden wall?

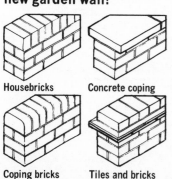

Housebricks   Concrete coping

Coping bricks   Tiles and bricks

The most convenient way to finish a garden wall would
be to lay a final course of housebricks across the width of
the wall. Alternatively, you could use special shaped
coping bricks laid in the same way. Coping bricks are
made to resist the rigours of weathering and are available in a choice of colours.

Ideally, copings should overhang the brickwork to
shed rainwater clear of the surface to reduce weathering
and staining. You can buy wide cast-concrete copings
for brick or stone walls, but real stone slabs are even
better. Alternatively, you can use a double course of
wide 'creasing' tiles under a course of coping bricks.

Is ready-mixed mortar as good as mortar you would mix yourself?

In terms of quality ready-mixed mortar is as good as any other and if you only need a small quantity for a job a bag of 'ready-mix' containing accurately mixed ingredients is a convenient way to buy it. However, it would not be cost effective for a large job. Because there is a tendency for the ingredients to settle during storage you should mix the entire contents of a bag or your mortar may not be consistent in quality.

What mortar mix should I use?

The mix will depend on the materials used for the mortar and whether the brickwork is to be constructed on an exposed or sheltered site. (See the chart below.)

The ingredients for a general-purpose mortar are cement, hydrated lime and builder's sand. The cement, and to some extent the lime, are hardening agents that bind the materials together. The lime also slows down the drying time, reduces shrinkage and generally makes the mortar easier to work. The sand gives extra body to the mortar.

Plasticizers are special additives that can be used as a substitute for lime. They produce an aerated mortar which is better for working in cold weather when freezing conditions could cause problems. Masonry cement already contains an aerating agent and only needs to be mixed with sand and water.

MORTAR MIXING PROPORTIONS	Cement/lime mortar	Plasticized mortar	Masonry cement mortar
General-purpose mortar (Moderate conditions)	I part cement I part lime 6 parts sand	I part cement 6 parts sand/ plasticizer	I part cement 5 parts sand
Strong mortar (Severe conditions)	I part cement ½ part lime 4 parts sand	I part cement 4 parts sand/ plasticizer	I part cement 3 parts sand

How much mortar will I need?

It will depend to some extent on whether the bricks or blocks are made with indentations or holes and also on how thick you lay the mortar. However, a typical single-brick thickness wall of plain bricks will require about ⅓cu m (11¾cu ft) of mortar for every 1000 bricks or 500 standard-size concrete blocks.

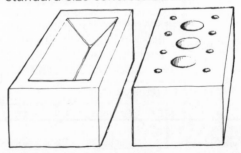

Some bricks have indentations (frogs), others are made with holes

What is the best way to cure squeaky floorboards and stairs?

Squeaks are caused by one piece of wood rubbing against another or rasping against fixing nails. To cure such problems with floorboards, drive the fixing nails in further using a nail punch and hammer, replace them with new slightly larger nails, or use special nails with serrated shanks for more grip.

Stairs can squeak where the tread or riser is jointed into the load-bearing string at each end, or where the tread meets the riser. Tighten the end joints by first removing the wedge from the offending joint and hammering it back in place after applying PVA glue. A tongued and grooved joint is commonly found between the riser and the tread, with glued blocks fitted inside the angle. Replace missing blocks and inject PVA glue into the joint. Drive a couple of countersunk screws through the tread to pull the joint together and provide extra support.

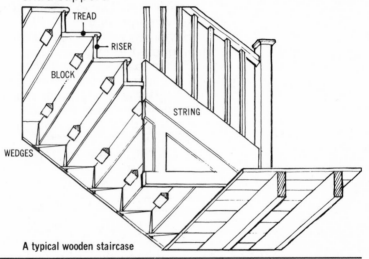

A typical wooden staircase

How can I lift a tongued and grooved floorboard?

This is more difficult than with ordinary butted floorboards because the jointed edges prevent the blade of a bolster chisel being inserted between the boards in order to prise them up. Use a tenon saw or special floorboard saw to cut along both sides of the board you want to lift. Tap a thin-bladed bolster chisel into one of the cuts and prise up the board, working progressively along its length. If you need to lift more than one board, prise up the remainder from underneath by placing the bolster between the boards and the floor joists.

When refitting the boards, first pull out the 'secret' fixing nails. Fix the boards with new nails driven in at an angle into the shoulder of the tongue. Fix the last boards with lost-head nails through the top surface.

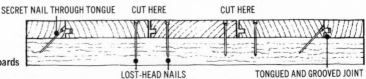

Fixing tongued and grooved boards

Can I replace my old floor-boards with chipboard?

If your floorboards need replacing you can use flooring-grade chipboard as an inexpensive, practical, if less attractive, alternative. Use only flooring-grade chipboard which is available as 18mm ($\frac{3}{4}$in) square-edged boards or 22mm ($\frac{7}{8}$in) tongued and grooved boards. You can use the 18mm ($\frac{3}{4}$in) thick boards over joists not more than 400mm (1ft 4in) apart, but use the thicker boards to span joists up to 600mm (2ft) apart. For areas such as bathrooms or kitchens where damp conditions are likely to occur, use a moisture-resistant variety of the flooring-grade board.

How do I lay chipboard flooring?

There are two methods, depending on whether you are laying square-edged boards or ones made with tongued and grooved edges.

All the edges of square-edged boards must be supported. Lay these boards with their long edges falling on the centre of a joist. You may have to cut them to width to achieve this. Nail 75×50mm (3×2in) softwood noggings (short crosspieces) between the joists to support the ends of the boards. Fix the boards with 50mm (2in) annular-ring nails spaced about 300mm (1ft) apart.

Lay tongued and grooved boards with their long edges across the line of the joists and with their short edges centred on joists. Support the edges of boards next to the walls with noggings.

Lay the first board in one corner, leaving a 10mm ($\frac{3}{8}$in) gap between it and the wall. The tongued edges should face outwards away from the wall. Nail the board in place. Apply PVA adhesive to the end tongue and lay the adjacent board in the row. Continue in this way, gluing the joints between each board until you have covered the whole floor area. Stagger the end joints in each row.

Although this type of flooring is intended to be covered with carpet or tiles you can seal it with two coats of polyurethane for an inexpensive finish.

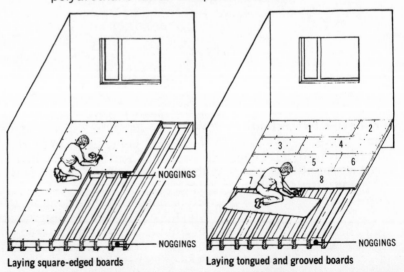

Laying square-edged boards   Laying tongued and grooved boards

How much concrete will I need?

Obtain the volume of concrete required for simple rectangular plots or pads by multiplying the length of the site by its width, then the resulting figure by the thickness.

Make a scale drawing of an irregular-shaped plot on squared paper, with each square representing one square metre. Calculate the volume of the whole squares as described above, then estimate the total area of the irregular portions to be able to calculate their combined volume.

How much sand, cement and aggregate will I need to mix concrete?

Calculate the volume of concrete required, then use the chart below to estimate the materials you will need. Three types of concrete mix are shown and the figures allow about 10 per cent for wastage. Read across the top of the chart to find the nearest figure in cubic metres, then read down the appropriate column to find the amount of ingredients you need. Use the ballast (combined sand and aggregate) figure as an alternative to the separate sand and aggregate figures.

CUBIC METRES OF CONCRETE	1.00	1.50	2.00	2.50	3.00	3.50	4.00	4.50	5.00
GENERAL-PURPOSE MIX									
Cement (50kg bags)	7.00	10.50	14.00	17.50	21.00	24.50	28.00	31.50	35·00
Sand (Cubic metres)	0.50	0.75	1.00	1.25	1.50	1.75	2.00	2.25	2.50
Aggregate (Cubic metres)	0.75	1·15	1.50	1.90	2.25	2.65	3.00	3.40	3.75
Ballast (Cubic metres)	0.90	1.35	1.80	2.25	2.70	3.15	3.60	4.05	4.50
FOUNDATION MIX									
Cement (50kg bags)	6.00	9.00	12.00	15.00	18.00	21.00	24.00	27.00	30.00
Sand (Cubic metres)	0.55	0.80	1.10	1.40	1.65	1.95	2.20	2.50	2.75
Aggregate (Cubic metres)	0.75	1.15	1.50	1.90	2.25	2.65	3.00	3.40	3.75
Ballast (Cubic metres)	1.00	1.50	2.00	2.50	3.00	3.50	4.00	4.50	5.00
PAVING MIX									
Cement (50kg bags)	9.00	13.50	18.00	22.50	27.00	31.50	36.00	40.50	45.00
Sand (Cubic metres)	0.45	0.70	0.90	1.15	1.35	1.60	1.80	2.00	2.25
Aggregate (Cubic metres)	0.75	1.15	1.50	1.90	2.25	2.65	3.00	3.40	3.75
Ballast (Cubic metres)	1.00	1.50	2.00	2.50	3.00	3.50	4.00	4.50	5.00

I'm having concreting sand, cement and aggregate delivered, but I can't start work until the weekend. How should I store them?

Keep loose sand and aggregate in separate piles on a firm base of concrete or thick plastic sheeting. To save space, bank them together with a deep separating board between them. Cover the piles with plastic sheeting if heavy rain is forecast.

Store bagged cement under cover in dry conditions. If you have to leave the bags outside, support them off the ground on boards covered with plastic sheeting, then cover them with more sheeting held down with bricks or stones.

When is it worth ordering ready-mixed concrete?

Ready-mixed concrete delivered to your site will save you a great deal of time and effort, but it is only worth considering for large jobs such as a patio or drive. Also, good access from the road is required for the delivery lorry to be able to deposit the load in a convenient spot, otherwise you will have to enlist the help of two or three 'labourers' to carry it in wheelbarrows from the road to the building site.

Allow about two hours to finish the work before the concrete begins to set. Working time can be increased by up to two hours by the addition of a retarding agent. You should discuss this possibility with the supplier when you order the concrete.

I want to lay a concrete drive. How thick should it be?

You must provide a sub-base of compacted hardcore to support a large slab of concrete such as a drive. This is usually a layer of broken bricks levelled with sharp sand. In most cases the thickness of the sub-base will be equal to that of the concrete itself, so be prepared to dispose of a lot of soil as you excavate the site.

Make the concrete slab for a drive or parking bay 100mm (4in) thick and lay a 100mm (4in) thick sub-base beneath it. If it will be used by relatively heavy vehicles such as delivery vans, increase the concrete thickness only to 150mm (6in).

A 100mm (4in) thick slab is adequate for a garage base, but thicken the edges to 200mm (8in) to provide support for the walls. Lay a 100mm (4in) thick sub-base.

You can use 75mm (3in) concrete without a sub-base for pedestrian pathways, but for larger pedestrian areas such as a patio, provide a 100mm (4in) thick sub-base for a 100mm (4in) thick concrete slab.

Do I need to build foundations for a garden wall?

Yes. All masonry walls should be built on firm footings (foundations). Dig a trench at least two bricks deeper than the footing itself so that the first two courses of masonry are below ground level. The recommended dimensions for footings are shown in the chart below.

Discuss special problems such as the location of service pipes, waterlogged ground, loose soil or tree roots with your local Building Control Officer.

RECOMMENDED DIMENSIONS FOR FOOTINGS			
Type of wall	Height of wall	Depth of footing	Width of footing
One brick thick	Up to 1m (3ft 3in)	100 to 150mm (4 to 6in)	300mm (1ft)
Two bricks thick	Up to 1m (3ft 3in)	225 to 300mm (9in to 1ft)	450mm (1ft 6in)
Two bricks thick	Over 1m up to 2m (Up to 6ft 6in)	375 to 450mm (1ft 3in to 1ft 6in)	450 to 600 mm (1ft 6in to 2ft)
Retaining wall	Up to 1m (3ft 3in)	150 to 300mm (6in to 1ft)	375 to 450mm (1ft 3in to 1ft 6in)

What sort of base will I need for a garden shed?

Garden sheds are relatively lightweight structures that can be supplied with or without wooden floors. When it has a floor you can build a shed on stout preservative-treated joists laid on well-compacted and drained earth stripped of vegetation.

A 75mm (3in) thick concrete slab, to be used with or without a floor, makes a more substantial base for a shed. To lay the base, first mark out the area with string 'lines'. Excavate the ground to twice the thickness of the concrete and about 150mm (6in) larger all round. Replace the lines and erect levelled formwork planks around the edges of the site to retain the concrete. Use wooden stakes to support the boards.

Having laid the sub-base, pour in the concrete, then compact and level it with a stout board scraped across the top edges of the formwork. Cover the slab with plastic sheet to retain the moisture and prevent cracking while the concrete sets.

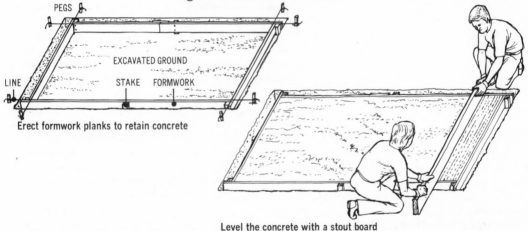

Erect formwork planks to retain concrete

Level the concrete with a stout board

We are thinking of laying a concrete patio, but I'm worried it will look cheap and boring. Is there any way to improve the appearance of concrete?

To improve upon the dull grey colour of concrete and add a pleasing texture, apply a layer of small stones to produce an exposed-aggregate finish.

Scatter well-washed pebbles, sold as fine aggregate for concrete mixes, onto freshly laid concrete. Tamp the pebbles into the concrete with a block of wood (stand on a wide plank laid on the concrete). Leave the concrete to partially set, then, using a fine water spray and a soft broom, brush the surface to expose the pebbles. Cover the concrete with plastic sheet for about 24 hours, then wash the surface again. Re-cover and leave the concrete to set hard.

I want to lay a vinyl floor-covering on a concrete floor, but the surface is very uneven. What can I use to level it?

You are right not to lay vinyl over an uneven floor as eventually the texture would show through the floor-covering. The best way to create a flat surface is to apply a proprietary self-levelling cement-based compound to the concrete.

Assuming your floor is sound and dry, first remove any loose dust. Mix the powdered compound with water to make a thin consistency following the manufacturer's instructions. Pour some of the compound in one corner of the room furthest from the door and spread it with a trowel to about 3mm ($\frac{1}{8}$in) thick, then leave it to find its own level. Work across the entire floor in the same way, joining one area of compound with another. You can walk on the floor after about an hour, but leave it for a few days to dry thoroughly before you lay any floorcovering.

I recently laid a concrete floor and now the surface seems to be breaking up. What should I do?

You probably overworked the concrete when you were levelling it with a trowel. This tends to leave a weak cement slurry on the surface which begins to break up after only a short period of time and does not provide a good base for a floorcovering. To stabilize the surface, collect all loose material with an industrial vacuum cleaner and apply two coats of PVA bonding agent thinned with five parts of water. If necessary, apply a self-levelling compound to reinstate a smooth surface.

The rendering on the outside of my house is cracked. Can I fill it with mortar?

Provided the movement that caused the crack has stabilized, you can make a repair using cement mortar or possibly exterior filler. Widen the crack with a cold chisel and club hammer. Dampen the wall and fill the crack with an exterior filler or, for a wide gap, use cement mortar made with 1 part cement to 4 parts builder's sand mixed with water plus a little PVA bonding agent to help it stick. After a few days paint the entire wall to avoid leaving a patchy appearance.

Last year I raked out and filled a crack in a smooth-rendered wall, but now a hairline crack has re-appeared. What can I do?

Filling a crack with mortar is usually sufficient to overcome the original problem, but in this case, reinforce the repair with fine scrim and bitumen. Fill the crack again and, when the mortar is dry, paint a 150mm (6in) band of bitumen base coat along the repair.

Embed strips of woven scrim (supplied with the base coat) into the bitumen and use a stippling action with a brush to press it home. Feather the edges of the bitumen with a foam paint roller. Allow 24 hours for the bitumen to harden, then apply a second coat and feather the edges. When the repair has set, apply two coats of reinforced exterior emulsion paint.

There is a crack running down the outside of my house. Does this neces-sarily mean serious structural failure?

No. Minor cracks in relatively new houses are often the result of shrinkage as the structure dries out, and they are not usually indicative of a serious fault. However, substantial cracks, particularly in older houses, may be the result of subsidence or heave which damage the foundations. Consult a builder or Building Control Officer for expert advice.

Cracks are appearing in the corner of my living room. Is that serious?

Cracks in interior surfaces are usually caused by differential movement where building materials expand or contract at different rates. These are not serious faults and you can repair them with cellulose filler. If cracks reappear you should get an expert opinion.

Alternatively, you can mask a crack along the corner where a ceiling meets a wall by applying a coving. Wooden, plaster and expanded-polystyrene covings, in various designs, are relatively simple to fit following the manufacturer's instructions.

Can I patch a hole in my roof lining?

Bitumen-felt roof linings are a secondary barrier to wind-driven rain or snow that might penetrate the roof-covering. Linings also provide some measure of insulation. They are supplied in rolled sheets and are laid across the rafters up from the eaves to the ridge so that each length overlaps the one below. Nailed tile battens hold the felt in place.

It is not really possible to make a successful repair from inside the roof although you can patch a tear in the lining temporarily with a square of felt stuck with mastic to the roof lining. The best course of action is to lift a small area of roofcovering in the vicinity of the tear and lay a large patch of felt over the hole. Tuck the top edge of the patch under the strip of felt above it and then replace the tile battens and roofcovering. This is really a job for a professional.

What is causing dark brown stains on the outside of my chimney stack?

This type of staining is caused by a breakdown of the chimney lining – a layer of cement rendering known as pargeting. Tar deposits are then able to migrate through the mortar of the brickwork to the outside.

The solution is to fit a flue liner in the chimney. It is possible to fit a sectional flue liner yourself, but it is a complicated procedure that requires the setting up of a safe working platform of scaffolding. It would be wiser to get quotations from specialists who can install a liner of lightweight concrete which is poured into the flue around an inflatable tube in the chimney. When the concrete has set, the tube is deflated and removed to leave a smooth-bored flue.

Can I patch a leaking flat roof?

You can repair splits in asphalt or roofing felt with little effort. For a small split, apply a gap-filling bituminous mastic applied with a filling knife. Spread the mastic about 1.5mm ($\frac{1}{16}$in) thick to cover the damage and at least 50mm (2in) all round. For splits more than 3mm ($\frac{1}{8}$in) wide, apply two layers of mastic with a strip of aluminium foil sandwiched between.

Alternatively, use a self-adhesive flashing tape. Apply the primer supplied with the tape following the manufacturer's instructions. Cut the tape to length, peel off the paper backing, then press it firmly in place.

Must I wait for dry weather before I can patch my flat roof?

Most repairs should be carried out in dry weather, but you can buy a trowel-on sealer that is specially formulated to provide an instant seal in wet conditions. Spread the sealant to fill the crack and leave it to set. Treat the surface with a compatible liquid-rubber waterproofer when the weather has improved.

I have patched my flat roof several times, but I can't afford to have it renewed yet. Is there some way I can extend its life?

You can buy brush-applied liquid waterproofer to extend the life of an old flat-roof covering. A bitumen-based waterproofer supplied with an open-weave glass-fibre reinforcing fabric would be suitable. First prepare the surface by removing all dirt and loose material. Treat traces of fungal growth with a fungicide and fill any splits with mastic.

Brush on the first coat of waterproofer and, while it's still wet, lay the fabric over it. Press the fabric into the waterproofer with a brush, using a stippling action. Where lengths of the fabric meet, overlap the edges by about 50mm (2in) and ensure they are well coated with waterproofer. After the first coat is dry, apply two more coats over the entire area, allowing each to dry in turn.

The cement-fillet flashing between the roof of my extension and the house wall is letting in water. What can I do about it?

Sometimes a cement fillet can detach itself from the wall due to thermal movement of the building materials. If the fillet itself is sound you can waterproof it by filling the gap with a gun-applied flexible caulking compound. Brush away any loose material, cut the tip off the cartridge nozzle to suit the width of the gap and inject the compound.

Fill the gap with compound

Is there a cost-effective way to repair our metal flashing?

You can use a self-adhesive aluminium-foil flashing tape that is sold in various widths. Choose one that will overlap the wall and roofing by at least 40mm (1½in).

Ensure the surfaces are dry and free from loose material. Cut the tape to the required length. Peel off the protective backing, about 1m (1yd) at a time, and press the tape down with a wooden seam roller or rub it firmly with a cloth pad.

Press the tape down firmly

How can I patch leaks in my conservatory roof?

If leaks occur along the glazing bars use a self-adhesive aluminium-foil tape to cover and seal the joints. Clean the surfaces thoroughly to ensure good adhesion. Work from the eaves up to the ridge. Cut the tape where one pane of glass overlaps another. Allow the cut end to overlap 50mm (2in) onto the pane of glass above and mould it into the stepped edge. Start the next strip overlapping the first by 50mm (2in).

If the glass is cracked, make a temporary repair with clear self-adhesive waterproofing tape. You can also use this tape to seal the overlapped edges of corrugated translucent plastic roofing.

How can I remove stains from marble?

Make a poultice from pulped blotting paper soaked in warm distilled water. Apply a 12mm ($\frac{1}{2}$in) thick poultice to the stained area and leave it to dry. As it does so the water is absorbed by the stone, loosens the dirt and is then reabsorbed into the poultice along with the dirt. Remove the poultice, then wash the surface with clean water and dry it with a soft cloth.

For oily stains, load a clean dry poultice pad with white spirit and apply it to the surface. After removing the poultice wash the marble with clean soapy water.

How can I protect the surface of marble against staining?

The simplest method is to apply a good-quality white wax polish with a soft cloth and burnish it.

For more porous stones, protect them against dirt by brushing on a coat or two of proprietary stone sealer.

How can I repair a broken cast-iron fire surround?

You might find a garage who will be willing to weld a broken cast-iron surround, but this is rather specialized work. However, if the break is clean and the parts fit perfectly you can make a satisfactory repair using a two-part epoxy glue.

Scrub the surround with hot soapy water to remove soot and dust, then clean the edges of the broken pieces with methylated spirits. Prop up the components of the surround so that gravity helps to hold the broken edges together, then apply the glue to the joint. As you fit the broken components, rock them slightly to help squeeze excess adhesive from the joint, then use cramps or strips of adhesive tape to bind the components to-gether. Clean glue from the surface of the surround with methylated spirits before it has time to set. If you feel it is necessary you can reinforce the inside of the repair with glass fibre.

Can I install a wood/coal effect gas fire?

There is no legislation to prevent you installing a gas fire and, provided you are competent and follow the manu-facturer's fitting instructions carefully, you could carry out the work yourself. However, it is advisable to hire a professional installer to make the actual connections to the gas supply. He or she will make the necessary tests on the gas supply, check the suitability and condi-tion of the flue and the provision for ventilation. You may also need expert assistance to make the electrical installations that are required for some appliances.

It isn't necessary to fit flue liners or chimney-pot terminals for most gas fires, but check with your local authority to see if this applies in your case.

Is it possible to repair a cracked fireback?

Cracks in an otherwise sound fireback can be filled with a fireproof cement. Remove the surface soot and rake out the cracks with the point of a trowel to provide a better key for the cement. Brush away all loose material and dampen the damaged area. Work the cement into the cracks with the trowel and fill them flush with the surface. Do not light a fire until the cement is dry.

What is the best way to seal off an unused fireplace?

Before you make the decision to seal off an unused fireplace consider whether there is a possibility that you might want to reinstate it as a working fireplace in the future. Reversing such a decision can prove to be an expensive operation. One option is to keep the fireplace as a purely decorative feature for the time being, otherwise the best solution is to remove it altogether and seal the opening.

Install a timber frame within the vacant opening and cover it with plasterboard or seal the opening with brick or lightweight concrete blocks. Cover the plasterboard or masonry with plaster to finish flush with the surrounding wall. Provide ventilation for the chimney with a plastic grille or an airbrick in the new closure.

How do I cut the bottoms off my doors to allow for the extra thickness of new carpet?

A carpet and underlay need a clearance of at least 12mm ($\frac{1}{2}$in). You can remove the door and trim the bottom edge with a power saw and electric planer. However, if there are a number of doors involved, it becomes economical to hire a carpenter who can cut the doors *in situ* using a special power saw.

I can't keep my door closed. What can I do?

A door that tends to spring open unless you apply force is probably 'hinge bound'. This occurs when, for one reason or another, the hinges are prevented from closing as intended.

Inspect the hinges to check if oversize countersunk screws have been used so that their heads are projecting. If so, replace them with similar screws of a smaller gauge. You will have to plug the old screw holes with wood and drill new pilot holes first.

Alternatively, the hinges may be set too deeply into the door or door frame. Remove the door and pack card behind the hinge leaves until they are flush with the surrounding wood and the door closes smoothly.

What knot should I use to tie a sash weight to its cord?

The cast-metal weights that counterbalance a sliding sash window are tied to the connecting cords with an especially secure knot.

Use only waxed sash cording and buy sufficient to replace both sides even if only one has broken. Make sure the new cording is the same thickness as the original cords.

Pass the end of the cord through the hole in the weight and make a loop about 75mm (3in) from the end. Take the end round the back of the cord to form a figure of eight, then pass the end through the first loop.

CORD

SASH WEIGHT

Sash-weight knot

One of my sliding sash windows is stuck. What can I do?

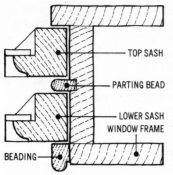

Section through sash-window mouldings

TOP SASH

PARTING BEAD

LOWER SASH
WINDOW FRAME

BEADING

If the sash is stuck with paint, work a filling knife between the sash and frame beading to break the seal. Open the sash and lightly rub the running surfaces with abrasive paper.

Alternatively, the wood may have swollen. This can be solved by lightly planing the edges of the sashes. Working from inside the room, prise off the beading on each side of the window frame. The lower sash can now be swung out from the frame, suspended on its cords, and the edges shaved with a block plane.

To do the same thing with the top sash also, prise out the parting beads from both sides of the frame. Pull the sash down and swing it clear of the frame.

Rub candle wax on the rubbing surfaces and reinstate the beadings.

Plane the edges of the lower sash

How do I take a door off its hinges?

Open the door and place a wedge under the bottom edge to support it. Clean out old paint that may be clogging the screws that hold the hinges in place. Remove the screws, starting with the bottom hinge. Steady the door as the last screw is extracted and get help to carry away a heavy door.

What is the best material to use for blocking off an unwanted interior doorway?

Cut blocks to match existing bonding

To block off a doorway, choose the same material used to construct the surrounding wall. These would be bricks or blocks for a masonry wall or wood for a timber-framed partition wall.

You can use plasterboard as a substitute for lath and plaster on a timber-frame wall, but fix it grey side out and coat it with finishing plaster to blend in with the old plaster around it.

Concrete blocks are convenient for infilling any masonry wall as their relatively large size makes them quick and easy to lay. To tie the infill into the wall, cut alternative courses of the blockwork into the sides of the old door opening to coincide with existing bonding.

My door is jamming against its frame. How can I cure it?

Check that the screws holding the top hinge have not worked loose, allowing the door to drop. Alternatively, the hinges may have become worn so that the pins are slack. You can buy new hinges or make the old ones last a little longer by swapping the top one for the bottom – this reverses the wear on the pins.

If the hinges seem to be in good condition, remove the door and skim the vertical stile with a plane.

As my door is opened, the bottom edge catches on the floor. How can I prevent it?

Fit rising butt hinges designed to lift the door as it swings open. If after fitting the door its top corner is scraping against the frame above it, plane a shallow bevel to provide a clearance.

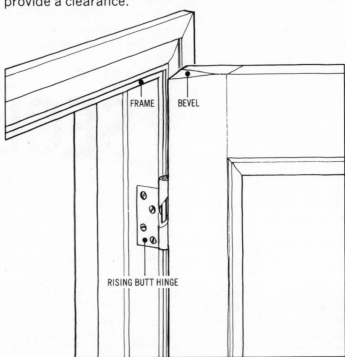

FRAME   BEVEL

RISING BUTT HINGE

Plane a bevel to clear the frame

HOME SECURITY

Each and every concerned householder will want to take reasonable precautions to protect themselves, their families and their home. If you are prepared to do the work yourself, home-security measures are not expensive, especially when compared with the costly repairs, replacements or rebuilding that could result from a break-in or even a small fire. The police and fire brigade appreciate the valuable contribution you can make to your own security and they are more than willing to offer advice and encouragement ●

Where can I get detailed advice on protecting my home?

Local authorities appoint a full-time Crime Prevention Officer who is available to give free advice on any aspect of home security. Telephone your nearest police station to make an appointment for the CPO to visit your home and suggest ways to improve your security measures. You can raise specific queries or simply ask the Crime Prevention Officer to inspect your property and make general recommendations.

Contact the Fire Prevention Officer at your local Fire Brigade Headquarters for similar advice on protecting your home and family against fire.

What is the best type of lock to fit on my front door?

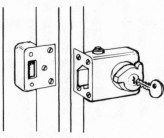

Automatic deadlocking rim latch

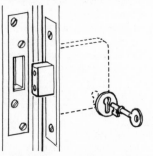

Mortise lock

Your final exit door, which is normally the front door onto the street, cannot be bolted once you have left the house. Consequently you must fit an especially strong tamper-proof lock.

Don't rely on a straightforward night latch – the type of lock that is operated by a latch key or a knob on the inside. A well-placed kick can burst its fixing screws from the woodwork and a thief can break a pane of glass to operate the latch from the inside or slide back its bolt with a plastic credit card. Either replace your night latch with an automatic deadlocking rim latch or provide additional security by fitting a mortise lock.

A rim latch locks automatically as the door is closed so that the bolt cannot be forced back without a key except by turning the knob on the inside. A turn of the latch key in the opposite direction prevents the lock being operated even from inside so that an intruder cannot walk out of your front door with your property.

The body of a mortise lock fits in a slot cut in the door itself where it is difficult to tamper with and cannot be displaced by force. A deadbolt is thrown by a key.

Choose a lock that conforms to British Standards (BS) 3621 which ensures that there are at least 1000 key variations and it will be impossible to cut through the bolts or drill into the body of the lock.

What type of lock can I use on a back door?

Mortise sash lock

A mortise sash lock is usually sufficient to secure a door that is not the final exit door from a house because additional bolts can be operated from the inside before you vacate the premises.

A mortise sash lock has a sprung latch bolt that is operated by a lever handle or a knob on each side of the door. A deadbolt that locks the door is thrown by a key from either side. Remember to remove the key, especially if the door is glazed. Make sure the lock is marked BS 3621.

Should I change my locks when I move into a new home?

You can never know who has a key to a new house and it is worth the expense of fitting new locks to all exit doors as soon as possible. If you buy identical locks they will fit snugly without having to recut the doors.

What is the most secure type of bolt I could fit to a door?

Mortise security bolt

A strong surface-mounted bolt with large fixing screws is acceptable, but a mortise security bolt is much better. This type of bolt fits into a hole drilled in the edge of the door and is operated by turning a special removable key. It is impossible to retract the bolt without a similar key and a considerable amount of force is required to break in. Fit one bolt near the top of the door and another near the bottom. One key will operate both bolts.

As my back door opens outwards, the hinges are on the outside. How can I prevent a thief driving out the hinge pins and removing the door?

Hinge bolt

You cannot prevent a thief dismantling an external hinge, but you can make sure he cannot remove the door afterwards. Fit a hinge bolt near the top and bottom of the door. A short metal 'bolt' driven into a hole in the edge of the door automatically locates in a reinforced hole in the surrounding frame as the door is closed.

Is it worth locking internal doors to hinder a burglar?

Once a burglar has broken into a house he can work undetected and locked doors will not deter him for long: not only will you have lost your property but you will be faced with a large repair bill.

If you live on your own there may be some value in locking yourself in your own bedroom, especially if you can call for assistance with a personal-attack button or telephone. However, leave the key in the door so that you can escape in the event of fire, and ensure there is an openable window in the room that will serve as a safe fire-escape route.

What type of lock can I fit to sash windows?

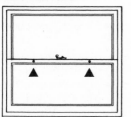

Fit two dual screws to a wide window

There are two-part sash-window locks that clamp the two meeting rails of the window together. The lock is operated by a removable key that should be stored to hand but out of reach of the window.

Dual screws are unobtrusive alternatives to a sash-window lock. A metal bolt, turned by a special key, passes through the front meeting rail and into a hole bored in the rail behind it, preventing either sash from sliding. Fit two dual screws in a large window.

If a sash window is never opened, the simplest solution is to screw the meeting rails together.

How can I leave a sash window open for ventilation without endangering a small child?

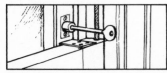

Sash stop

Sash stops allow a sash window to be opened to leave a slight gap at the top or bottom but prevent it being opened fully. This not only protects children from a potentially dangerous situation, but also prevents a burglar gaining access via the window.

A metal bolt is withdrawn from the upper-sash frame with a key, and a small metal plate protects the top edge of the lower sash. Fit a sash stop on each side of a wide window.

Is it necessary to lock small hinged fanlights?

It is worth locking a hinged fanlight even though you might consider it too small for a burglar to use. A thief can squeeze through any gap larger than the average human head, and many burglars use child accomplices. There are various simple locks for this type of window including those that bolt the metal stay to the frame.

Should I fit locks to upstairs windows?

If a window can only be reached with a ladder it is probably safe to use a simple catch, especially if that window is clearly visible from other houses. But fit a cheap key-operated lock to be certain. If a window, including roof skylights, can be reached via drainpipes, fences, walls or flat roofs it should be locked securely like any downstairs window.

How should I secure hinged casement windows?

There are many excellent locks for metal and wooden casement windows. Although these locks must be opened by means of a removable key, choose a type that locks with a simple push bolt or the turn of an integral catch. This alleviates the temptation to leave a window unlocked if you cannot locate the key.

I have fitted locks to my home, but one very vulnerable window has been broken twice. What else can I do?

A local blacksmith or garage can make a set of metal bars to protect an especially vulnerable window, but few people would welcome the feeling of living in a prison. A more unobtrusive solution is to fit a ready-made sliding metal grille that is folded away behind the curtains when not in use.

How can I secure louvre windows?

Glass-louvre windows have proved to be especially vulnerable to burglary. By folding back the soft-metal tabs that hold the louvre strips in place, all the glass in the window can be removed silently. In addition to fitting a special louvre-window lock, glue the glass strips in place with epoxy-resin glue.

How can I deter a burglar from climbing up my downpipe?

Paint the pipe with an 'anti-climb' paint that remains permanently slippery. To protect your pets and clothing don't paint the first 2.5m (8ft) of drainpipe.

I'm afraid to answer my front door to callers. What can I do?

The first thing you should do is fit a wide-angle viewer that fits in a 12mm ($\frac{1}{2}$in) hole drilled through the door. This will allow you to see a caller without opening the door. Fit a porch light so that you can identify a caller after dark.

Fit a security chain or a restraint bar to the door to prevent it being opened more than a few centimetres (inches). With the chain in position you can check the credentials of callers with confidence.

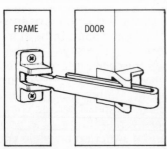

Restraint bar

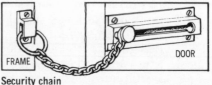

Security chain

Is double glazing a deterrent to burglars?

Double-glazed sealed units are relatively tough and will deter burglars to some extent but don't rely on double glazing alone as a security measure.

Is there a burglar-proof glass?

You can buy wired glass with a fine steel mesh incorporated during its manufacture. The mesh holds the glass together to prevent it disintegrating when broken.

Toughened or tempered glass is heat-treated to make it four to five times stronger than ordinary glass. This type of glass must be cut before the toughening process, but there are standard-size panes available from good joinery suppliers.

Laminated glass is made with a sheet of tough plastic sandwiched between two sheets of glass. The plastic helps absorb the energy from an object hitting the glass.

How can I decide what burglar-alarm system is best for my home?

From the cheap DIY variety to the expensive professionally monitored system, there are so many types of burglar alarm that it can be difficult to decide what is best for your situation. Reliability is an extremely important factor: your neighbours are likely to become less vigilant if they are constantly subjected to false alarms. In this respect a simple well-tried system is often the best, and make sure it meets with British Standards (BS) 4373 if it is to be professionally installed or BS 6707 if it is a DIY system.

Your local Crime Prevention Officer can suggest the type of system that would suit you best and specialist advice should also be available from your insurance company.

What is a passive burglar-alarm system?

A passive burglar-alarm system incorporates scanning devices that use infra-red, ultrasonic or radio waves to detect movement or the presence of a human being. A passive system is usually relatively simple to install and is especially suitable for small flats or open-plan dwellings. Passive systems must be designed by the installer to ensure that pets and small children who may leave their bedrooms during the night do not inadvertently set off the alarm. These systems are ideal for protecting premises that are empty during the day or perhaps vacated for extended periods. However, they can restrict your own movements to some extent and cannot normally be active while you and your family are awake.

What is a perimeter burglar-alarm system?

A perimeter system protects all the likely means of entry – basically the doors and windows – and sounds the alarm if they are breached or tampered with. This type of alarm system is usually backed up by one or two internal detectors of one sort or another in case the perimeter detectors are bypassed by a skilful burglar. Many people prefer a perimeter system to a passive system because it is designed to prevent a burglar even setting foot in your premises and the system can be switched on while you continue with your normal activities indoors.

What is a monitored alarm system?

The majority of systems rely on neighbours calling the police in response to an alarm, but there are inevitable delays especially if your neighbours are used to hearing false alarms. A break-in may occur when your neighbours are not at home or perhaps they live too far from your house to hear the alarm bell or siren.

The very best systems transmit a warning directly to a police station or to a professionally manned monitoring centre that can check your alarm call is genuine and respond immediately.

What is a personal-attack button?

Most alarm systems incorporate a personal-attack button or switch that can be situated near the front door or in a bedroom so that you can trigger the alarm manually if you are subjected to a physical attack or there is the threat of a break-in. The button will activate the alarm even when the rest of the system is switched off.

How can I be sure a burglar-alarm installer is reliable?

Although a Crime Prevention Officer cannot recommend an individual company or installer, he or she will give you a list of reputable firms that will design an alarm system to suit your requirements and supply you with a quote for installation.

Alternatively, you can contact the National Supervisory Council for Intruder Alarms who will send you a list of approved installers.

What sort of security lighting is worth installing?

There are two types of security lighting that are worth considering for a domestic situation – one type convinces a burglar that you are at home and the other type is designed to detect the presence of someone approaching your house.

In the first category there are light-sensitive switches that you can install in place of an ordinary wall-mounted switch. As darkness falls the switch turns on a light automatically and can be programmed to turn it off again up to eight hours later.

External security lighting is equipped with infra-red sensors to detect and illuminate a person or vehicle approaching the house and the light will remain on for approximately five minutes. The operational sequence is cancelled by daylight. Not only is this type of light an effective security measure but it also helps you park a car, find your door key and negotiate steps or pathways.

What can I do to identify my property?

A thief will find it difficult to sell stolen property that is marked indelibly with some form of personal identification and you will find it easier to reclaim marked property should it be found by the police. The method of marking you choose will depend on the nature of the property and whether you can mark it without spoiling its appearance. There are simple engraving or etching tools, and invisible-marking pens that leave telltale signs only under ultra-violet light. Inexpensive marker kits are available from stationers or your Crime Prevention Officer can arrange the loan of equipment. The best form of identification is your postcode followed by the number of your house/flat or the first two letters of its name.

If you cannot mark an object take a coloured photograph of it against a contrasting background and lay a ruler in the picture as a guide to the scale of the object.

How can I be sure a smoke detector will be reliable?

Only buy a smoke detector that conforms to British Standards (BS) 5446 Part 1.

Can I install a smoke detector myself?

The majority of smoke detectors are battery operated and all you have to do is screw them in place. Choose a detector with a test button to check periodically that the battery is charged (replace the battery annually) and the alarm is in working order. Other features to consider are a pause button for cancelling a false alarm (the detector resets itself after a few minutes) and a light that can lead you to a safe exit.

Where should I install a smoke detector?

The optimum position for a smoke detector is on the landing outside the bedrooms. Screw it to the ceiling or high up on a wall, but not in a corner where the 'dead-air' space can delay the efficient working of the alarm.

A smoke detector in my kitchen keeps sounding the alarm due to nothing more than ordinary cooking fumes and steam. What can I do?

You should replace it with a detector that has a built-in photo-electric cell that can differentiate between steam and smoke.

Will a smoke detector tell me if there is a gas leak in my home?

A smoke detector is not sensitive to gas fumes, but there are special alarms that will detect gas in a room before it reaches a dangerous concentration. Gas alarms are connected by means of a three-pin plug to the mains electricity supply.

Fit a gas alarm in the room where your boiler, cooker or fire are installed. Screw it to the wall about 300mm (1ft) from the ceiling to detect natural gas. If you are using bottled gas, install an alarm about 300mm (1ft) from the floor.

In the event of an alarm sounding, open doors and windows and do not smoke or operate an electrical switch. Check quickly to see if there is an obvious reason for the gas leak – pilot light blown out, gas tap turned on – and if a cause cannot be identified, leave the house immediately and ring the local gas supplier to report an emergency.

How should I deal with a chip-pan fire?

Never attempt to move a chip pan containing burning fat or oil. Turn off the source of heat and smother the fire with a proprietary fire blanket (BS 6575) or a pan lid. If you have nothing else, soak a towel in water, wring it out and drape it over the burning pan. Let the pan cool for at least 30 minutes before removing the blanket.

Never use a fire extinguisher or water to put out a chip-pan fire and if possible replace your frying pan with a thermostatically controlled fryer with a lid.

What is the best general-purpose fire extinguisher for my home?

For domestic premises and home workshops, choose a fire extinguisher containing dry powder. It can be used to tackle most small fires including those caused by electrical faults. Don't attempt to extinguish burning gas – turn off the gas supply and then tackle the fire. If the gas supply cannot be turned off safely, leave the fire brigade to put out the fire.

Don't attempt to tackle any fire if there is a possibility that your escape route might be cut off by flames or smoke. If gas cylinders are threatened by fire or the fire continues to spread, retreat calmly closing doors behind you. Call the fire brigade.

What should I do if my chimney catches fire?

Phone the fire brigade immediately, then stand a fire-guard in the fireplace to prevent burning material falling into the room and, if possible, remove hearth rugs. Leave the room, closing windows and doors behind you, and get everyone out of the house.

9

WORKING
OUTDOORS

Many a householder who lacks the confidence to repair or decorate the house
seems to find the idea of working in the
garden far less intimidating. Perhaps
there's the feeling that the level of
accuracy demanded to lay paving or build
a low wall is not the same as that required
to carpet the living room or plaster the hall-
way. Whatever the motivation, working
outdoors is often seen as a more pleasur-
able and relaxed activity, but it's one that
generates just as many queries ●

I'm concerned about a tree growing near my house. Should I have it cut down?

If a large tree appears to be in danger of falling you should seek the advice of a qualified tree surgeon to avoid the possibility of it damaging the house or injuring passers-by.

A tree growing very close to a building can absorb moisture from the site causing the foundations to subside as the supporting earth collapses. However, felling a tree can be just as damaging because surrounding soil swells with excess water that was once taken up by the tree's root system. The upward movement known as heave can distort foundations and crack masonry as effectively as subsidence.

Some trees are protected by a preservation order and you could be prosecuted if you were to have them cut down without permission. It is always worth seeking professional advice from a tree specialist and/or a structural surveyor before felling trees close to your home.

I am planning to plant several new trees. How far from the house should I plant them?

Try to ascertain the likely spread of a tree's root system before planting it close to a building or underground drainage pipes. As a rough guide make sure there is a distance of at least two thirds of a tree's mature height between it and nearby buildings, and in the case of poplars, elms and willows, their full mature height.

Do I have to erect a fence with the 'good' side facing my neighbour?

There is no legislation that could be used to force you to construct a fence facing in a particular direction, but the unwritten rule suggests that a good neighbour always erects the posts and rails facing his or her own property. However, check the line of the boundary so that you do not encroach upon your neighbours' property, and get permission to trespass on their side of the boundary during the construction of the fence.

My fence panels are in good condition, but several posts have rotted at ground level. Must I replace them or is there some way to extend their usefulness?

To save buying new fence posts you can brace what's left with a concrete spur – a short post that is bolted to the upper section of the original wooden fence post.

Having removed the rotted post stump from the ground, lower the spur into the hole, positioning it against the post. Pack hardcore around the base of the spur, bolt it to the post, then infill with concrete.

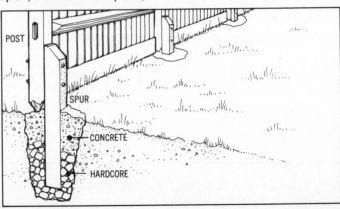

Concrete spurs support rotted posts

Is it safe to grow ivy on a house wall?

If you allow ivy to grow on an old wall with weak mortar joints or broken rendering, then there is a risk that the plant's aerial roots will invade the material, searching for moisture. However, if the wall is in good condition with sound pointing, the plant will flourish without harming the masonry. Don't allow ivy to block your gutters or grow onto the roof.

How can I protect new fence posts from rot?

Most wooden fence posts are pre-treated to prevent rot. However, you can provide additional protection by soaking the base of the post in a bucket of preservative for one hour.

As wooden fence posts tend to rot are there any alternatives I could consider?

There are angle-iron posts for chain-link wire mesh fencing, but they do not make for an attractive garden fence.

Reinforced-concrete posts are marginally better. There is a variety of 100mm (4in) square posts for different styles of fence. There are pre-drilled posts for chain-link fencing, mortised posts for arris rails and grooved posts to take pre-fabricated fence panels.

There are also plastic posts, but most of them have to be reinforced with wooden inserts for fences over 750mm (2ft 6in) in height.

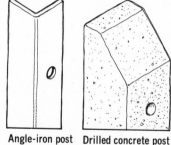
Angle-iron post   Drilled concrete post

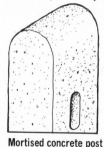
Mortised concrete post

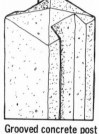
Grooved concrete post

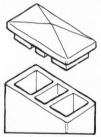
Capped plastic post

Will a freshly creosoted fence harm my plants and shrubs?

Creosote is harmful to plants, but there are several general-purpose wood preservatives that are specifically formulated for use on horticultural woodwork. Apply three brush coats to a fence or leave timber immersed for an hour if it is to be buried below ground.

I have a closeboard fence with broken arris rails. Can I repair them or must they be replaced?

When a closeboard fence is buffeted by high winds, the horizontal arris rails take much of the strain and frequently break, usually where the rails enter the posts but sometimes in the middle of a rail. You can buy galvanized-metal brackets to repair this type of rail.

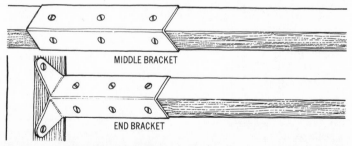
MIDDLE BRACKET

END BRACKET

Repair arris rails with brackets

I want to construct a side-entrance gate beside my house. What sort of gate should I be looking for?

Side-entrance gates are designed to prevent intruders gaining easy access to the rear of the building. Consequently, look for a gate that is 2m (6ft 6in) in height and sturdily built. Good-quality wooden gates are made from cedar or oak and are constructed with stout sections of timber that are braced with strong diagonal members to keep them rigid. A vertically boarded gate – tongued and grooved or closeboarded – is relatively difficult to climb.

You can close off a side-entrance with a wrought-iron gate, but make sure it is not designed in such a way that it forms a ladder.

What bricks are suitable for use outside?

The names attributed to bricks such as London Stocks, Leicester Reds, Blue Staffs and so on usually reflect their place of origin where an indigenous clay imparts a particular colour to a brick. Alternatively, such names may be chosen by a manufacturer to suggest an association with a reputable brick-making tradition, and as such cannot be relied upon as a guide to their suitability for a specific use or location.

Look for a range of 'facings', bricks that are suitable for any type of exposed brickwork. They are both water resistant and frost resistant, and as facings are intended to be visible, they are available in a wide range of colours and textures.

There are 'special-quality' bricks that will withstand extreme weathering and exposure, but 'ordinary-quality' bricks are suitable for most external locations.

The term 'seconds' refers to second-hand rather than second-rate bricks and are much sought after for their subtle colouring that blends with existing structures. As a result high prices are sometimes asked for seconds.

What size posts should I use for hanging a gate?

You can use standard 100mm (4in) hardwood fence posts for a small garden gate, but use 125mm (5in) posts for a 2m (6ft 6in) high side-entrance gate.

Hang wide gates across a driveway from 150 to 200mm (6 to 8in) square posts.

Brick piers should be at least 325mm (1ft 1in) square and built on a flat concrete footing. For heavy gates, reinforce the hinge pier with a metal rod or scaffold pole anchored in the concrete footing and rising vertically through the centre of the pier.

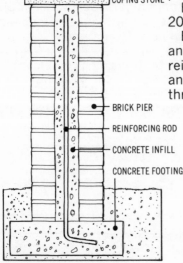

COPING STONE

BRICK PIER

REINFORCING ROD

CONCRETE INFILL

CONCRETE FOOTING

A reinforced brick pier

I want to terrace my garden with stone retaining walls. How do I go about it?

A series of low retaining walls can be used to divide a steeply sloping site into several terraces. Cut the site into steps, excavating the soil at the base of each bank to lay a 100mm (4in) deep concrete footing.

Lay stone blocks on beds of mortar, staggering the joints to form a 'bonded' wall with a wide base but tapering towards the top.

Allow for drainage to prevent the soil behind the wall becoming waterlogged, putting unnecessary pressure on the masonry. Embed 22mm ($\frac{3}{4}$in) plastic pipes in the mortar on top of the first course of stone. Place the pipes at 1m (3ft) intervals and ensure they slope slightly down towards the face of the wall.

Allow the mortar to set for a day or two, then lay hardcore behind the base of the wall to cover the drainage pipes. Pack shingle against the wall as you infill with soil, finishing with a generous layer of topsoil if you intend to plant up to the wall.

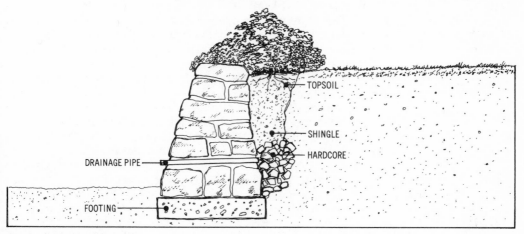

A natural-stone retaining wall

How should I prepare the ground for laying paving slabs?

Use pegs and string to mark out an area for paving slabs. Allow for a 6mm ($\frac{1}{4}$in) gap between slabs unless they are made with integral spacers, and plan to use whole slabs whenever possible to avoid having to cut them.

For a straightforward patio or path, excavate the topsoil to allow for the thickness of the slabs plus a 25mm (1in) layer of sharp sand. Compact the soil with a garden roller before spreading the sand with a rake and levelling it with a long straightedge.

To support heavier loads, or if the soil is composed of clay or peat, lay a 100mm (4in) deep compacted-hardcore base below the sand. Increase the depth of hardcore to 150mm (6in) if you plan to park a car on the paved area.

What degree of slope should I allow for drainage when laying a patio?

A paved area next to a house should have a fall (slope) of 1 in 100 away from the building. For a drive, provide a crossfall of 1 in 40 to ensure puddles of rainwater do not collect on the surface.

Should patio paving be set above or below the surface of an adjacent lawn?

If grass is to grow up to the edge of the patio, set the slabs 18mm ($\frac{3}{4}$in) below the level of the lawn to avoid damaging the mower. If you wish to step up onto a raised patio, create a 150mm (6in) gravel margin between the lawn and patio.

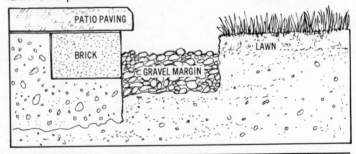

Allowing for a raised patio

What is the recommended method for laying paving slabs?

Set up string lines to form a right angle as a guide to laying two rows of edging slabs. Starting from one corner, lay the slabs on a levelled bed of sand until you are satisfied they are accurately aligned and fit the shape you have in mind, then lift each one and replace it on a bed of firm mortar (1 part cement: 4 parts sand). For paths and patios, place a fist-size mound of mortar under each corner of a slab and a fifth mound under its centre. For a parking space or drive, lay slabs on a continuous 50mm (2in) deep bed of mortar.

Gauge the level of the slabs with a long straightedge and a builder's spirit level, using a wooden block and a club hammer to tap the slabs in place.

Lay the remaining slabs in similar rows, starting each time from the internal corner to keep the joints square and aligned. Use wooden spacers to help create accurate joints, but remove them before the mortar sets.

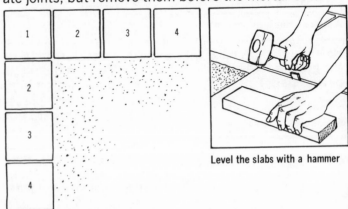

Level the slabs with a hammer

Lay paving slabs from one corner

How should I fill the joints between paving slabs?

Allow the bedding mortar to set for a day or two before you walk on paving slabs, then fill the gaps between them with a dry mortar mix composed of 1 part cement: 3 parts sand. Brush the mix into the joints and sweep the surface clean before sprinkling the paved area with a fine spray of water to consolidate the mortar.

What is the best way to cut heavy concrete paving slabs?

Hire a portable angle grinder with a stone-cutting disc. Having marked the line with chalk or a soft pencil, score a deep groove across the face of the slab and down both edges with the grinder. Protect your eyes with goggles and wear a face mask. Lay the slab on a bed of sand and tap along the groove with a bolster to produce a crack.

Cut paving slabs with a grinder

Is it easier to lay crazy paving than regular concrete slabs?

Laying irregular crazy-paving slabs or stones avoids the necessity of achieving the geometric accuracy required with square or rectangular slabs. However, a good eye for shape and proportion is required to create an attractive jigsaw effect with reasonably narrow gaps between the stones.

Lay a 25mm (1in) bed of sharp sand over compacted soil or hardcore, and arrange an area of stones or slabs on the sand. Select fairly large stones or slabs for the perimeter of a paved area as small ones are likely to break away. Use a wooden mallet to bed each stone into the sand, checking its alignment with a builder's level. If necessary, lift a stone to remove or add sand to achieve a flat surface. Lay a crazy-paving parking space or drive on an additional bed of mortar.

Once the main area of the paving is level, fill remaining gaps with small stones, shaping them with a bolster chisel as required.

Brush dry sand into all the joints between stones or fill them flush with an almost dry mortar mix. Use a trowel and an old paintbrush to smooth mortared joints.

Can I use ordinary housebricks to pave a garden path?

Although there is a risk that ordinary housebricks may crack or spall in freezing conditions, these slight flaws will only add to the overall colour and texture of brick paving, especially if it is composed of seconds. However, housebricks are not strong enough for driveways and parking spaces. For these areas you should consider using concrete paving bricks.

What is the minimum recommended width for a driveway?

Allow a minimum width of 3m (10ft) for an average car, making sure there is room to open the doors if you have to park beside a building, wall or fence. Make sure that the entrance to the drive is wide enough for easy access and unobstructed by fences or shrubs that would obscure your view of traffic when pulling out.

I have several storm-blown trees. Any ideas for using the wood?

Arrange logs on end to form a path

If the wood is not valuable enough to sell to a timber merchant you can make charming and original garden paths with logs. Saw large-diameter logs into 150mm (6in) lengths and soak them in preservative.

Excavate the area of the pathway to a depth of 200mm (8in) and spread a 50mm (2in) layer of gravel mixed with sharp sand across the bottom of the trench.

Arrange the logs on end, packing them closely together and bedding them into the sand-and-gravel ballast until their tops are aligned with the top of the trench. Pour more ballast between the logs and brush it in all directions until it is flush with the logs.

We are wearing a bald strip across our lawn on the way to the garage, but we don't really want to lay a pathway. Is there an alternative?

You can form a row of stepping stones across a lawn using natural-stone or concrete paving slabs. Lay individual stones on the grass and cut around them with a trowel. Lift the cut turf and scoop out soil to allow for the thickness of each stone plus 18mm ($\frac{3}{4}$in), and a 25mm (1in) layer of sharp sand. Tap the stones into the sand until they are level and stable.

Cut around a stone with a trowel

What is a gravel garden and how is it laid?

An area of fine gravel makes an attractive background for certain plants, especially heathers and conifers, while restricting the growth of weeds.

Excavate the topsoil to allow for a 25mm (1in) layer of gravel. Having spread the gravel with a garden rake, scrape it back to reveal small areas of soil for planting. Replace the gravel, sprinkling it around individual plants.

Lay a brick or stone edging to a gravel garden to contain the small stones and prevent them spreading into an adjacent lawn or flower bed.

I like the idea of a cobbled area in my garden. Should I set the stones in concrete?

Cobbles for a decorative area in a garden can be set in mortar, but use a concrete mix over hardcore for a cobbled drive or parking space. Spread a 50mm (2in) layer of dry concrete or mortar mix, then press the cobbles into it, packing them closely and projecting above the surface. Use a stout wooden batten to lightly tamp the cobbles level. Use a fine spray to sprinkle the entire area with water to consolidate the mortar or concrete.

Tamp cobbles level with a batten

What is the best way to break up old concrete paving?

Save yourself a great deal of hard labour by renting heavy breaking equipment from a tool-hire company. Use a demolition hammer for relatively thin concrete up to 100mm (4in) thick. These tools are small electrically powered versions of the familiar road drills. Larger breakers are available for demolishing concrete pads up to 300mm (1ft) thick. Wear goggles and hearing protectors when breaking up concrete.

I want to construct some steps in my garden. How high should each step be?

The proportion of the tread (horizontal part of a step) in relation to the riser (the vertical part) is perhaps more important than the actual dimension of garden steps. You should aim to construct a flight of steps that can be climbed or descended with an easy steady rhythm. As a rough guide, the depth of the tread plus twice the height of the riser should equal 650mm (2ft 2in). For example, 350mm (1ft 2in) treads would require 150mm (6in) risers. Never construct garden steps with treads that are less than 300mm (1ft) deep or risers that are higher than 175mm (7in).

What is a good size for a garden pond?

The volume of water plays a most important part in creating a pond with a perfectly balanced ecosystem with clean clear water and healthy plants and fish. A pond with a surface area of up to 9sq m (100sq ft) should be at least 450mm (1ft 6in) deep. Larger ponds should be 600 to 750mm (2 to 2ft 6in) deep. It is very difficult to maintain a balanced system in a pond with a surface area of less than 3.75sq m (40sq ft).

Where is the best place to dig a pond in my garden?

Dig a pond in an open area of the garden away from overhanging trees where it will receive plenty of sunlight. Although sunlight will promote algae growth in a newly stocked pond, it is also essential to encourage the spread of plants that will oxygenate the water. Mature floating plants and tall marginal growth will eventually provide the shade necessary to keep the water clear and protect fish from direct sunlight.

Check that you can reach a pond with a hosepipe and that you can run power to pond lighting and pumps.

Is it easier to construct a pond with a rigid liner or a flexible one?

There is no real difficulty with using either type of liner. The rigid plastic-moulded liners come ready-made and are lowered into a hole that roughly approximates the shape of the moulding. As the liner is filled with water, finely sifted soil or sand is used to infill around it.

A flexible-sheet liner faithfully follows the shape of the hole you dig, therefore a much more accurate excavation is required. To prevent the liner being punctured by sharp stones or tree roots, the excavation is lined with damp sand. With the liner draped across the hole and held in place with bricks all round its perimeter, the pond is gradually filled with water from a hose. As the water level rises, the liner is stretched and hugs the sides and bottom of the excavation.

What is the best type of flexible pond liner?

Polyethylene liners are cheap but relatively fragile and are only worth considering for temporary fish-keeping ponds, and even then, a double thickness of plastic is recommended.

PVC liners, especially those reinforced with nylon, are usually guaranteed for a minimum of five years.

The very best liners are sheets of synthetic rubber based on butyl with a life expectancy of up to 50 years. A good butyl liner will be sold with something like a 20-year guarantee.

Liners are available in a range of standard sizes, but larger ones or special shapes are often made to order.

What type of stone should I lay around the edge of a pond?

You can edge a garden pond with broken concrete paving slabs, but for the best effect use 50mm (2in) thick natural riven stone.

Bed the slabs in mortar laid over the edge of the pond liner, arranging them so that they project over the water by about 50mm (2in) to cast a deep shadow line around the edge of the pond.

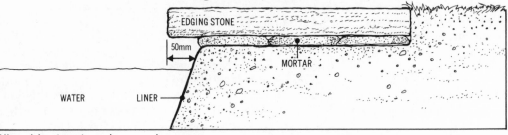

Allow edging stones to overhang a pond

How can I introduce plants to a pond?

You can buy perforated plastic planting crates from any aquatic-garden centre. Depending on the species of plant you are growing, crates are placed on the bottom of the pond or on marginal shelves moulded or cut into the walls.

Line a crate with close-weave hessian or a proprietary liner and fill it with finely sifted soil free from fertilizer, manure and weedkillers. Spread a layer of washed gravel on top of the soil to prevent fish from disturbing the plant roots.

What size should marginal shelves be to accommodate planting crates?

A marginal shelf should be about 225mm (9in) wide and 225mm (9in) below the surface of the water. Slope the sides of a pond to an angle of about 20 degrees to prevent excessive creasing of the liner as it clings to the contour of the excavation.

Slope the sides of a garden pond

I want a very natural-looking pond. Can I cover the bottom with a layer of soil instead of using planting crates?

Once plants become established and a pond matures you can hardly detect planting crates, but if you prefer you can spread a layer of chemical- and fertilizer-free soil across the bottom of the pond. You can also create soil-filled planting pockets for marginal plants. Make 600mm (2ft) wide but shallow pockets for bog plants and dig deeper 300mm (1ft) wide pockets for those rushes or irises that need to grow in 75 to 125mm (3 to 5in) of water. Oxygenating plants will spread quickly in this type of environment and their growth must be controlled to prevent them choking the pond.

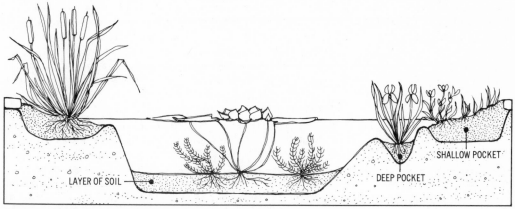

Creating a natural-looking pond

How can I build a pond on a sloping site?

Build up the low side of the pond with soil and lay turf up to the paved edge. Cut back the high side and build a low retaining wall or construct a rockery to hold the bank in place.

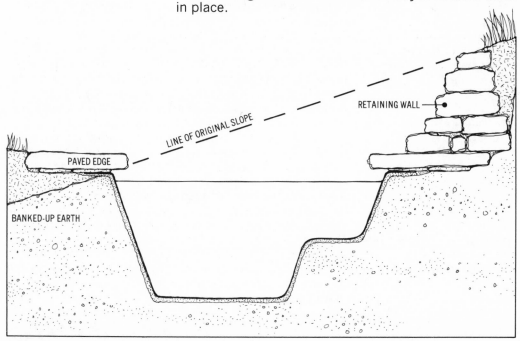

Accommodating a sloping site

What can I do to prevent a pond overflowing?

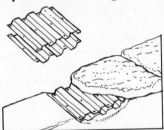

Place a drain beneath edging stones

The surface of the water in a pond should be 25mm to 50mm (1 to 2in) below the stones that surround it. However, if you forget to turn off the tap when topping up the water level, it can overflow and flood areas of the garden. To prevent an overflow, construct a shallow drain beneath one of the edging stones to direct excess water into a soakaway dug alongside the pond.

Two pieces of corrugated plastic roof sheeting, pop-riveted together, make an ideal drain. Scrape sand and soil from beneath the edge of a flexible pond liner to accommodate the drain, then cover it with mortar before placing the edging stone on top.

How can I stop my pond turning green?

Pond water turns green due to an over-abundant growth of algae. Although it's not harmful to fish or other wildlife, algae spoils the appearance of a pond. Once oxygenating plants get established they will compete with the algae for mineral salts in the water and eventually the water will become clear and remain so provided the balanced ecosystem of the pond is maintained. You can speed up the operation somewhat by adding a proprietary water conditioner available from any good aquatic-garden centre.

How long should I wait before introducing fish to a new pond?

Leave newly planted oxygenating plants to establish themselves for at least two weeks before introducing fish to a pond.

How can I calculate the amount of water in my pond?

Before adding chemical water conditioners it is important to be able to calculate the amount of water contained in a garden pond. First, calculate its volume, allowing for shallow water over marginal shelves, then allow 27 litres (6$\frac{1}{4}$ gallons) for every 30cu cms (1cu ft).

How many fish can live comfortably in a pond measuring 1.5 × 1.2m (5 × 4ft)?

As a rough guide to stocking a pond with fish, allow for 50mm (2in) 'length of fish' for every 300sq mm (1sq ft) of water-surface area. A pond measuring 1.5 × 1.2m (5 × 4ft), for example, can support twenty 50mm (2in) long fish or ten 100mm (4in) long fish, and so on.

Can fish survive in a frozen pond?

Fish will survive in a frozen pond provided a small area is kept free from ice to permit toxic gases from rotting vegetation to escape. Install a small electric pond heater, or stand a saucepan of boiling water on a frozen pond every morning to melt a small hole in the ice.

I want to build a large rockery. Where can I buy natural stone at a reasonable price?

Buying individual rocks from a garden centre is prohibitively expensive if you are planning to build an impressive rockery. It is much cheaper to buy stone by weight directly from a quarry. Normally you can select blocks of stone from the site and either have them delivered or loaded onto your own transport.

There are bats living in my loft. What can I do about them?

Bats prefer to inhabit farm buildings, caves, unused tunnels and mines, but they will occasionally roost in domestic buildings. Although many people are alarmed by bats they are in fact harmless. They do not constitute a health hazard, they do not gnaw woodwork and may even be an advantage in a loft as they will feed on woodworm beetles.

As bats are now relatively rare, it is illegal to injure them, disturb their roost or block their means of access. If you feel unable to live in close proximity to a colony of bats, contact the Nature Conservancy Council for assistance.

What is the best way to trap mice?

There are humane traps designed to capture mice so that they can be released away from the house. Alternatively there are the familiar spring-loaded snap traps. Bait traps with flour, chocolate or porridge oats.

Place traps every 2m (6ft) or so along mouse runs (regular routes indicated by droppings, gnawed timber, half-eaten food and so on), and especially against skirting boards.

As an alternative to traps, proprietary ready-poisoned bait can be sprinkled onto sheets of paper left along recognized mouse runs: uneaten bait can be wrapped and discarded safely. Only use poisoned bait where it cannot be found by children or pets.

How can I rid my out-buildings of rats?

Rats can be killed with anti-coagulant poisons, following the manufacturer's instructions for mixing and depositing bait. As rats can be a serious health hazard, contact your Environmental Health Department for advice as soon as you suspect infestation.

What can I do to control a colony of ants?

Locating an ant's nest is normally quite easy. It will inevitably be situated under a pathway or patio within 6m (20ft) of the house. There will almost certainly be ant activity around the nest entrance which will be surrounded by excavated soil or sand. Flood the nest with boiling water or, if that would harm plants, spray insecticide into the nest entrance.

If you cannot locate a nest, prevent ants invading the house by treating door and window frames, ventilators and wastepipes with an insecticide.

Getting up in the middle of the night I found cockroaches in my kitchen. What can I do about them?

Cockroaches are nocturnal feeders which is why you rarely see them during the hours of daylight when they are hiding in cracks and crevices, under cupboards and especially in warm environments close to cookers, refrigerators and central-heating pipes.

Your local Environmental Health Department will give you professional advice and help, or you can lay an insecticidal-powder barrier between suspected cockroach haunts and food. Use an old paintbrush to stipple insecticide under skirting boards. Take care to ensure insecticide does not contaminate food or water.

How can I destroy a wasps' nest?

Wasps are beneficial to a gardener in the spring when they are feeding on garden pests, but the presence of a nest near the house or even in the loft itself can be alarming, especially with small children in the family.

You can sprinkle insecticidal powder at the entrance to the nest where the wasps alight so that they gradually distribute the powder deep inside. Alternatively, you can ignite a smoke pellet in the entrance, then seal it immediately.

However, approaching a wasps' nest can be hazardous; if wasps are aroused they may attack *en masse*. For professional help, contact your local Environmental Health Department. They may employ a pest-control unit that will deal with the nest for a fee.

What timber preservative is safe to use on a dog kennel?

You should always check with the manufacturer of a preservative that their particular product is safe to use. Tell them the size of the dog that will inhabit the kennel because small animals are at greater risk. A water-based product might be the safest, but in every case, wait until the preservative has dried thoroughly and all fumes have evaporated before introducing a dog to the kennel. If a dog begins to chew the woodwork, ask your vet for advice.

10

REPAIRING CHINA AND GLASS

It may not be valuable, but why discard your favourite china and glassware just because you knocked the handle off a cup or broke a wineglass stem? They may no longer be suitable for everyday use, but at least you've preserved them for the display cabinet. The same goes for what might pass for junk at the local market. Broken or damaged pieces are sold for a fraction of the price of perfect pieces, but they can be almost as attractive after a few hours' work ●

Is there a way to remove ugly stains from old china?

With patience, stains can be bleached from old china. Ordinary household bleach may remove light staining, but in all probability you will have to buy a stronger bleach such as hydrogen peroxide (100 volume) from a pharmacist.

Make a solution of 1 part bleach to 3 parts water plus a drop or two of ammonia. Always wear protective gloves and old clothing or an apron when you are handling strong bleach. Use water to wash spilled bleach from your skin immediately.

Soak the stained china in water prior to bleaching, then use tweezers to dip balls of cotton wool in the bleach solution and lay these swabs on the stain. Seal the china in a plastic bag and leave the bleach to react for a couple of hours. If necessary, repeat the process until the stain disappears, then wash the china in water.

There is a white lime-scale ring on the inside of a ceramic bowl. What will dissolve it?

Lime scale can be dissolved with hydrochloric acid (spirits of salt), available from a pharmacist. Hydrochloric acid must be handled with great care. Always wear protective gloves and goggles while you are handling it, and keep all such chemicals locked away where children cannot reach them.

Pour water into the bowl to cover the stain, then slowly add acid to the water until the lime scale begins to bubble. *Always add acid to water – never add water to acid or they will react violently!* Leave the solution to dissolve the lime scale, adding more acid at a later stage if necessary. When the bowl is clean, pour the solution into a drain and wash the china thoroughly.

I have an antique plate that was once repaired with what looks like dark brown glue. How can I dismantle the plate to make a neater repair?

A great deal of broken china was repaired in the past with woodworking animal glue or shellac (French polish). Both substances will normally dissolve in hot water.

Lower the plate into a bowl of warm water, then gradually increase the temperature by adding hot water from a kettle.

Leave the glue to soften, examining the plate from time to time to see if there is any movement between the broken pieces. You can try inserting the point of a blade into a crack to encourage the joint to open.

As the pieces separate, use an old toothbrush to scrub the glue from the edges.

If hot water has no effect on the glue, lay cotton-wool swabs dipped in methylated spirits along the joints. Methylated spirits will dissolve shellac.

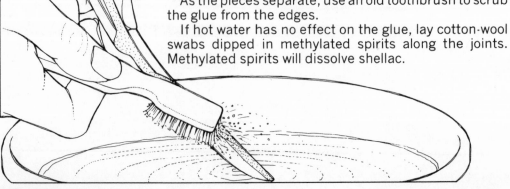

Scrub the edges with a toothbrush

What will dissolve a modern adhesive that has been used to repair china?

If you have to dismantle broken china that has been repaired with a modern adhesive, try soaking it in hot water, but if that is unsuccessful, brush paint stripper along both sides of the joints. When the glue softens, prise the pieces apart and scrub them in hot water. Wear protective gloves and goggles for this stage of the work.

If the china is decorated, check before you apply stripper that there is no paintwork applied to the surface of the glaze. If so, brush stripper on the undecorated side of the china only, and take great care not to smear stripper onto the paint when washing the broken pieces.

Is it possible to remove a row of old metal reinforcing staples?

Copper or iron staples, better known as 'rivets', were used by earlier restorers to reinforce cracks or joints in heavy china plates or bowls. The ends of each rivet fit in holes drilled in the china and were held in place with plaster of Paris.

If you want to remove old rivets in order to make a neater repair, lay a swab of cotton wool dipped in hot water over each one to soften the plaster. Change the swabs frequently, picking out plaster from around the rivets as it begins to soften.

Finally, remove each rivet with pliers, gently twisting it from side to side as you pull. You must take care not to damage the china further by using excessive force at this stage.

What is the best glue to use for repairing broken china?

Cyanoacrylate water-clear adhesive is ideal for gluing hard fine porcelain, especially as small pieces can be hand held while the glue sets in 10 to 15 seconds.

White PVA woodworking glue is an excellent adhesive for thick earthenware and pottery. Soak the broken edges with water before applying the glue.

Two-part epoxy glue is the most versatile adhesive for ceramics. Leave the tubes of glue and hardener on a radiator to encourage them to flow before mixing them with a little titanium dioxide – a fine white powder that prevents yellowing of the glue. Titanium dioxide is available from a pharmacist.

Is it possible to repair cracked china?

Very low-viscosity cyanoacrylate glue is designed to flow into hairline cracks.

Alternatively, cracked china can sometimes be repaired with epoxy glue by warming the piece in an oven or on a radiator, then opening the crack slightly with the point of a knife blade: take great care not to break the china in two by forcing the crack apart. Spread a little epoxy glue along the crack (the heated china will draw it in), then remove the blade and strap the repair with strips of adhesive tape stretched across the crack. Wipe glue from the surface using a cloth dampened with methylated spirits.

How can I replace a broken cup handle?

Don't attempt to replace the handle on a cup from which you intend to drink hot liquids. The repair may last for months, even years, but it could suddenly break down without warning, causing a painful accident.

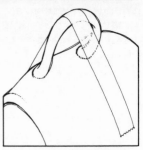

Hold a glued handle with tape

Apply epoxy glue to the broken ends of a cup handle, then press it in place, rocking it gently to squeeze excess glue out of the joints. Strap it to the cup with one strip of adhesive tape stretched taut across the handle from one side to the other. Reinforce the strapping with two more strips stretched diagonally across the handle. Check the handle is upright and put the cup aside until the glue has set.

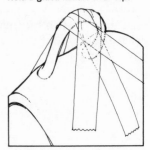

Reinforce repair with strips

What is the best method for repairing a broken plate?

Prepare a broken plate for reassembly by cleaning the edges with a piece of silk dipped in acetone.

Cut strips of adhesive tape beforehand for strapping the pieces of china together.

Apply epoxy adhesive to one half of a broken joint, then push both halves together while rocking them slightly to squeeze out excess glue and encourage the edges of the china to mate accurately. Stretch adhesive tape across the joint on both sides of the plate, making sure the tension is evenly applied.

Run a thumbnail across a joint to make sure both halves are aligned perfectly, and make any necessary adjustments before cleaning glue from the surface of the plate with methylated spirits. Don't attempt to remove glue that has spread under the tape – simply scrape it off with a knife when it has set. Stand the plate upright in a plate rack for the prescribed setting time.

I want to repair a bowl that has been broken into dozens of pieces. How can I make sure all the pieces are going to fit accurately?

The first stage of a complicated repair is to make a 'dummy run' by taping the pieces together without glue. Make a note of the order of assembly by numbering each piece with a wax pencil. You might have to make several attempts until you find a particular sequence that does not prevent you inserting the last pieces of china. When you are satisfied with a sequence, carefully dismantle the broken china piece by piece and clean each one ready for assembly.

Don't attempt to glue all the pieces together at one time. Instead, assemble two or three of the larger pieces, put them aside to set and assemble two or three more. When these subassemblies have hardened thoroughly, join them one to another to complete the job.

Is there some way to reinforce a glued repair on a heavy pottery dish?

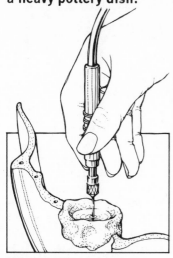

Make a modelling-clay reservoir

You can reinforce a joint with narrow stainless-steel pins, but you will need some rather specialized equipment to do it. Ceramics are too hard for ordinary drill bits so you must acquire one or two fine diamond-tipped drill bits from a dental supplier. To facilitate the delicacy required for this type of drilling, you should fit each drill bit in a flexible-drive attachment designed for connecting to an ordinary electric drill.

Make the reinforcing pins by first roughening the surface of a stainless-steel rod with a file, then having cleaned it with acetone, cut the rod into short lengths with a hacksaw.

Mark the position of each pin with spots of paint along the edge of one half of the dish, then assemble the joint to transfer the marks to the other half. Drill holes in the centre of each mark. To keep the drill bit cool, model a small reservoir around the edge of the dish and fill it with water.

Use epoxy adhesive to glue reinforcing pins in one half of the dish only. Glue and assemble the pieces and strap them with tape until the adhesive sets.

The glued joints I have made to repair broken china are still apparent. Is there something else I can do to disguise the repair?

If you use a magnifying glass to examine the repair you will discover minute chips along the edges that tend to exaggerate the width of what, in reality, might be a hairline crack. Make an epoxy putty to fill these chips flush with the surrounding surface.

Mix the two parts of epoxy glue with titanium dioxide to turn it white, then gradually add talcum powder until you can knead it into a putty-like consistency. Use a knife blade to scrape this filler across the crack, then dip the blade in methylated spirits and draw it along the repair to smooth the filler. Leave it to harden, then use a sharp blade to scrape the filler flush with the china. Use a small patch of very fine silicon-carbide paper to gently smooth the repair.

Can I rebuild a chipped edge to a broken ceramic vase?

Small semi-circular or 'shell' chips can be found along the edges of vases, plates, bowls and many other pieces of china and pottery. This type of damage is relatively simple to repair using a home-made epoxy putty. Apply a thin film of neat epoxy glue (coloured with titanium dioxide) to the surface of the chip, then mix talcum powder with the remaining glue to make a putty. Mould some of this putty into the chip, shaping it with your fingers to approximate the intact edge of the vase. When the putty is hard, shape it with a fine file and finish the job with fine silicon-carbide paper.

Is it possible to regild the edges of porcelain cups and saucers?

Gilding was widely used to decorate antique chinaware. Worn gilding can be retouched with metallic powders mixed with a little cold-cure lacquer. Metallic powders can be bought from artists' suppliers and most good modelling shops.

What paints should I use to retouch repaired china?

Artist's acrylic paints are easy to acquire and relatively simple to apply. Mix a white paint that matches the colour of the china's background, and use it to camouflage a repair made with epoxy putty. Don't leave a sharp edge to the paintwork, however, but feather the paint with a soft artist's brush.

Retouch areas of colour to match a pattern. Leave the paint to dry, then cover it with a clear glaze.

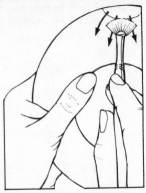

Feather paint with light strokes

What can I use to reglaze repairs in china?

The surface of acrylic paint used to disguise epoxy fillings has a matt surface that stands out against the shiny glaze that covers most items of china. There are professional glazes that are cured in an oven, and although the finished results are almost indistinguishable from the original glaze, it is a difficult process to master. Provided the china you are working on is for display only, you can reglaze a repair using cold-cure lacquer that is sold for varnishing woodwork.

Use a wide soft artist's brush to apply the clear lacquer over the repair, then feather the edge of the newly glazed area with the brush dampened with thinners. Cover the piece with a box or suspend plastic sheeting over it to prevent airborne dust settling on the lacquer before it sets hard after about 12 hours.

Protect wet glaze with plastic sheeting

How can I clean a stained glass decanter?

Many an old decanter is stained with wine or by calcium-carbide deposits (lime scale) left by hard water. Hydrochloric acid will dissolve these stains using the method described for cleaning stained china, but as strong acid can etch some old glassware first try soaking the stain with a mild acid like white vinegar. Pour the vinegar into the decanter and leave it for several days. If the stain has disappeared, wash the decanter with warm water before using it.

Is it possible to regrind the chipped rim of a drinking glass?

Provided the damage is very minor you can regrind the rim of a drinking glass with ordinary wet-and-dry paper. Use progressively finer grades of paper as the work progresses.

Lay a sheet of wet-and-dry paper face up on a perfectly flat surface. Dip the rim of the glass in water and rub it upside down across the abrasive surface.

When you have ground away the damage, round over the sharp edges with a piece of wet-and-dry paper wrapped around a pencil or short length of wooden dowel. The rim is left with a slightly matt texture, but it is quite safe to use for drinking or display.

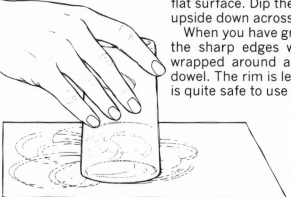

Regrind the rim of a glass

What glue can I use for repairing glassware?

Use a water-clear ultraviolet-curing anaerobic glue specially made for gluing broken glassware. As soon as a glued joint is closed the adhesive begins to set due to the action of the ultraviolet present in daylight. In bright sunlight the glue sets hard in a few seconds, but on an overcast day it might take a couple of minutes. Clean excess glue from the surface of the glass with acetone.

A perfectly glued joint will be practically invisible, but air trapped in the joint shows as a silver line in the glass. To rectify it, run a little glue along each side of the closed joint and blow hard to force the adhesive into the crack.

How can I repair a broken wineglass stem?

Stand the bowl of the glass upside down and, having attached the broken stem with anaerobic adhesive, support the base on columns of children's modelling clay. When the stem is perfectly balanced, open the window curtains to expose the repair to sunlight.

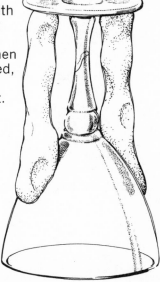

Support a wineglass stem with modelling clay while glue sets

Can I use anaerobic glue to mend coloured glass?

If glass is opaque or the colour is very dense, ultraviolet light may not be able to penetrate to set anaerobic glue. If that proves to be the case, remove the glue with acetone and use a cyanoacrylate adhesive instead.

Can I fill a small chip in a glass vase?

There are no clear fillers for badly chipped glassware, but you can disguise minute chips with drops of anaerobic glue. Let the 'beads' of adhesive stand proud of the surface until they harden – this may take up to 24 hours. If they sink, fill the chips a second time. Finally, pare the glue flush with the glass using a very sharp knife, then polish the surface with a metal polish.

11

FIXINGS AND FITTINGS

A job that may have kept you busy for a
whole weekend could have been finished
in half the time if only you had known there
was some little gadget that would have
solved all your problems. There is now a
steady supply of ingenious fixings and
fittings for the DIY trade, some of which
were only available to furniture manufacturers or professional kitchen fitters up
to a few years ago ●

I am finding it difficult to hold very small panel pins while hammering them. Any tips?

Push a small nail through a piece of thick paper which will hold it upright. Tap in the nail, then tear the paper free before driving the nail home.

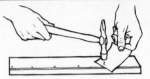

Hold a small nail with paper

Can I hide nail fixings?

You can hide sunken nail heads using a colour-matched wood filler. Alternatively, lift a flap of wood with a gouge, drive the nail in under the flap and sink its head with a nail punch. Glue the flap back in place and clamp it until the glue sets.

Hide a nail under a flap of wood

How can I remove a screw that is stuck fast?

First of all choose a screwdriver that fits snugly in the screw slot. Before you attempt to remove painted-over screws, tap the tip of a screwdriver sideways along the slot to cut out the paint. If the screw slot has become damaged you may have to drill out the head. Mark the centre of the head with a punch and use progressively larger drill bits until the screw head breaks off.

What is the best nail to use to avoid splitting the wood?

Oval nails driven in with the widest face parallel with the grain reduce splitting to a minimum. Another tip is to blunt the point of a nail with light hammer blows. The blunted point punches its way through the timber without forcing the wood fibres apart.

Can I use carpet tacks for upholstery?

Carpet and upholstery tacks are similar in appearance, but carpet tacks would probably split all but the largest wooden upholstery frame. Tacks used for upholstery are not more than 16mm ($\frac{5}{8}$in) long. Improved upholstery tacks are used to fix webbing and hessian seat platforms. The slimmer, fine tacks are generally used to attach lining and top-cover fabrics.

What fixing should be used to nail up plaster-board?

Use galvanized nails such as large-headed clout nails or purpose-made plasterboard nails which have a jagged shank for extra grip. Use 32mm ($1\frac{1}{4}$in) long nails for standard 9.5mm ($\frac{3}{8}$in) thick plasterboard.

I want to build some rough shuttering and I want to dismantle it afterwards. What fixing should I use?

Use duplex-head nails for temporary fixings. These nails have extended heads designed to provide a grip for a claw hammer in order to extract them.

Duplex-head nail

What nail can I use to hold corrugated plastic-sheet roofing?

Use plated nails fitted with plastic collars to fit the crests of corrugated plastic sheet. The nails supplied for the purpose usually have twisted shanks for extra grip.

Corrugated-roofing nail

What can I use to fix upholstery braid?

Many upholsterers use glue to attach decorative fabric trimmings known as braid, but there are also very fine tacks known as gimp pins that are specially designed for the purpose. Choose gimp pins from a range of available colours that will merge with the general colour of the braid you intend to use.

What nails can I use for a stronger-than-average fixing?

For extra-strong fixings, use ring-shank nails made with serrations along the first half of the shank to grip the wood securely.

Ordinary woodscrews keep pulling out of chipboard. Are there any alternatives?

You can use special twin-threaded chipboard screws that grip fibrous particle boards better than conventional woodscrews. They can also be driven into the edges of chipboard without splitting the board.

Alternatively, you can use nylon inserts with ordinary woodscrews. Inserts are tapped into pre-drilled holes in the edge of a board. A screw driven into an insert expands it to grip the chipboard and make a firm fixing.

Chipboard connectors are coarse-threaded blunt screws designed to be driven directly into pilot holes drilled in the edge of a board.

Chipboard screw

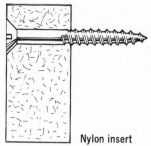

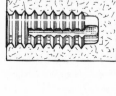

Nylon insert

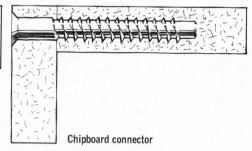

Chipboard connector

How should I fix a door frame in its opening in the wall?

You could measure and pre-plug the wall for screw fixings, but an easier method is to use a special frame fixing which eliminates the need to measure and pre-drill the holes. Position the frame and wedge it in place, then drill right through it into the wall. Insert the frame fixing, consisting of a long plastic plug and a plated screw, and tighten it.

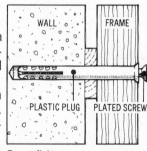

Frame fixing

What is a security screw?

Security screw

A security or clutch-head screw is used for fixing locks or for securing valuable objects. They are often used, for example, to attach framed paintings to the wall. The head of the screw is designed to be turned one way only. The screw 'slot' is shaped to grip an ordinary straight-tipped screwdriver while the screw is being driven into the work, but if the screwdriver is turned anticlockwise to remove the screw, the tip slips out of the slot.

What are the advantages of using twin-threaded screws?

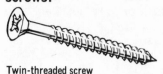

Twin-threaded screw

These relatively new screws have twin helical threads which extend along three quarters of their length, and their shanks are narrower than the width of the threads. When compared with conventional woodscrews, the twin threads provide more grip and the relatively narrow shank is less likely to cause splitting, particularly in man-made boards. The steep pitch of the threads also pulls the screw quickly into the wood.

How should I decide what size screw to use for a job?

Screws are designated by length and diameter or 'gauge'. The length is always specified as a true measurement, usually in inches, but the gauge is specified by numbers from 0 to 20 – the higher the number the larger the screw.

As a general rule to selection, the length of a screw should be about three times the thickness of the component it is fixing. Choose the largest possible gauge for a given length, but it should never be more than one tenth of the width of the wood into which it is driven.

Is there some way to smarten up a screw fixing?

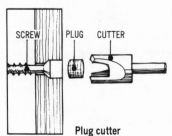

Plug cutter

If you want to make a neat feature of a visible screw fixing you could use a metal screw cup that forms a 'collar' around the head of a countersunk or raised-head woodscrew.

You can also get plastic covers to mask screw heads. One type snaps over a mating screw cup, while another is simply made to be a friction fit in the slots of a cross-head screw.

To hide a screw head completely, drill a hole to form a recess, insert the screw, then fill the hole with a matching wooden plug. Plug-cutting tools are available for use with an electric drill.

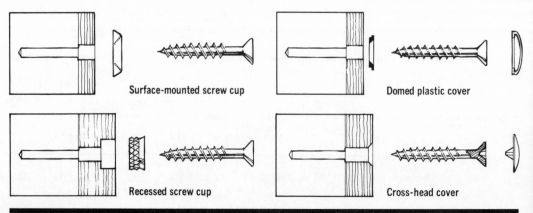

Surface-mounted screw cup

Domed plastic cover

Recessed screw cup

Cross-head cover

What can I use to hold two lengths of kitchen worktop together?

You can get a fitting called a panel connector that is designed to pull two parts of a worktop together. A large-diameter stopped hole is drilled in the underside of both panels and a groove is cut between them to accommodate a connecting bolt. Tightening a nut closes the joint between the two halves of the worktop. You need two fittings for a standard 600mm (2ft) wide kitchen worktop and you should insert locating dowels in the edges to help keep the surfaces flush.

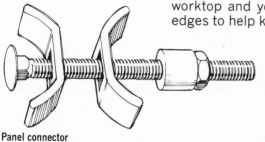

Panel connector

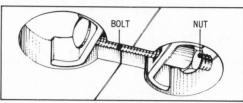

The fitting pulls worktops together

Is there a fixing that will make a strong table that can be dismantled when I decide to move?

A metal corner-plate fitting is available for assembling a table with four legs and rails. The corner plate itself holds two rails together at a right angle. Flanges on each side of the plate locate in saw cuts across the rails and the plate is held in place with woodscrews. Each fitting is supplied with a threaded bolt that is screwed into the chamfered inside corner of a table leg. This bolt passes through a hole in the plate and is secured with a wing nut that pulls the leg against the square-cut ends of the rails. One corner plate is required for each leg of the table.

Corner-plate fitting

CORNER PLATE THREADED BOLT
WING NUT
RAIL   RAIL
LEG

The fitting clamps a table leg in place

Are traditional fibre wall plugs better than plastic ones?

In terms of performance there is little difference between plastic wall plugs and fibre ones, but the individual moulded plastic plugs are more convenient to use. You don't have to cut them to length and one size will take a range of screws of different gauges.

Can plastic wall plugs soften with heat?

Yes. Where there is a possibility that heat might affect plastic plugs, substitute special metal frame fixings or bolt-type anchors.

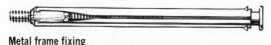

Metal frame fixing

Bolt-type anchor

What can I use to fix cupboards to a stud-partition wall?

It is always best to make screw fixings directly into the wooden studs rather than into hollow parts of a partition wall. Where this is impossible you can use special cavity fixings, but only for light to medium loads. Various types and sizes are available such as spring toggles, gravity toggles and collapsible anchors, all of which open out on the inside of the wall panel to form a fixing and spread the load.

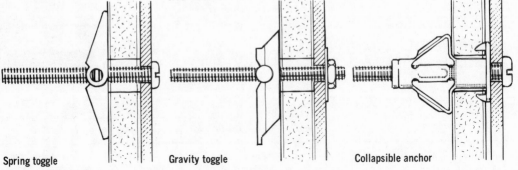

Spring toggle   Gravity toggle   Collapsible anchor

12

REPAIRING FURNITURE AND WOODWORK

You don't need the skills of a cabinet-maker in order to save a lot of money restoring old furniture and repairing wood-work around the home. Jobs that would once have required special preparation or hours of practice can now be tackled using readily available products straight off the shelves at the DIY store, and some tech-niques are so simple that you can achieve professional-looking results even if you have never set foot in a workshop ●

Can you still get old-style animal glue?

Traditional woodworking glue made from animal skins and bone is still available, usually in a granular form which has to be liquified by heating it in a special glue pot with water. There is also a jelly-like animal glue sold in cans. This type of glue can be liquified by standing the can in hot water.

Is a modern woodworking adhesive better than a traditional glue?

Generally speaking a modern adhesive is stronger than a traditional animal glue although the latter is normally perfectly adequate unless it becomes damp, in which case it dissolves. Animal glue is particularly good for veneering where its thermoplastic qualities are especially advantageous.

Most modern adhesives are very convenient to use. White PVA glue, for example, is ready to use straight from its container, while some glues require no more than mixing with water. Others are supplied as two components that are mixed prior to application.

What is the best glue to use for veneering?

There are several excellent adhesives for applying thin wooden veneers although traditional animal glue is perhaps the most versatile. The technique for hand-laying veneers with animal glue requires some practice, but as the glue can be melted by warming the veneer with a heated iron, faults are easily corrected. If necessary this can be undertaken days after the glue sets.

A more convenient glue is sold as a thin film which is laid between the veneer and its groundwork (backing material). The application of a warm iron melts the glue film, bonding the veneer in place.

Specially developed contact glues are also available for veneering. A thin coat of glue is brushed or spread onto both the veneer and groundwork and left to dry. When the two glued surfaces are brought together they bond instantly.

How can I protect my furniture against woodworm?

Polish furniture with a wax polish that contains an insecticide to protect it against woodworm infestation. Brush a clear preservative that kills woodboring insects onto unpolished wooden surfaces such as the backs of cabinets, drawer bottoms and runners.

Can I fill woodworm holes?

You can fill any small holes, even fine cracks, with a proprietary wood filler mixed with a little stain to match the colour of the timber. Press it well into the holes and leave it overnight to harden. Sand the filler flush with fine abrasive paper, then polish the area with a good wax furniture polish.

For a few holes only, melt some coloured wax crayons into a small container using the tip of a small soldering iron. Mix several colours together to achieve the required shade. Press some scrapings of the cooled wax into the woodworm holes with a knife and burnish the repair with the smooth back of a piece of abrasive paper. A light dressing of wax polish finishes the job.

Can I treat an outbreak of woodworm myself or should I hire a professional?

There is nothing to prevent you treating woodworm yourself unless the outbreak is serious and a mortgage company insists you hire a professional eradicator. This makes perfect sense in any case because you would want a professional guarantee that the house has been treated when you come to sell it at a later date. However, remedial treatment is relatively straightforward and curing woodworm in furniture is positively simple.

Provided the timber is still sound, the woodworm can be eradicated or the timber protected from future attack by soaking it with a proprietary preservative. Preservatives can be applied to bare wood with a brush or you can buy aerosols that are especially convenient for treating wickerwork. It might be worth hiring spray equipment to treat household timbers so that, having lifted a few floorboards, you can insert the spray lance to treat all the joists and the undersides of floorboards.

Follow manufacturers' recommendations when using chemical preservatives and wear protective gloves, goggles and a facemask, especially when spraying.

How can I remove a white ring left on my polished table?

There are proprietary blemish removers formulated to deal with white rings and stains left on a polished surface by water or alcohol. Basically they are all mild abrasives that are used on a soft cloth to burnish the stain out of the polish. Car-paint cleaner and even liquid metal polish will often work just as well.

Is there a simple way to remove inkstains inside an antique desk?

First you should have the desk valued because a certain amount of staining, minor dents and scratches are only to be expected on antique furniture. To remove these clues to its genuine antiquity could reduce the value of the piece.

Provided the ink has not penetrated the wood you might be able to burnish it out of the polish using a white-ring or stain remover. Alternatively, try a little methylated spirits on a cloth to dissolve the surface of French polish and lift out the ink at the same time.

If the ink is actually in the wood itself you will have to strip the polish locally and bleach the stain. Use wood stain to colour the bleached area to match the surrounding timber, then apply a polish.

Is it possible to get a dent out of a piece of wood?

Apply the tip of a heated soldering iron to a damp cloth laid over the dent. The steam generated by the heat causes the wood fibres in the dent to swell until they lie flush with the surrounding timber. Allow the wood to dry before sanding it smooth.

Use a soldering iron to generate steam

How can I disguise a scratch in a polished surface?

There are special wax sticks, in a range of wood-like colours, that are used to fill and colour scratches or cigarette burns in polished, varnished or lacquered surfaces. The technique couldn't be simpler. Rub a stick back and forth across the blemish until you have built up a layer of wax that is slightly proud of the surface. Use a small piece of flexible plastic (credit card) to scrape the wax flush, then buff the area with a wax polish or the proprietary polish supplied with some kits.

Is there an easy way to upgrade my plastic-laminated kitchen cupboards in order to give them a genuine-wood appearance?

The easiest way to upgrade plastic-laminated cupboards is to cover the doors with self-adhesive veneers. These are incredibly thin hardwood veneers sold in continuous rolls that can be cut with a sharp knife or scissors. Peeling off a backing paper exposes the ready-glued surface which, when pressed against the workpiece, produces an instant bond.

The corners of my veneered chest of drawers are chipped. How can I repair them?

This is a common problem with some veneered furniture where the exposed edges of veneers get broken away to reveal bare areas of groundwork.

Take a piece of the original veneer to a veneer supplier so that you can buy a close match in colour and grain pattern. Try to find a veneer that is slightly thicker than the original or stick two pieces together to make up the required thickness.

Tape a small piece of veneer over a damaged area, aligning the grain pattern as best you can, and allow the veneer to overhang the corner of the chest. Cut a V-shaped patch through both veneers down to the groundwork, then use a chisel to cut out the old veneer and scrape the groundwork clean. Glue the patch in place and, when the adhesive has set, trim off the overhang before sanding the veneer flush. Finally stain and polish it to match the surrounding veneer.

Cut through both veneers at once

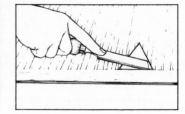

Clean the groundwork with a chisel

There is a blister in the centre of a veneered table top. What can I do about it?

An old table will almost certainly have been veneered using animal glue, in which case you may be able to re-activate the glue with heat. You will probably have to repolish the table after treatment.

Use a sharp knife to slit the blister along the grain to release air trapped inside it. Lay a damp cloth over the blister and apply a heated iron to soften the glue and flatten the veneer. The glue may adhere without further treatment, but to make sure, clamp a block of wood over the previously blistered area.

I have seen some beautifully shaded marquetry veneers. How is that done?

Shaded veneers are used to create traditional three-dimensional marquetry effects such as shells or fans. The graded tonal effect that ranges from dark to light is created by scorching, each piece of veneer being partially dipped in hot sand. Heat a small metal tray of silver sand and use a pair of tweezers to insert a slightly oversize piece of veneer, on edge, in the sand. Leave it for 10 to 12 seconds depending on the degree of shading you require. Having achieved the desired result by trial and error you can repeat the process as many times as necessary.

Is it possible to bleach discoloured timber?

Darkened timber, caused by stripping with caustic soda or ammonia for example, can be made lighter in tone by applying a proprietary two-part kit comprising bleach and neutralizer. Wood bleach is a potent chemical and you should follow the manufacturer's instructions carefully, wearing protective gloves, goggles and old clothes whenever you handle it.

Apply an even coat of bleach to the wood using a clean white rag or nylon brush. Check the reaction every 20 minutes or so until the wood reaches the required tone, then wash the surface with neutralizer. After about four hours, wash the wood with clean water and leave it to dry naturally.

Can I dismantle the joints of an old dining chair in order to repair it?

Weak joints can sometimes be tapped apart with a hammer, using a block of softwood to protect the chair. If the joints are sound you can soften old animal glue with steam. Make yourself a steam generator using an old-fashioned kettle you can stand on a gas or electric ring, a cork bug, a length of silicone-rubber hose and two short lengths of brass tube.

Fill the kettle about three-quarters full with water and heat it until steam begins to escape. Wearing protective gloves, play the brass nozzle around the shoulders of the joints until the glue becomes soft enough to pull them apart. If the joints won't budge, drill a hole through the underside of the chair rail into the joint and direct steam into it.

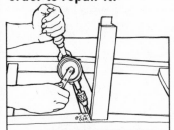

Drill a hole into a joint

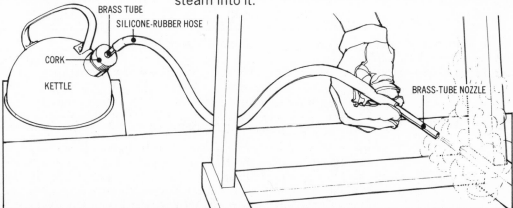

BRASS TUBE
SILICONE-RUBBER HOSE
CORK
KETTLE
BRASS-TUBE NOZZLE

Play steam around a joint to soften the glue

What is the best way to level table legs?

If a four-legged table rocks badly you can trim the legs to make it stable. Stand the table on a sheet of chipboard or some other surface you know to be flat. Pack pieces of veneer under the shortest leg until the table no longer rocks, then have an assistant hold the table steady while you use the pack of veneers to mark the other three legs. Trim each leg to the marked line with a fine saw, chisel or block plane.

One door is hanging off my cupboard because the wood has split behind one of the hinges. How can I repair it?

A heavy cupboard door can cause the wooden frame to split, and before long the screws pull out. Remove the door and flex the damaged frame in order to work some PVA glue into the split using a knife blade. Clamp the split closed with a G-cramp and clean the glue out of the screw holes with a damp tissue wrapped around a matchstick. When the glue has set, replace the door using the original screws.

How can I cure a drawer that sticks?

A sticking drawer can often be corrected by rubbing a wax candle along the running surfaces, including the drawer runners inside the cabinet. If that is unsuccessful look for shiny patches that indicate areas of friction along the sides of the drawer and skim them with a finely set plane.

Can I revive a dull-looking polish?

Old furniture often looks dull and lifeless due to the gradual accumulation of dirt and wax. Make up a mixture of 4 parts white spirit to 1 of linseed oil and use a piece of sacking to rub the mixture along the grain. Quite vigorous action may be required to remove a heavy layer of dirty wax. You may even have to resort to using very fine wire wool dipped in the cleaning mixture, but use light pressure only to avoid cutting through to the wood. Wipe the surface with a rag, then burnish it with one of the preparations manufactured to remove white rings or similar stains.

What exactly is French polish?

French polish is a wood finish made from shellac dissolved in industrial alcohol. It was introduced to Britain from France in the early part of the nineteenth century and was popular throughout the Victorian era.

What is the difference between French polish and button polish?

French polish usually refers to the standard grade of shellac polish as supplied by manufacturers. Button polish refers to a superior grade named after the fact that the shellac was left to cool in the form of thin translucent discs that could be viewed against the light by prospective buyers in order to verify its purity. Even button polish is now normally sold in flake form.

French and button polish are brown in colour, but there is also a polish made from bleached shellac (white polish) for use on pale woods, and a clear polish made by removing the natural wax suspended in shellac polish. Garnet polish is a dark red-brown shellac polish for use on mahogany and similarly coloured timbers.

Is it easy to learn how to French polish?

Traditional French polishing is a skill that requires practice before one can hope to become proficient. A ball of cotton wadding soaked in shellac is wrapped in cloth to make a polisher's rubber. By rubbing it across the wood using circular and figure-of-eight strokes, shellac is squeezed out of the rubber, gradually building a layer of polish on the surface.

If you are a complete beginner it might be easier to try a brushing French polish – shellac with an additive to slow the drying time and allow the polish to be brushed onto the surface. Fifteen to twenty minutes after applying the first coat, rub down with fine silicon-carbide paper and brush on a second coat. Up to three coats can be applied in the same way. Finally, apply a generous coat of wax polish with a ball of very fine wire wool, and five minutes later, burnish the wax with a soft cloth.

What type of stain is best for colouring wood?

Wood stains can be used to alter or modify the colour of practically any timber. The chemical composition of the different types of stain determines their properties.

Water-based stains flow well and consequently it is easy to get an even distribution of colour. However, being water based, this type of stain tends to raise the grain of the timber leaving a rough surface unless you wet the wood and sand it smooth before staining. Any finish can be applied over a water-based stain.

Methylated-spirits based stains will not raise the grain, but because they dry so fast the effect is often patchy unless the stain is sprayed onto the wood. However, the colour may bleed through a subsequent coat of French polish.

Oil-based stains evaporate relatively quickly, but there is still plenty of time to achieve a satisfactory result even when using a brush or rag to apply them. These stains will not raise the grain but will be dissolved by the white spirit in polyurethane varnishes and wax polishes. It is best to seal an oil-stained surface first with two coats of shellac sanding sealer.

What is the difference between a wood stain and a stained varnish?

Wood stains are very fluid and are meant to penetrate the timber to which they are applied. Stains are merely colouring agents and must be overlaid with a clear protective finish such as varnish or French polish.

Stained varnish is both a colouring agent and a hard-wearing finish. However, since the coloured pigments are suspended in the varnish, scratches and scuffs tend to show as relatively obvious blemishes because some of the colour has been removed. A coat of clear varnish over the stained variety will protect it from scratching. Stained varnish is particularly useful for changing the colour of a workpiece that is already varnished rather than having to strip the piece down to the bare wood in order to apply a wood stain.

Can I use teak oil on woods other than teak?

Teak oil is the traditional finish for oily woods such as teak and afrormosia that tend to reject other finishes. However, it is a suitable finish for practically any timber, especially open-grain woods such as oak. Oil is a durable finish for exterior woodwork and it effectively re-nourishes sun-bleached timber. Don't use oil to finish the insides of cupboards and drawers, however, where it could stain the contents.

What is the best wax polish for wood?

Some professionals believe that the only way to obtain a good wax polish for wood is to make it oneself by dissolving beeswax and hard carnauba wax in turpentine. However there are some excellent ready-made polishes that are more than adequate.

Liquid or cream wax polishes are brushed onto the wood or rubbed into the grain with a soft cloth. To prevent the initial coat being absorbed too deeply into the grain, seal the wood first with a shellac sanding sealer or French polish. Rub it down with fine silicon-carbide paper before applying a liberal coating of wax. An hour later buff the surface vigorously, then apply a second but thinner coat with a rag, rubbing in the direction of the grain. Buff again and add a third coat. Leave the wax to harden for several hours, then burnish it with a soft cloth.

If you prefer to use one of the thicker paste polishes, apply two coats with a ball of very fine wire wool, rubbing with the grain only. Leave the wax to harden between coats, then buff it with a soft cloth.

Avoid using wax polishes that contain silicones. If they sink into the timber they will repel practically any finish that is applied should the workpiece ever have to be restored in the future.

What is the best varnish to use for a stripped wooden floor?

A two-part cold-cure lacquer is one of the most hard-wearing clear finishes for a stripped wooden floor.

What is the best clear finish to use on stripped-pine furniture?

For a really hardwearing finish use a polyurethane varnish, but cut back the 'glassy' look of a gloss finish by rubbing it in the direction of the grain with fine wire wool, then give it a dressing of wax polish. Oil endows pine with a rich amber colour and it is also a tough water-resistant finish.

I've just finished varnishing a table only to find dust particles stuck to it. What can I do?

Let the varnish harden, then rub the surface in the direction of the grain with fine wire wool dipped in wax polish. Finally, buff it with a soft cloth.

Is there a suitable paint for an old piano?

If an instrument is valuable it should be refinished by a professional, but to renovate a run-of-the-mill piano use a glossy black cold-cure lacquer.

13

CLEANING METALWARE

We all think we know how to clean metalware, but for even such a seemingly straightforward task there are still easier or more efficient ways of going about it. Many of the polishes on the market are based on formulae developed in the days when domestic servants were expected to keep the household silver and brass gleaming. These products are tried and tested, but it helps to know which is the right one to use and for what purpose ●

We don't use our silver tableware very often. How should I store it to prevent tarnishing?

Make sure you have washed all silverware thoroughly to remove corrosive foodstuffs such as egg, salad dressings, olives, fruit juices and especially salt. Silver saltcellars should be emptied before you store them and remember to remove the glass insert (found in most saltcellars) before you wash it to ensure grains of salt are not trapped between the glass and silverware.

Dry washed silverware thoroughly, then wipe it with a cloth impregnated with long-term silver polish to restore the lustre and inhibit tarnishing. You can buy impregnated cloths or you can make one by adding a tablespoon of household ammonia and a dessertspoon of long-term silver polish to a cup of water. Pour the solution over a clean tea towel and leave it to drip dry. Use the cloth to dry your washed silver.

Newspaper and brown paper will tarnish silver, so wrap clean silverware in acid-free tissue paper available from a jeweller. Never use rubber bands to bind wrapped silver – they can tarnish silver through several layers of tissue paper.

What is the best polish to use on solid silver?

Don't use any of the abrasive polishes made for cleaning relatively hard metals like brass and copper. A silver polish comprises a very fine powder suspended in a liquid medium to minimize the loss of metal caused by buffing the surface of silverware. 'Long-term' silver polishes contain an additive that leaves an invisible chemical barrier to inhibit the natural tarnishing of silver. As a result there is no need to polish silver quite so frequently.

A dry residue from silver polishes can become caught up in intricate engraving and embossing. For this type of decorated silverware use a mild foaming silver polish that is applied with a damp sponge before rinsing the clean metal under running warm water.

Polishing wadding, impregnated with silver polish, is slightly more abrasive than liquid polishes and should be used with care on fine silverware, especially silver-plated items.

Silversmith's gloves (traditionally used by butlers when silver dinner services were in daily use in many households) are very convenient for cleaning tableware and other large silver items. Being impregnated with silver polish, the gloves are simply rubbed across the silver to impart a shine. They can be bought with a supply of dry silver polish for reimpregnation. Similar gloves can be used with a brass and copper polish, but mark them clearly so that they are not used inadvertently to clean silverware.

What can I use to clean silver-plated items?

Any silver polish can be used to clean plated silverware, but as the layer of precious metal is extremely thin the abrasive nature of most polishes eventually wears through the silver to reveal base metal. However, when a silver-plating polish is rubbed onto the surface, it not only removes tarnishing, but deposits a coating of pure silver. You can even restore worn items by applying a silver-plating formula in a similar way. If the metal has been lacquered it must be stripped using acetone (nail-varnish remover) before a silver-plating formula can take effect.

How should I clean precious-metal jewellery?

Gold or silver chains, rings, brooches and other jewellery that is too delicate to clean with metal polishes can be immersed in a mild chemical dip that removes soap deposits, dust and make-up while chemically removing the tarnish from the surface of the metal. Jewellery, arranged in a small perforated container, is lowered into a proprietary 'dip' for two minutes, then removed and dried with a soft cloth or hair dryer. Don't immerse gold and silver together in the same dip and do not use it on pearls, opals, turquoises or other porous stones such as coral or jade.

How can I clean heavily corroded brass?

Neglected brass develops a thick dark brown patina that shrugs off metal polishes. Break down this heavy corrosion with half a lemon. Sprinkle salt onto the cut surface and rub it vigorously over the brass until the corrosion begins to soften. Alternatively, gently wash the corroded brass with a very fine wire-wool pad dipped in a solution of one level tablespoon of salt mixed with a tablespoon of vinegar in half a pint of hot water.

Once you have removed the worst of the corrosion, burnish the metal with a brass polish.

How should I clean brass handles on an antique sideboard?

If possible, remove the handles and clean them with a long-term brass or copper polish. Use an old toothbrush to clean out awkward crevices. If you cannot remove the handles, use masking tape to protect the surrounding woodwork and polish the metal *in situ*.

What is the best way to clean brass inlay in an old table top?

Make a paste of lemon juice mixed with salt and spread it thinly onto the brass. After about five minutes remove the paste with a damp cloth, then rub the inlay gently with long-term silver polish. Finally, polish the table top, including the inlay, with a good-quality wax polish.

What is the recommended method for cleaning copper cooking utensils?

If the copper utensils are for decoration only, polish them with a long-term brass and copper polish. If you use them for cooking don't reheat food left standing in a copper pot as the acid content of the food can react with the metal to form toxins. (Copper pans are often lined with tin to prevent this.) You can even polish them if they are used infrequently, but wash them in hot soapy water before you cook the next time.

Is it possible to lacquer polished metal to protect the shine?

A special acrylic-resin lacquer is made to protect polished metal. It is applied with a soft artist's paint-brush, working fairly quickly to avoid leaving brush marks in the setting lacquer. If this is unavoidable, stand the lacquered metal on a warm radiator – the heat sometimes causes the marks to flow out.

Lacquering protects a polished surface indoors for a number of years, but when it finally needs repolishing, remove the lacquer with acetone first.

I know one shouldn't polish antique pewter, but how is one supposed to keep it clean?

The soft-grey patina of old pewter should be preserved at all costs and the metal requires no more than an occasional dusting with a soft cloth.

Heavy corrosion can be removed by immersing pewter in paraffin for a day or two before washing it first in methylated spirits, then warm soapy water. Rinse and dry the metal thoroughly.

New pewter tankards can be kept clean with a long-term foaming silver polish.

What can I use to polish a cast-iron insert and grate?

Traditionally, cast-iron fireplaces are polished with a thick black paste that produces a beautiful gunmetal sheen. Spread this grate polish (black lead) onto the surface of the metal with a cloth and use an old tooth-brush to scrub it into decorative details and crevices. Burnish the paste by rubbing vigorously with a soft cloth. You will have to renew the polish regularly to maintain the finish.

CHAPTER 1

REPAIRING BOOKS AND PICTURES

Restoring pictures and conserving valuable documents and books are highly skilled specialized professions, but some of the techniques employed are surprisingly simple. With care and patience, amateur restorers can improve the appearance of old books and pictures, often with materials that are readily to hand. However, it pays to have a dealer examine a book or picture before you restore it yourself just in case you are lucky enough to have stumbled across something rare ●

Can I clean an old print without damaging it?

You can safely clean, even bleach, most old black-and-white prints of which there are many thousands in circulation. However, you should check beforehand that the print in question is not valuable.

Coloured prints should be examined by an expert before you attempt to clean them because a great many are hand coloured, and some quite recently. Hand-coloured prints are relatively delicate and may require expert treatment.

Take extra care with prints on very thin paper – it is all too easy to wear a thin patch or even a hole while trying to remove a dirty mark.

How can I clean a grubby print?

Surface dirt and scuffs can usually be removed from a black-and-white print using one of a number of erasers, but make sure you are not dealing with a pencil, charcoal, pastel or chalk drawing. There is no guarantee that these materials have been 'fixed' adequately by the artist and you might begin to erase the artwork itself.

Make a simple eraser by kneading soft white bread into a small ball. Discard bread crusts and do not use wholemeal bread containing actual wheat kernels. Hold the print down on a flat surface with the fingertips of one hand and erase the blemish with short straight strokes in one direction, away from you.

For more persistent marks, buy a 'putty rubber' from an artists' supplier. Knead this soft eraser into a ball, then use it to stipple the blemish to pick up much of the dirt before removing what's left in the same way as with a bread eraser.

Professionals use a very fine abrasive powder known as document cleaner that is available from specialist conservation-materials suppliers. Document cleaner is supplied in an open-weave bag which you squeeze to sprinkle a little powder onto the dirty area before rubbing it with the bag itself.

Is it possible to remove brown spots from a print?

These brown spots known as foxing are found on many an old print. Foxing is the result of fungal growth and is easily eradicated with bleach, but this process should be adopted for sturdy black-and-white prints only.

Make a mild solution of 1 part household bleach to 12 parts of cold water in a shallow plastic tray. Lay the print face up on a piece of glass and slide it gently under the surface of the bleach solution. As soon as the foxing disappears (it should take a few minutes only) pour the solution away and refill the tray with clean water. Change the water four times at five-minute intervals, then lift the glass and print from the tray and lay the print only face down on a sheet of blotting paper to dry. Take care when handling fragile wet paper.

I have a print that has been folded in half. How can I remove the crease?

Even if you cannot lose the crease completely, you can at least improve the appearance of the print. Run a damp cotton-wool swab along the back of the crease, then, with the print sandwiched between sheets of blotting paper, press it with a warm iron.

Is it possible to remove a grease stain from a print?

A professional picture restorer may be able to remove the grease with chemicals, but inexpert treatment can spread the grease over a wider area. Try placing the print between two sheets of blotting paper and warm the grease stain with an iron. If the heat appears to be drawing the grease into the blotting paper, apply a clean sheet and repeat the process.

Is there an alternative to using clear self-adhesive tape for repairing torn paper?

Ordinary self-adhesive tape is only suitable for utilitarian repairs. In time the adhesive becomes brittle and turns brown, staining the paper to which the tape is applied. Torn documents, books, prints and ink, pencil or pastel drawings require less obtrusive and more permanent methods of repair.

Special self-adhesive document-repair tape can be obtained from conservation-materials suppliers. This tape is much thinner than the common variety and the glue is stable. When pressed in place, document-repair tape is practically invisible, and a printed page beneath it is still perfectly legible.

As paper normally tears with feathered edges it is possible to glue them back together again. Mix up a little lightweight-wallpaper paste containing fungicide and use a fine artist's brush to paint it along the feathered edges only. Carefully bring the feathered edges together and, with the paper between sheets of polyethylene, press the repair flat with the back of a spoon.

Can I patch holes bored by insects through an old print?

Cut a very thin strip of paper from one edge of the damaged print and make it into papier-mâché in a saucer with hot water. Lay the print on a smooth piece of hardboard and, having dampened the area of the damage with a cotton-wool swab, press a little papier-mâché into each hole with a spoon handle so that the fibres of the wet paper and pulp interlock. Press the filled area flat with a warm iron and leave it to dry.

What is the professional way to replace a loose page in a book?

Lay the loose page on a flat surface and cover it with a sheet of paper that masks all but a 3mm ($\frac{1}{8}$in) strip along the bound edge. Paint thinned PVA glue across the exposed strip, brushing away from the mask. Replace the page in the book with all edges carefully aligned and lightly rub down the glued strip. Insert polyethylene, close the book and leave the glue to set.

Is there a simple way to revive dull leather book bindings?

It depends on the condition of the leather. If it's just dirty, you can wash leather with saddle soap sold in flat tins by conservation-materials suppliers, hardware shops and some shoe repairers. Work up a lather with a small damp sponge and wash the leather with tight circular strokes. Wipe the lather off with cotton wool, leave the binding to dry, then buff it with a soft cloth.

If the leather is also in a very dry condition, wash it with a flour-and-water paste. Dip a damp sponge in the paste and rub it into the leather with overlapping circular strokes. The next day apply a proprietary leather dressing available from a conservation-materials supplier. Soak a pad of cotton wool in the honey-like dressing and wring it out until it is almost dry, then rub it across the binding with small circular and figure-of-eight strokes. Twenty-four hours later buff the leather with a soft cloth.

Whatever method you use, protect the pages with polyethylene or waxed paper.

Should I have an oil painting cleaned by a professional?

In most cases the answer is yes, especially if it is necessary to strip old discoloured varnish. The methods employed are not difficult in themselves, but patience and concentration are required to avoid damaging a painting. If you have never attempted this type of work before it is prudent to restrict yourself to removing surface dirt only, and then only if the paint and varnish are sound. Paintings with crazed or flaking surfaces should always be taken to an expert.

Turn the painting round and tuck folded strips of newspaper between the canvas and the wooden stretcher to cushion the canvas during cleaning processes.

Dip a small ball of cotton wool in clean, preferably distilled water and squeeze it almost dry, then rub a small area near one corner of the painting with circular strokes. Inspect the surface of the swab to see how much dirt, if any, is being removed. If the treatment appears to be successful, work slowly across the painting, cleaning one small area at a time and blotting it immediately with dry cotton wool. Make sure you keep the back of the canvas dry throughout the process or you could seriously damage the painting.

What varnish should I use to protect an oil painting?

Although you can buy relatively cheap synthetic varnishes, it is advisable to use a natural copal, damar or mastic varnish on an old painting. Picture varnishes are available from artists' suppliers.

Work in good light in a warm, clean and dry environment. With the painting lying face up on a table, apply the varnish with a wide artist's brush.

Is there some way to reduce the reflection from framed pictures?

A lightly textured picture glass can be ordered from any framer. Non-reflective glass is relatively expensive and some people object to its slightly 'milky' quality, claiming that it has a detrimental effect on the appearance of the artwork. This is really only noticeable if the artwork is framed with a thick cardboard window mount.

15

REMOVING STAINS

Having to remove stains of all kinds from upholstery, carpets and rugs is practically an everyday occurrence. We are well served by manufacturers who supply an assortment of general-purpose shampoos and cleaners, and there are also proprietary removers that are formulated to deal with a specific type of stain. Even so, the next time you knock over a glass of wine or someone treads tar into your carpet there may not be a commercial stain remover in reach, and that's when it's handy to know what your grandparents used ●

How can I check a fabric is colourfast before trying to remove a stain?

Always check that colours will not run if they are subjected to a particular solvent or cleaning fluid. Use a cotton-wool swab to apply a sample of the solvent to an inconspicuous part of a carpet, upholstery or other fabric. There may be no reaction immediately, but after a few minutes press clean cotton wool or blotting paper against the test area. If the paper or cotton wool is clean you can proceed with removing the stain.

Also, check that a solvent does not harm an acetate or viscose fabric.

How can I prevent a stain spreading when I try to remove it?

Whatever you are cleaning, avoid spreading a stain over a wider area by applying the solvent in a circle around the outside of the stain, then work inwards towards the centre. Place a pad of absorbent rag or paper tissues under the stain while you clean it and, if possible, work from the back of the fabric.

Mop up spillage on a carpet immediately, then place a pile of absorbent tissues over the area and stand on them. Your weight helps to draw still more spillage out of the carpet before it has had a chance to leave a permanent stain. Try to lift that area of the carpet so that it can dry from both sides.

How can I get urine out of a carpet?

Wash the area with water containing a little disinfectant, but do not soak the carpet. If a stain develops, clean the carpet with a proprietary shampoo. There are spray-on liquid shampoos that are convenient for cleaning small areas of carpet. Alternatively, try a dry-powder carpet cleaner that you scrub into the pile with a stiff-bristle brush, then 30 minutes later pick up the powder with a vacuum cleaner.

Discourage pets from urinating in the same place by sprinkling the area with grated orange peel and cloves.

How can I get mud off my carpet?

Don't try to remove the mud if it's still damp. Leave it to dry thoroughly, then sweep the area with a stiff-bristle brush before using a vacuum cleaner to pick up the loose dirt that remains.

How can I remove grass stains?

Use clear methylated spirits on a clean cloth to remove grass stains. Clear meths can be obtained from a pharmacist, but if you have difficulty obtaining some, try using white spirit.

How can I remove soot from my carpet?

If you rub soot into a carpet it will cling to the pile and be be more difficult to remove. Hold the nozzle of a vacuum-cleaner hose just above the surface of the carpet to lift as much loose soot as possible, then vacuum the pile thoroughly before applying a carpet shampoo.

You may be able to shift a stubborn soot stain with a proprietary oil and grease solvent.

What will remove black grate polish from my fireside rug?	White spirit will dissolve grate polish (black lead).
How can I get chewing gum off my upholstery?	Before you attempt to remove chewing gum, freeze it by applying a plastic bag containing ice cubes. When the gum is hard, pick it off with your thumbnail or a blunt table knife. Wipe away the residue with a proprietary grease solvent or try a specific-stain remover.
How can I remove candle wax?	Pick off any large lumps of wax, then place blotting paper over the residue (on both sides if possible). Apply a warm iron. As the wax is absorbed into the paper, apply a clean piece and heat again. Finally, use cotton wool moistened with white spirit to clean the area.
How can I lift stains left by children's crayons?	Treat as for candle wax, but if you cannot remove all the colour with white spirit, try using clear methylated spirits.
How can I remove ballpoint ink?	There are specific-stain removers made for removing this type of ink. Alternatively, try using acetone (nail-varnish remover).
How can I remove fountain-pen ink?	Water, or an appropriate carpet or upholstery shampoo, may be enough to remove fountain-pen ink. You can try loosening it first by applying a paste of lemon juice and salt for ten minutes.
How can I remove stains left by felt-tip pens?	Use a specific-stain remover or clear methylated spirits. Some felt-tip inks are water-based and may wash out.
How can I remove black drawing ink?	This type of ink often leaves indelible stains, but you may be able to remove it with clear methylated spirits if you act quickly.
How can I remove blood stains?	If the stain is fresh, clean the fabric with cold water containing a few drops of household ammonia. Dried blood often responds to lemon juice plus salt. Alternatively, try a specific-stain remover.
How can I remove make-up from fabric?	Most cosmetics are greasy and can be removed with clear methylated spirits or try using a proprietary oil and grease solvent.
How can I remove wine stains?	Act quickly to prevent red wine staining. Blot the spillage with absorbent tissues, rinse with water, then blot again. Sprinkle salt liberally onto the area to act as an absorbent and one hour later pick it up with a vacuum cleaner or brush and dustpan. If there is still a hint of colour try a specific-stain remover.
How can I remove beer stains?	Beer will not stain if you blot a spillage quickly and sponge the area with warm soapy water. Add a few drops of ammonia to the water to remove a dried stain or try swabbing it with white vinegar.

How can I remove spirit stains?	Treat spilled spirits like beer, but use clear methylated spirits to loosen an old stain before rinsing with water.
How can I remove shoe polish?	Lift shoe polish with white spirit, then wash with an appropriate carpet or upholstery shampoo.
How can I remove tar stains?	Pick up any solid lumps of tar with a blunt table knife, then clean the stains with white spirit or a specific-stain remover.
How can I remove tea and coffee stains?	Wash tea and coffee stains with warm soapy water or use a suitable shampoo.
How can I remove chocolate?	Remove the heaviest stains with a proprietary grease solvent, then wash with warm soapy water.
How can I remove fruit juices?	Mop up a fruit-juice spillage with warm soapy water containing a little ammonia.
How can I remove grease stains?	Use a proprietary grease solvent to remove stains left by substances such as butter, cooking fats and oil.

16

WHAT TOOLS SHOULD I USE?

If you were to own all the tools listed in this chapter you could probably handle most of the jobs that are likely to crop up around the house. However, to assemble such a tool kit would cost you a small fortune. Good tools are expensive, but poor-quality tools are a waste of money. It pays in the long run to buy a few at a time but get the very best tools you can afford and, for the time being, hire those tools that you need for one job only ●

Adjustable spanner

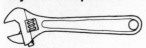

Having a movable jaw, an adjustable spanner is not as strong as an open-ended or ring spanner but is often the only tool that will fit a large or overpainted nut. Make sure the spanner fits the nut snugly by rocking it slightly as you tighten the jaws. Grip the nut with the roots of the jaws. If you use just the tips they can spring apart slightly under force and the spanner will slip.

Beam-compass cutter

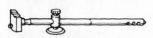

A beam-compass cutter is for scoring circles on glass – when, for example, you need a round hole in a window pane to fit a ventilator. The cutting wheel is mounted at the end of an adjustable beam that turns on a centre pivot which is fixed to the glass by suction.

Belt sander

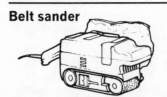

A belt sander has a continuous loop of abrasive paper passing round a drum at each end. The flat plate between the revolving drums presses the moving abrasive against the wood.

Bending springs

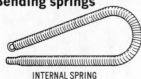

INTERNAL SPRING

You can bend small-diameter pipes over your knee, but their walls must be supported with a coiled spring to prevent them buckling.

Push an internal-type spring inside the pipe or an external-type one over it. Either type of spring must fit the pipe exactly.

Bevel-edge chisel

A bevel-edge chisel is used for paring, especially in trimming undercuts like dovetail joints or housings. Its bevels enable the blade to work in tight spaces that would be inaccessible to a thick firmer chisel. It is not as strong as a firmer and may break if it is used for heavy work. If a little extra force is needed to drive the chisel forward, use your shoulder or the ball of your hand.

Bolster chisel

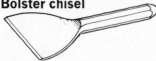

The wide bit of a bolster chisel is for cutting bricks and concrete blocks. It's also useful for levering up square-edged floorboards.

Box spanner

A box spanner is a steel tube with its ends shaped into hexagons – an excellent tool for reaching a nut in a confined space. Turning force is applied with a tommy bar slipped into a hole drilled through the spanner. Don't use a very long bar. Too much leverage may strip the thread of the fitting or distort the thin walls of the box spanner.

Brace

Use a brace for drilling the larger diameter holes. The bit is driven into the wood by the turning force on the handle plus pressure on the head of the tool.

A good brace will have a ratchet for turning the bit in only one direction when working in confined spaces where a full turn of the handle isn't possible.

Brace bits

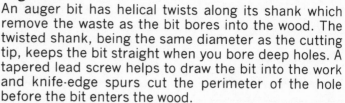

Brace bits have square-section tangs that fit into the jaws of tool's chuck.

Auger bit

An auger bit has helical twists along its shank which remove the waste as the bit bores into the wood. The twisted shank, being the same diameter as the cutting tip, keeps the bit straight when you bore deep holes. A tapered lead screw helps to draw the bit into the work and knife-edge spurs cut the perimeter of the hole before the bit enters the wood.

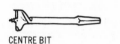

AUGER BIT

Centre bit

A centre bit is fast-cutting because it has no helical twists to create friction, but it tends to wander off line. It's best for drilling man-made boards in which the holes are never very deep. Its relatively short shank makes it useful for working in confined spaces.

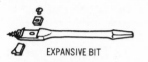

CENTRE BIT

Expansive bit

This bit has an adjustable spurred cutter for making holes of up to 75mm (3in) in diameter.

EXPANSIVE BIT

Bricklayer's line

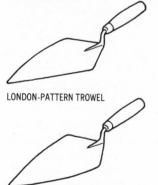

Use a bricklayer's line as a guide for laying bricks or blocks level. It is a length of nylon string stretched between two flat-bladed pins that are driven into vertical joints at the ends of a wall. There are also special line blocks that hook over the bricks at the ends of a course. As a makeshift you can stretch a string between two stakes driven into the ground outside the line of the wall.

Brick trowel

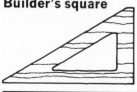

LONDON-PATTERN TROWEL

CANADIAN-PATTERN TROWEL

A brick trowel is for handling and placing mortar when laying bricks or concrete blocks. A professional might use one with a blade as long as 300mm (1ft), but such a trowel is too heavy and unwieldy for the amateur, so buy one with a fairly short but wide blade.

The blade of a **London-pattern trowel** has one curved edge for cutting bricks, a skill that needs much practice to perfect. The blade's other edge is straight, for picking up mortar. This type of trowel is made in right-handed and left-handed versions, so be sure to buy the right one for you. A right-handed trowel has its curved edge on the right when you point it away from you.

A **Canadian-pattern trowel** is symmetrical, so it's convenient when people with different left-hand and right-hand preferences want to share the one trowel.

Builder's square

A large set square is useful when you set out brick or concrete-block corners. The best ones are stamped out of sheet metal, but you can make a serviceable one by cutting out a thick plywood right-angled triangle with a hypotenuse of about 750mm (2ft 6in). Cut out the centre of the triangle to reduce the weight.

Cabinet screwdriver

A cabinet screwdriver has a shaft ground on two sides to produce a flat square tip. It may have a hardwood handle, strengthened with a metal ferrule, or a plastic one moulded onto the shaft.

Carpenter's mallet

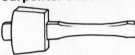

A carpenter's mallet is for driving a chisel or gouge into wood. Its striking faces are angled so as to deliver square blows to the end of the chisel. A loose mallet head is tightened by tapping the top of the tapered shaft on the bench.

Centre punch

A centre punch is for marking the centres of holes to be drilled in metal.

Chain tools

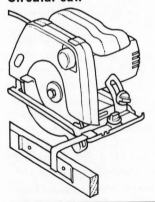

CHAIN-LINK CUTTER

CHAIN WRENCH

Chain-link cutter
Cut large-diameter pipes with a chain-link cutter. Wrap the chain round the pipe, locate the end link in the clamp and tighten the adjuster until the cutter on each link bites into the metal. Work the handle back and forth to score the pipe and continue, tightening the adjuster intermittently to cut deeper, until the pipe is severed.
Chain wrench
A chain wrench does the same job as a stilson wrench but it can be used on very large-diameter pipes and fittings. Wrap the chain tightly round the work and engage it with the hook at the end of the wrench, then lever the handle towards the toothed jaw to apply turning force.

Circular saw

When you buy or hire a circular saw choose one with a 190mm (7½in) blade. Its motor will be powerful enough to give a blade speed that can cut thick timber and man-made boards without straining the saw or scorching the work. There are blades designed just for ripping and others for crosscutting, but for general use choose a combination blade. This will cut efficiently both along and across the wood grain and is suitable for sawing man-made boards. There are also special blades and abrasive discs for cutting metal and stone.

On a good saw you can adjust the angle of the blade for cutting bevels.

Claw hammer

ADZE-EYE HAMMER

METAL-SHAFT HAMMER

A claw hammer is a heavy-weight general-purpose tool, probably the most useful hammer to have in a tool kit. The split claw at the back of the head is for levering out nails, and to withstand the strain of this the head must be fixed firmly to a strong shaft. The traditional adze-eye head has a deep square socket driven and wedged onto a tough but flexible hickory shaft. The all-metal hammer is an even better tool. Its tubular steel shaft won't bend or break, and the head can't work loose. The rubber grip is comfortable and shock-absorbing.

Club hammer

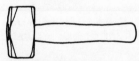

A heavy club hammer is used for driving cold chisels and for various demolition jobs. It is also useful for driving large masonry nails into walls.

Cold chisel

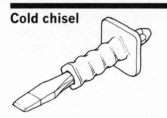

Cold chisels are made from solid steel hexagonal-section rod. They are primarily for cutting metal bars and chopping the heads off rivets, but a builder will use one for cutting a chase in plaster and brickwork or chopping out old brick pointing.

Slip a plastic safety sleeve over the chisel to protect your hand from a misplaced blow with the club hammer.

Combination square

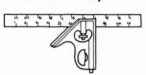

A combination square is a very versatile tool. Essentially it is a try square, but instead of a fixed blade it has a calibrated rule that slides in the stock to make a blade of any length up to 250mm (10in). This works as a useful depth and marking gauge. The head has an angled face for marking mitres and incorporates a small spirit level for checking vertical and horizontal surfaces.

Coping saw

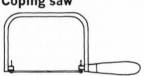

A coping saw has a frame that holds a fairly coarse but very narrow blade under tension for cutting curves in wood or man-made boards.

Corner roller

You cannot paint into a corner with a standard roller, so unless there are to be different adjacent colours, paint the corner first with a shaped corner roller.

Craft knife

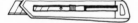

RETRACTABLE-BLADE KNIFE

Use a knife to trim paper round light fittings and switches and to achieve perfect butt joints by cutting through overlapping edges of paper. The knife must be extremely sharp to avoid tearing the paper, so use one with disposable blades that you can change easily when one gets blunt. Some craft knives have short double-ended blades clamped in a metal or plastic handle. Others have long retractable blades that can be snapped off in short sections to leave a new sharp point.

Cranked spanner and basin wrench

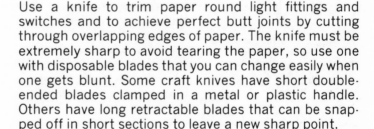

CRANKED SPANNER   BASIN WRENCH

A cranked spanner is a special double-ended wrench for use on tap connectors.

A basin wrench, for the same job, has a pivoting jaw that can be set for either tightening or loosening a fitting.

Crosscut saw

Unlike ripsaw teeth, which are filed square with the face of the blade, those of a crosscut saw are filed at an angle to form points that score lines along both edges of the kerf before removing the wood between them. This allows the saw to cut across the grain of solid timber without tearing the fibres.

Cross-head screwdriver

Always use a matching cross-head screwdriver to drive screws with cruciform slots. Using a flat-tip one instead invariably damages the screw.

Cross-peen hammer

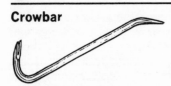

For those jobs too delicate for a heavy claw hammer use a medium-weight cross-peen one. Its wedge-shaped peen is for setting (starting) a nail held between finger and thumb.

Crowbar

A crowbar, or wrecking bar, is for demolishing timber framework. Force the flat tip between components and use the leverage of the long shaft to prise them apart. Choose a bar that also has a claw at one end for removing large nails.

Cutting-in brush

The filling of a cutting-in brush, or 'bevelled sash tool', is cut at an angle for painting moulded glazing bars right up into the corners and against the glass, though most painters make do with a 12mm ($\frac{1}{2}$in) flat brush.

Disc sander

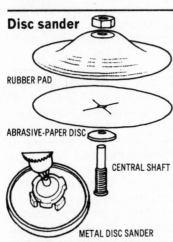

RUBBER PAD

ABRASIVE-PAPER DISC

CENTRAL SHAFT

METAL DISC SANDER

Disc sanding is not suitable for fine woodwork. It inevitably leaves swirling scratches that have to be removed with a finishing sander or cabinet scraper before a clear finish can be applied. The sander removes old paint very successfully and is handy for cleaning up old floorboards that are inaccessible to a large floor-sanding machine.

The simplest disc sander has a flexible rubber pad with a central shaft that is gripped in the chuck of an electric drill. An abrasive-paper disc is bolted to the face of the pad.

Metal disc sander

A superior type has a rigid metal plate on a ball-and-socket joint that lets the disc stay flat on the work while in use.

Dovetail saw

Because the tails and pins of a dovetail joint run with the grain the teeth of a dovetail saw are like miniature ripsaw teeth. Use this saw for fine cabinet work.

Drain auger

A flexible drain auger of coiled wire will pass through small-diameter wastepipes to clear blockages. Pass the corkscrew-like head into the pipe until it reaches the blockage, clamp on the cranked handle and turn it to rotate the head and engage the blockage. Push and pull the auger until the pipe is clear.

Drain rods

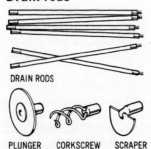

DRAIN RODS

PLUNGER   CORKSCREW   SCRAPER

You can hire a complete set of rods and fittings for clearing main drains and inspection chambers. Traditionally the rods are of flexible cane and wire, but modern ones come in 1 m (3ft 3in) lengths of polypropylene with threaded brass connectors. The clearing heads comprise a double-worm corkscrew fitting, a 100 mm (4 in) rubber plunger and a hinged scraper for clearing the open channels in inspection chambers.

Dusting brush

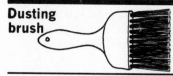

A dusting brush has long soft bristles for clearing dust out of mouldings and crevices just before painting wood-work. You can use an ordinary paintbrush if you keep it clean and reserve it for the job.

Electrician's screwdriver

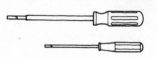

An electrician's screwdriver has a long, slim cylindrical shaft ground to a flat tip. For work on the terminals in sockets and larger appliances buy one with a plastic handle and a plastic insulating sleeve on its shaft. Use a smaller driver with a very slim shaft to work on ceiling roses or to tighten plastic terminal blocks on small electrical fittings.

Electronic mains tester

An electronic mains tester has a light in its handle that glows when its screwdriver-like tip touches a 'live' elect-rical wire or terminal. You have to place a fingertip on the tool's metal cap for the light to work, but there is no danger of a shock. A small test button on the handle tells if the tool is in working order.

Engineer's pliers

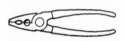

For general-purpose work buy a sturdy pair of engineer's pliers. The toothed jaws have curved sections for gripping round stock and side cutters for cropping wire.

Files

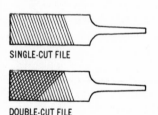

SINGLE-CUT FILE

DOUBLE-CUT FILE

The working faces of a file are composed of parallel ridges, or teeth, set at about 70 degrees to its edges. A file is classified according to the size and spacing of its teeth and whether it has one or two sets.

A *Single-cut file* has one set of teeth virtually covering each face. A *double-cut file* has a second set of identical teeth crossing the first at a 45-degree angle. Some files are single-cut on one side and double-cut on the other.

The spacing of the teeth relates directly to their size: the finer the teeth the more closely packed they are. Degrees of coarseness are expressed in numbers of teeth per 25mm (1in). Use progressively finer files to shape a component and gradually to remove marks left by coarser ones.

File classification
Bastard file – coarse grade (26 teeth per 25mm) – For initial shaping. *Second-cut file* – Medium grade (36 teeth per 25mm) – For preliminary smoothing. *Smooth file* – Fine grade (47 teeth per 25mm) – For final smoothing.

Filling knife

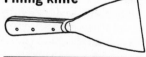

A filling knife looks like a paint scraper but has a flexible blade for forcing filler into cracks in timber or plaster. Patch large areas of damaged wall with a steel float or plasterer's trowel.

Finishing sander

The finishing sander produces a surface that needs only a light further hand finishing. On the machine, a strip of abrasive paper is stretched across a flat rubber pad which is moved by the motor in a tight, rapid orbital pattern. Use only light pressure or the paper will leave tiny swirling marks on the wood.

Firmer chisel

A firmer chisel has a strong, flat rectangular-section blade for chopping out waste wood. It is strong enough to be driven with a mallet or hammer – though hammers must not be used on wooden handles.

Flat paintbrush

The filling is set in rubber – or occasionally in pitch or resin – and bound to the wooden or plastic handle by a pressed-metal ferrule. You will need several sizes up to 50mm (2in) for painting, varnishing and staining woodwork.

A bristle filling is ideal for paintbrushes because each hair tapers naturally and splits at the tip into even finer filaments that hold paint well. Bristle is also tough and resilient. Synthetic 'bristle', usually of nylon, is made to resemble the characteristics of real bristle, and a good-quality nylon brush will serve the average painter as well as a bristle one.

Floorboard saw

If you prise a floorboard above its neighbours you can cut across it with an ordinary tenon saw, but a floorboard saw's curved cutting edge makes it easier to avoid damaging the boards on either side.

Foam drum sander

This is a flexible plastic-foam drum covered by an abrasive-paper band and attached to a power drill by a central shaft. The foam drum will deform against irregularly curved workpieces.

The abrasive bands are easy to take off and replace.

Force pump

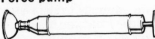

With the rubber mouth of the tool over a sink or basin outlet, water is forced along the wastepipe to clear a blockage by pumping the handle. A similar tool is available for clearing a blocked toilet.

Frame and mitre cramps

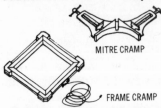

MITRE CRAMP

FRAME CRAMP

The four plastic corner blocks of a simple frame cramp contain the glued corners of a mitred frame. A strong cord pulled taut round the blocks applies equal pressure to all four joints, holding the frame perfectly square while the glue sets.

A cast-metal mitre cramp holds one joint at a time, clamping the two mitred members against a right-angle fence. The joint can be glued or nailed.

Frenchman

A Frenchman is a specialized tool for cutting excess mortar away from brickwork jointing. You can make one by heating and bending an old table knife.

Garden rake

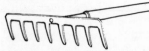

Use an ordinary garden rake to spread gravel or level wet concrete, but be sure to wash it before any concrete sets on it.

G-cramp

A G-cramp has a screw that grips the work between a shoe attached to its end and the cast-metal frame. You will need at least one 150mm (6in) and one 300mm (1ft) G-cramp.

Gents saw

This cheap alternative to a dovetail saw has a straight wooden handle.

Glass cutter

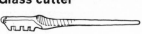

A glass cutter doesn't really cut glass but scores a line in it. The scoring is done by a tiny hardened-steel wheel or a chip of industrial diamond mounted in the pen-like holder. The glass will break along the scored line when pressure is applied to it.

Gouges

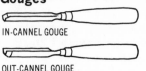

IN-CANNEL GOUGE

OUT-CANNEL GOUGE

An in-cannel gouge is one whose cutting edge is formed by grinding the inside of the curved blade. It is used for trimming rounded shoulders. An out-cannel gouge is ground on the outside so that the blade will not be driven deeper into the wood when it is scooping out shallow depressions.

Hacking knife

A hacking knife has a heavy steel blade for chipping old putty out of window rebates so as to remove the glass. Place its point between the putty and the frame and tap its thickened back with a hammer.

Hacksaw

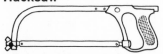

A modern hacksaw has a tubular steel frame with a light cast-metal handle. The frame is adjustable to blades of different lengths, which are tensioned by tightening a wing nut.

Hand drill

For small-diameter holes use a hand drill, also called a wheelbrace. Some have cast bodies enclosing their drive mechanisms to keep gear wheels and pinions dust-free. Fit standard twist drills.

Hawk

A small square board with a handle underneath for carrying wet plaster or mortar. Professionals often use all-metal hawks.

Hole saw

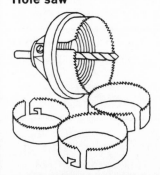

You can buy a set of hole-saw blades for cutting perfectly round holes of different diameters. They clip into a backing plate clamped to a central twist drill which fits in the chuck of a power drill. Place the tip of the twist drill at the centre of the required hole and, with the power tool at slow speed, slowly push the revolving saw against the wood. Always place a piece of scrap timber behind the work to stop the saw breaking out the back.

Hook scraper

A hook scraper's disposable blade slides into a clip at the end of a wooden handle. Use the scraper by pulling it towards you along the grain of the wood, applying light pressure.

Hot-air stripper

The gas blowtorch was once the professional's tool for softening old paint so as to strip it, but the modern electric hot-air stripper is much easier to use. It is as efficient as a blowtorch, but involves little risk of scorching woodwork. Early models were heavy and tiring to use, but today's are light enough to be used for long periods without fatigue. On some strippers the air temperature can be adjusted. Others have interchangeable nozzles shaped to concentrate the heated air or direct it away from glass panes.

Jack plane

A jack plane 350 to 375mm (1ft 2in to 1ft 3in) long is a good all-purpose tool. If you can afford only one bench plane choose a jack plane, which is light enough to cope with most planing without tiring you.

Jigsaw

A portable jigsaw is primarily for making curved cuts in timber and man-made boards. Most such saws have guide fences for straight cutting, but they are rarely sturdy enough to stop the blade wandering. Discard jigsaw blades when they get blunt and keep some spares handy. As blades are fairly cheap it's worth buying some of the special ones for cutting plastics, metal, plasterboard and even ceramics.

Jointer

A jointer is shaped for making 'V' or concave joints between bricks. The narrow blade is dragged along the mortar joint and the curved front end used for shaping the verticals.

Jointer plane

The jointer is the longest bench plane, with a sole up to 600mm (2ft) long. It is designed for truing up the long edges of boards that are to be glued together, and for levelling large flat panels. Its long sole bridges minor irregularities until the blade shaves them down. A shorter plane would simply follow the uneven surface.

Joist brace

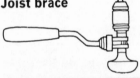

A joist brace has a chuck that takes standard brace bits but its side-mounted handle and ratchet mechanism allow drilling in the restricted space between floor and ceiling joists.

Junior hacksaw

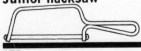

Use a junior hacksaw for cutting small-bore tubing and thin metal rod. In most types the blade is held under tension by the steel frame.

Kettle

To carry paint to a work'site, decant a little into a cheap, lightweight plastic paint kettle.

Marking gauge

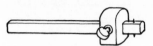

With a marking gauge you can score a line parallel to an edge. Set the movable stock the required distance from the pin in the beam. Press the face of the stock against the edge of the timber, tilt the gauge to an angle, the pin touching the wood's surface, then push the tool away from you to scribe the line.

Marking knife

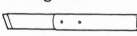

Before sawing timber, mark the cutting lines with a knife. It is more accurate than a pencil and prevents the grain breaking out when you saw. The blade of a marking knife is ground on only one side, and its flat face is run against a try square.

Mastic guns

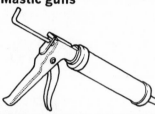

Non-setting (permanently flexible) mastic is for sealing gaps between masonry and wooden frames, and other joints between materials whose different rates of expansion will eventually crack and eject a rigid filler. You can buy mastic that is squeezed direct from its plastic tube like toothpaste, but it is easier to apply from a cartridge in a spring-loaded gun or an aerosol can with a special pointed nozzle.

Mattock

The wide blade of a mattock is ideal for breaking up heavy clay soil,and it's better than an ordinary pickaxe for ground that's riddled with tree roots.

Mortise chisel

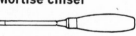

A mortise chisel has a thick blade, rectangular in section, for chopping and levering the waste out of mortise joints. Mallets are always needed to drive mortise chisels, so many of them have a shock-absorbent leather washer between the blade and the ferrule.

Nibblers

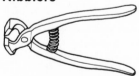

It is impossible to snap a very narrow strip off a ceramic tile. Instead score the line with a tile cutter, then break off the waste little by little with tile nibblers. They resemble pincers but have sharper jaws of tungsten-carbide that open automatically when you relax your grip on the spring-loaded handles.

Open-ended spanner

A set of the familiar open-ended spanners is essential to a plumber or metalworker. In most situations pipework runs into a fitting or accessory and it is not possible to use anything but a spanner with open jaws. Most spanners are double-ended, perhaps in a combination of metric and imperial sizes, and sizes are duplicated within a set for when two identical nuts have to be manipulated simultaneously, as on a compression joint, for instance.

Padsaw

Also called a keyhole saw, this small saw has a narrow tapered blade for cutting holes in timber.

Paint pads and trays

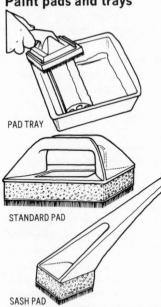

PAD TRAY

STANDARD PAD

SASH PAD

Pads and trays are normally sold as sets, but if you buy a separate tray get one with a loading roller that distributes paint evenly onto the sole of a pad drawn across it. Paint pads are a fairly recent development aimed at helping inexperienced painters to apply oil and emulsion paint quickly and evenly. They are not universally popular, but no one disputes their value in painting large flat areas. They cover quickly and are unlikely to drip paint if they are loaded properly.

Rectangular pads
There is a range of rectangular pads for painting walls, ceilings and flat woodwork. They have short mohair pile on their painting surfaces and handles on their backs.

Edging pad
To paint a straight edge – between a wall and a ceiling, for instance – use an edging pad with small wheels or rollers that guide it parallel to the adjacent surface.

Sash pad
A sash pad has a small mohair sole for painting glazing bars. Most sash pads have plastic guides on their backs to prevent them straying onto the glass.

Paint rollers

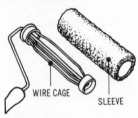

WIRE CAGE   SLEEVE

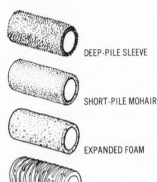

DEEP-PILE SLEEVE

SHORT-PILE MOHAIR

EXPANDED FOAM

MOULDED PVC

A paint roller is efficient for painting large areas quickly. On the better type the cylindrical sleeve that applies the paint slides onto a revolving sprung-wire cage on a cranked handle. The sleeves on this type of roller are easily changed. Don't buy one whose sleeve is held in place by a small nut and washer. Even if the nut doesn't get lost, corroded or paint-clogged it's much too fiddly.

Sleeves for standard rollers range from 175mm (7in) to 337mm (1ft 1½in) in length, but there are smaller rollers for painting narrow strips of wall or woodwork.

There are roller sleeves of various materials to suit different paints and surface textures. Most are of **sheepskin** or **synthetic fibre,** both of which suit emulsion paint and leave an even finely textured finish. Use a **deep-pile** sleeve to paint a heavily textured surface, a **medium-pile** one for smooth walls and ceilings.

Short-pile roller sleeves, usually of mohair, are made for use with oil paints.

The cheap **plastic-foam** sleeves are unsatisfactory both with oil and emulsion paints. They leave tiny air bubbles in the painted surface and the foam often distorts as it dries after washing. But they are cheap enough to be thrown away after use with finishes – like bituminous paint – which would be hard to remove even from a short-pile roller sleeve.

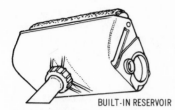

Use a **coarse expanded-foam** sleeve for applying textured coatings. There are also **moulded PVC** rollers with embossed surfaces to pattern all kinds of textured paints and coatings.

Extending a roller

If your roller has a hollow handle you can plug it onto a telescopic extension handle so as to reach a ceiling from the floor. Loading an extended roller can be tricky, but you can buy one with a built-in reservoir that keeps the roller charged and holds enough paint for a large area.

BUILT-IN RESERVOIR

Paint shield and scraper

There are various plastic and metal shields for protecting glass when window frames and glazing bars are being painted, and glass that does get spattered can be cleaned with a razor blade clipped in a special holder.

Panel saw

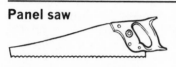

The teeth of a panel saw are set and shaped like those of a cross-cut but are smaller and closer together. They cut a finer kerf. The saw is used for cutting thin man-made boards like plywood and hardboard.

Paperhanger's brush

This is a brush used for smoothing wallcovering onto a surface. Its bristles should be soft, so as not to damage delicate paper, but springy enough to provide the pressure to squeeze excess paste and air bubbles from beneath the wallcovering. Wash the brush in warm water when you finish work to prevent paste hardening on the tips of the bristles.

Paperhanger's scissors

Any fairly large scissors can be used for trimming wallpaper to length, but proper paperhanger's scissors have extra-long blades to achieve a straight cut.

Paste brush

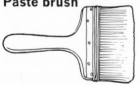

Apply paste to the back of wallcovering with a wide wall-brush. Alternatively use a short-pile mohair roller. Clean either tool by washing it in warm water.

Pasting table

Though you can paste wallcoverings on any convenient flat surface a proper pasting table is ideal. It stands higher than the average dining table and is only 25mm (1in) wider than a standard roll of wallpaper, making it easier to apply paste without spreading onto the work surface. The underframe folds flat and the top is hinged, so the table can be carried from room to room and stowed in a small space.

Pickaxe

Use a medium-weight pickaxe to break up heavily compacted soil, especially if it contains a lot of buried rubble.

Pin hammer

A small lightweight pin hammer is perfect for tapping in fine panel pins and tacks.

Pipe roller

A pipe roller has two narrow sleeves, mounted side by side, which locate over cylindrical pipework to paint it.

Plasterer's rule

A plasterer's rule is simply a straight wooden batten used for scraping plaster and rendering undercoats level.

Plasterer's trowel

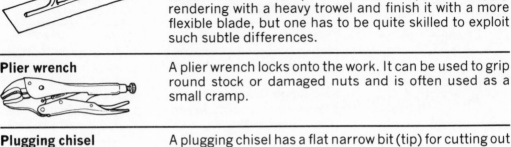

A plasterer's trowel is a steel float for applying plaster and cement rendering to walls. It is also dampened and used for 'polishing', stroking the surface of the material when it has firmed up. Some builders prefer to apply rendering with a heavy trowel and finish it with a more flexible blade, but one has to be quite skilled to exploit such subtle differences.

Plier wrench

A plier wrench locks onto the work. It can be used to grip round stock or damaged nuts and is often used as a small cramp.

Plugging chisel

A plugging chisel has a flat narrow bit (tip) for cutting out old pointing. It's worth hiring one if you have a large area of brickwork to repoint.

Plumb line

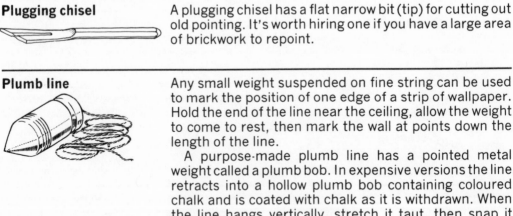

Any small weight suspended on fine string can be used to mark the position of one edge of a strip of wallpaper. Hold the end of the line near the ceiling, allow the weight to come to rest, then mark the wall at points down the length of the line.

A purpose-made plumb line has a pointed metal weight called a plumb bob. In expensive versions the line retracts into a hollow plumb bob containing coloured chalk and is coated with chalk as it is withdrawn. When the line hangs vertically, stretch it taut, then snap it against the wall like a bowstring to leave a chalked line.

Pointing trowel

The blade of a pointing trowel is no more than 75 to 100mm (3 to 4in) long, designed for repairing or shaping mortar joints between bricks.

Post-hole auger

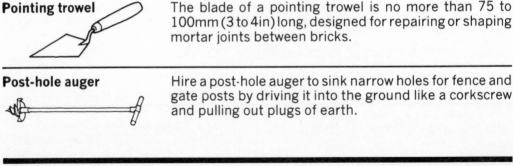

Hire a post-hole auger to sink narrow holes for fence and gate posts by driving it into the ground like a corkscrew and pulling out plugs of earth.

Power drill

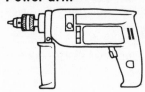

Buy a well-made drill that can cope with all the tasks you may have to tackle now and later. Choose one with a powerful motor – up to 600W – especially if you plan to use it with power-tool attachments. Continuously using a circular saw for a long time will burn out an under-powered drill. Most drills now have plastic bodies that are lighter than metal ones and will protect you from electric shock. A few drills are battery-powered and have plug-in rechargers.

Selecting useful features

Before you choose an electric drill note down the features that would be of most use to you and list them in order of priority in case you can't find a tool that has them all.

Drill speed

A power drill with one fixed speed is too limiting for general use. Some drills have from two to four fixed speeds and a switch for selecting the one appropriate to a given job. A slow speed uses the drill's power to produce more torque (turning force) for drilling such materials as masonry and metal; a high speed gives a clean cut when drilling wood.

Run power-tool attachments at the speeds recommended by the manufacturer.

A variable-speed drill can be operated at any speed throughout its range by varying pressure on the trigger or setting a control dial. This lets you select the ideal speeds for drilling various materials, and is essential also if you want to use a screwdriver bit in a power drill.

Trigger lock

A trigger lock button sets the drill for continuous running when it is used to drive attachments.

Chuck size

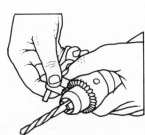

Operating a chuck
Most chucks are operated with a key as shown here. A straight pull opens a fast-action chuck.

The chuck's size refers to the maximum diameter of drill shank or attachment spindle that it can accommodate. A 10mm ($\frac{3}{8}$in) chuck is adequate for most purposes, though there are drills with a chuck size of 13mm ($\frac{1}{2}$in). You can drill holes of greater diameter than the chuck size by using special drill bits with cutters larger than their shanks.

Percussion or hammer action

By operating a lever you can convert some drills from smooth rotation to a hammer action that delivers several hundred blows per second to the revolving chuck. This is required only for drilling masonry, when the hammer vibration breaks up hard particles ahead of the special toughened bit before the debris is cleared by the helical flutes on the bit.

Reverse rotation

If you want to use a screwdriver bit with your electric drill make sure that its rotation can be reversed so that you can take screws out as well as insert them.

Handgrips

Most power drills have a pistol-grip handle and a second handgrip for steadying the drill. Some manufacturers provide a handle that bolts onto the rear of the drill so that it can be controlled with both hands when pressure is needed directly behind the chuck.

Power-drill bits

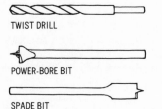
TWIST DRILL

POWER-BORE BIT

SPADE BIT

COUNTERSINK BIT

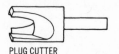
SCREWDRIVER BIT

PLUG CUTTER

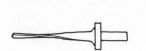
DOWEL BIT

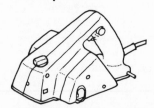
DRILL AND COUNTERSINK BIT

A variety of bits can be used in a power drill, depending on the kind of hole you want to bore.

Twist drill
You can use standard twist drills of any size to the maximum opening of the chuck. To bore larger holes use reduced-shank drill bits.

Power-bore and spade bits
With a power-bore bit or a spade bit you can drill holes of up to 38mm (1½in) in diameter. Either bit produces minimal friction. Place the sharp lead point of the bit on the centre of the hole before pressing the trigger of the power drill.

Countersink bit
To sink the head of a countersunk woodscrew flush with the surface of the work, make a tapered recess in the top of the clearance hole with a 'rose' or countersink bit. These bits can be used in hand drills and braces, but a high-speed electric drill forms a neater recess.

Except with a vertical drill stand, the countersink bit 'chatters' if the hole has already been drilled, producing a rough recess. When you have to use the drill 'freehand' it's best to make the recess first, then drill the hole itself.

Screwdriver bit
With slotted-head or cross-head screwdriver bits you can use your electric drill as a power screwdriver. The drill must be capable of slow speeds.

Plug cutter
This special bit cuts cylindrical plugs of wood for concealing the heads of screws sunk below the surface of the workpiece.

Dowel bit
This is a twist drill with a sharp lead point and cutting spurs that help to keep it on line when holes are bored for dowel joints.

Drill and countersink bit
This bit makes the pilot hole, clearance hole and countersink recess for a woodscrew in one operation. As it is matched to one specific screw size it is worth purchasing only when you plan to use a fair number of identical woodscrews.

Power plane

A power plane is useful for smoothing and shaping large structural timbers. Its revolving two-cutter or three-cutter block can be used for planing rebates if guided by a side fence.

Profile gauge

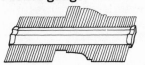

A profile gauge is for copying the shapes of pipework or door mouldings to provide a pattern for fitting soft floor-coverings, for example. As you press the steel pins of the gauge against the object you wish to copy they slide back, mirroring the shape. When you want to copy another shape press the needles against a flat surface to reposition them in a straight line.

Pump-action screwdriver

The tip of a pump-action screwdriver is turned by a thrusting action on the handle. The spring-loaded shaft moves in and out of a hollow handle containing a ratchet mechanism that controls the direction of rotation. Interchangeable cross-head and flat-tipped bits fit into a chuck on the end of the shaft.

Putty knife

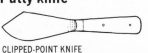

CLIPPED-POINT KNIFE

The blunt blade of a putty knife is for shaping and smoothing fresh putty. You can choose between spearpoint, clipped-point and straight blades according to your personal preference.

Radiator brush and roller

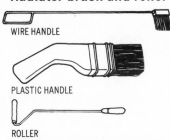

WIRE HANDLE

PLASTIC HANDLE

ROLLER

Unless you take a radiator off the wall for decorating you need a special brush to paint the back of it and the wall behind it. There are two kinds: one with a standard flat paintbrush head at right angles to its long wire handle, the other like a conventional paintbrush but with a cranked plastic handle.
Radiator roller
This is a thin roller on a long wire handle for painting behind radiators and pipes.

Ratchet screwdriver

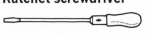

By using a ratchet screwdriver you can insert and remove screws without having to replace the tip in the slot after each turn or shifting your grip on the handle. You can select clockwise or anti-clockwise rotation or lock the ratchet and use the tool like an ordinary fixed screwdriver.

Ring spanner

Being a closed circle, the head of a ring spanner is stronger and fits better than that of an open-ended one. It is specially handy for loosening corroded nuts if it can be slipped onto them from above.

Ripsaw

The ripsaw is made specifically for cutting solid timber along its length ('ripping down'). Each of its teeth is like a tiny chisel that slices the timber along its grain. Alternate teeth are bent outward in opposite directions (set) so that the groove (kerf) cut in the timber is slightly wider than the thickness of the blade. Most saws are set in this way, or they would jam in the kerf.

Roller tray

A paint roller is loaded from a sloping plastic or metal tray whose deep end acts as a paint reservoir. Load the roller by rolling paint from the deep end up and down the tray's ribbed slope once or twice so as to get even distribution on the sleeve.

Sash cramp

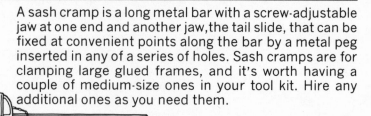

A sash cramp is a long metal bar with a screw-adjustable jaw at one end and another jaw, the tail slide, that can be fixed at convenient points along the bar by a metal peg inserted in any of a series of holes. Sash cramps are for clamping large glued frames, and it's worth having a couple of medium-size ones in your tool kit. Hire any additional ones as you need them.

Saw file

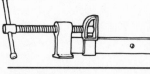

A saw file has a bent metal frame that holds the thin wire rod under tension. The rod is coated with particles of tungsten-carbide hard enough to cut through ceramic tiles. Circular in section, the file will cut in any direction, so it can cut curved and straight lines with equal ease.

Seam roller

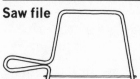

Use a hardwood or plastic seam roller to press down butted joints between adjacent strips of wallpaper, but not on embossed or delicate wallcoverings.

Serrated trowel

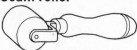

Make a ridged bed of adhesive for ceramic tiles by drawing the toothed edge of a plastic or steel tiler's trowel through the material.

Shavehook

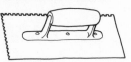

This is a special scraper for removing old paint and varnish. A straight-sided triangular one is fine for flat surfaces, but one with a combination blade can also be used on concave and convex mouldings. You pull a shavehook towards you to remove the softened paint.

Sheet-metal cutter

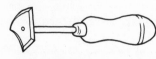

Unlike tinsnips, which will distort a narrow waste strip on one side of the cutting line, a sheet-metal cutter removes a narrow strip as perfectly flat as the larger sheet. It is also suited to cutting rigid plastic sheet, which can crack if it is distorted by tinsnips.

Shovel

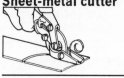

You can use a spade for mixing and placing concrete or mortar, but the raised edges of a shovel retain it better.

Sink plunger

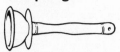

This is a simple but effective tool for clearing a blockage from the trap. A pumping action on the rubber cap forces air and water along the pipe to disperse the blockage.

When you buy a plunger make sure that the cup is big enough to surround the waste outlet completely.

Sledgehammer

Hire a big sledgehammer if you have to break up hard-core or paving. It's also the best tool for driving stakes or fence posts into the ground, though you can make do with a club hammer if the ground is not too hard.

Slip-joint or waterpump pliers

The special feature of slip-joint pliers is a movable pivot for enlarging the jaw spacing. The extra-long handles give a good grip on pipes and other fittings.

Smoothing plane

A finely set smoothing plane is used for putting the final surface on a piece of timber after it has been reduced to size with a jack plane or jointer plane.

Smoothing roller

RUBBER ROLLER   FELT ROLLER

There are rubber rollers for squeezing trapped air from under wallcoverings, but use a felt one on delicate and flocked wallpapers.

Soft mallet

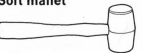

Soft mallets have heads of coiled rawhide, hard rubber or plastic. They are used for bending strip or sheet metal, which would be damaged by a metal hammer.

Soldering irons

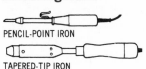

PENCIL-POINT IRON

TAPERED-TIP IRON

Successful soldering needs the work to be made hot enough to melt the solder and cause it to flow; otherwise the solder will solidify before it can completely penetrate the joint. The heat is applied with a soldering iron.

There are simple irons that are heated in a fire, but an electric iron is much handier to use and its temperature is both controllable and constant. Use a low-powered pencil-point iron for soldering electrical connections and a larger one with a tapered tip to bring sheet metal up to working temperature.

Spade

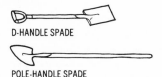

D-HANDLE SPADE

POLE-HANDLE SPADE

Buy a good-quality spade for excavating soil and mixing concrete. One with a stainless-steel blade is best, but alloy steel will last fairly well if it is looked after. For strength choose a D-shaped handle whose hardwood shaft has been split and riveted with metal plates to the crosspiece, and make sure that the shaft socket and blade are forged in one piece.

Square blades seem to be the most popular, though some builders prefer a round-mouth spade with a long pole handle for digging deep trenches and holes.

Spear-point glass drill

A glass drill has a flat spearhead-shaped tip of tungsten carbide on a toughened steel shaft. The shape of the tip reduces friction that would otherwise crack the glass, but it needs lubricating with oil, paraffin or water during drilling.

Spirit level

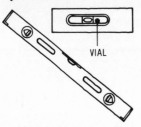

VIAL

A spirit level is a machine-made straightedge incorporating special glass tubes or vials that contain a liquid. In each vial an air bubble floats. When a bubble rests exactly between two lines marked on the glass the structure on which the level is held is known to be properly horizontal or vertical, depending on the vial's orientation. Buy a wooden or lightweight aluminium level 600 to 900mm (2 to 3ft) long. A well-made one is very strong, but treat it with care and always clean mortar or plaster from it before they set.

Spokeshave

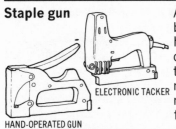

A spokeshave is a miniature plane for shaping curved edges in wood. Use one with a flat base to shape a convex curve, one with a bellied base for a concave curve. When you use either tool, shape the curve from two directions so as to work with the grain all the time. Sharpen a spokeshave cutter as you would a plane blade.

Squeegee

A squeegee has a blade of hard rubber mounted in a wooden handle. Use one for spreading grout into the gaps between ceramic tiles.

Staple gun

ELECTRONIC TACKER

HAND-OPERATED GUN

A staple gun is used for fixing mineral-fibre tiles to battens attached to a ceiling. The hand-operated type has a trigger that works a spring-loaded striker, which drives two-pronged staples into the work. It can be tiring to use with an outstretched arm. An electronic tacker makes light work of the largest ceilings and is much more powerful than the hand-operated tool, though its force is adjustable to suit various materials.

Steam wallpaper stripper

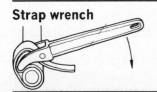

To remove wallpaper quickly, especially thick wall-covering, buy or hire an electric steam-generating stripper. All such strippers work on the same principle, but follow any specific safety instructions that come with the machine.

Stilson wrench

The adjustable toothed jaws of a stilson wrench are for gripping pipework. As force is applied, the jaws tighten on the work.

Straightedge

Any length of straight, fairly stout timber can be used to tell whether a surface is flat or, used with a spirit level, to test whether two points are at the same height.

Strap wrench

With a strap wrench you can disconnect chromed pipework without damaging its surface. Wrap the smooth leather or canvas strap round the pipe, pass its end through the slot in the head of the tool and pull it tight. Leverage on the handle will rotate the pipe.

Surform files

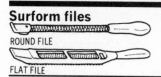

ROUND FILE

FLAT FILE

A round Surform file has a detachable handle and thumb-grip at the tip. A flat Surform has a disposable blade that fits into a hollow metal frame.

Tank cutter

Use a tank cutter to make holes for pipework in plastic or metal storage cisterns.

Tape measure

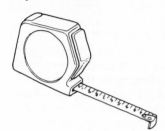

A modern retractable steel tape measure can take measurements up to about 5m (16ft), including internal ones using the tip of the tape and back of the case. The tape can be locked open at any point. Avoid letting a spring-loaded tape snap back into its case or the riveted hook on its end will become loose.

An ordinary retractable steel tape measure is adequate for most purposes but, if you need to mark out or measure a large plot, hire a wind-up tape up to 30m (100ft) in length.

Tenon saw

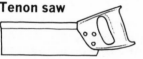

A tenon saw has fine teeth shaped and set like those of a crosscut saw. It is the perfect saw for general-purpose woodworking and is especially useful for cutting some of the large joints used in house construction.

Tile cutter

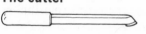

A tile cutter is a square-section rod of steel with a pointed tungsten-carbide tip. The tip is for scoring the glazed surface of a ceramic tile so that it will snap cleanly along the scored line. Other cutters have steel wheels like glass cutters.

Tile-cutting jigs

FLOOR-TILE JIG

A tile-cutting jig greatly simplifies the cutting and fitting of border tiles to fill the edges of a field of tiles. With the one tool you can measure the gap, score the tile and snap it along the scored line.

Floor-tile jig

Large cutting jigs for floor tiles can be hired or bought from good DIY stockists.

Tinsnips

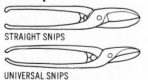

STRAIGHT SNIPS

UNIVERSAL SNIPS

Tinsnips are heavy-duty scissors for cutting sheet metal. Straight snips have wide blades for cutting straight edges. If you try to cut curves with them the waste gets caught against the blades, though it's possible to cut a convex curve by removing small straight pieces of waste and working down to the marked line. Universal snips have thick narrow blades that will cut a curve in one pass and will also make straight cuts.

Try square

A try square is used to check the accuracy of square joints and planed timber. It is also for marking out timber which is to be sawn or cut 'square' to its edge. Look for a try square with its blade and stock (handle) cut from one L-shaped piece of metal. One with a straight blade riveted to the stock may lose its accuracy. Some try squares have the top of the stock cut at 45 degrees for marking out mitre joints. Buy the largest square you can afford. They come with blades up to 300mm (1ft) long.

Tube bender

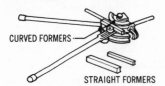

CURVED FORMERS

STRAIGHT FORMERS

In a tube bender, pipe is bent over one of two fixed curved formers that give the optimum radii for plumbing. Each has a matching straight former which is placed between the pipe and a steel roller on a movable lever. When this lever is moved towards the fixed one the pipe is bent over the curved former. The formers support the pipe walls during bending.

You can get extra leverage by clamping the fixed lever in a vice and using both hands on the movable one.

Tube cutter

A tube cutter will cut the ends of pipes at exactly 90 degrees to their length. The pipe is clamped between the cutting wheel and an adjustable slide with two rollers, and is cut as the tool is revolved around it and the adjusting screw tightened before each turn. Keep the cutter lightly oiled when you use it.

Universal saw

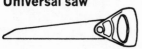

A universal or general-purpose saw is designed to cut wood, metal, plastics and building boards. Its short frameless blade has a low-friction coating and is stiff enough to make straight cuts without wandering. The handle can be set at various angles. The saw is particularly useful for cutting second-hand timber, which may contain nails or screws that would blunt an ordinary woodsaw.

Vinyl gloves

Most people wear ordinary 'rubber' gloves to protect their hands when washing down or preparing paintwork, but tough PVC work gloves are more hardwearing and will protect you from a great many harmful chemicals.

Wallbrush

To apply emulsion paint by brush use a 150mm (6in) flat wallbrush or a two-knot brush of the kind favoured by continental painters and decorators.

Wallpaper or paint scraper

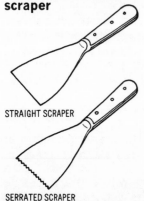

STRAIGHT SCRAPER

SERRATED SCRAPER

The wide stiff blade of a scraper is for removing softened paint or soaked wallpaper. The best scrapers have high-quality steel blades and riveted rosewood handles. One with a 100 to 125mm (4 to 5in) wide blade is best for stripping wallpaper, but a narrow one, no more than 25mm (1in) wide, is useful for removing paint from window or door frames. A serrated scraper will score impervious wallcovering so that water or stripping solution can penetrate it faster. If you use one, try not to damage the wall behind the covering.

Water level

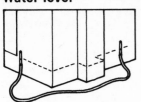

You can make a water level from a garden hose with short lengths of transparent plastic tube plugged into its ends. Fill the hose with water until it appears in both tubes. As water level is constant the levels in the tubes are always identical and so can be used for marking identical heights even over long distances and round obstacles and bends.

WC auger

The short coiled wire WC auger, designed for clearing WC and gully traps, is rotated by a handle in a hollow rigid shaft. A vinyl guard prevents scratching of a WC.

Web cramp

A web cramp acts like a frame cramp, forming a tourniquet round large frames. Its nylon webbing is tensioned by adjusting a ratchet mechanism with a spanner or screwdriver.

Wheelbarrow

The average garden wheelbarrow is not really strong enough for work on building sites, which entails carrying heavy loads of wet concrete and rubble. Unless the tubular underframe is rigidly strutted the barrow's thin metal body will distort and perhaps spill its load as you cross rough ground. Check, too, that the axle is fixed securely. Cheap wheelbarrows often lose their wheels when their loads are being tipped into excavations.

Wire brushes

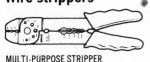

HANDBRUSH

CUP BRUSH

A handbrush with steel wire 'bristles' will remove flaking paint and rust particles from metalwork before repainting. The job is easier with a rotary wire cup brush in a power drill, but wear goggles or safety glasses.

Wire strippers

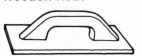

MULTI-PURPOSE STRIPPER

To remove the colour-coded insulation from electrical cable and flex, use a pair of wire strippers with jaws shaped to cut through the plastic without damaging the wire core. There is a multi-purpose version that can both strip the insulation and crop the wires to length.

Wooden float

A wooden float is for applying and smoothing cement renderings and concrete to a fine attractive texture. The more expensive ones have detachable handles so that their wooden blades can be replaced when they wear, but the amateur is unlikely to use a float often enough to justify the extra cost.

REFERENCE
SECTION

PRODUCT BRAND NAMES	168
GLOSSARY OF TERMS	182
INDEX	186

DECORATING

PAINT AND VARNISH STRIPPERS

BRAND NAME	MANUFACTURER/SUPPLIER	DESCRIPTION
All Purpose Paint Remover	Nitromors	*Gel-like stripper. Ideal for removing paint from large vertical surfaces.*
Colron Hard Finish Remover	Sterling Roncraft	*Removes polyurethane varnishes, paints and other finishes.*
Craftsman's Paint Remover	Nitromors	*Free-flowing liquid paint stripper for intricate work and veneers.*
Peel Away	Langlow	*Poultice-type stripper that removes paints from a range of surfaces including plaster and brickwork.*
Safer Stripper	Langlow	*Paint and varnish stripper that does not burn skin and does not emit harmful fumes.*
Strypit	Rustins	*General-purpose stripper for paints and varnishes.*
Textured Paint Remover	Nitromors	*Removes vinyl and acrylic resin-bonded textured paint from ceilings and walls.*

PREPARATIONS AND CLEANERS

BRAND NAME	MANUFACTURER/SUPPLIER	DESCRIPTION
Klean'n'Key	Nitromors	*Chemically impregnated pad for preparing paintwork for redecoration.*
Knotting	Rustins	*Shellac-based sealer for knotty timber.*
Knotting Solution	International Paint	*As above.*
Liquid Sander	International Paint	*Chemical cleaner that prepares paintwork for decoration.*
Patent Knotting	Langlow	*Shellac-based sealer for knotty timber.*
Pre-Paint Wipes	Nitromors	*Lifts dust and dirt created by preparing paintwork.*

FILLERS

BRAND NAME	MANUFACTURER/SUPPLIER	DESCRIPTION
Exterior Polyfilla	Polycell	*Filler for cracked masonry, cement render and concrete.*
Multi Purpose Ready Mixed Filler	UniBond	*As above.*
Polyfilla	Polycell	*Cellulose filler for plaster and woodwork.*

BRAND NAME	MANUFACTURER/SUPPLIER	DESCRIPTION
Polyfilla Advanced Formula Woodfiller	Polycell	*Flexible woodfiller.*
Ronseal Wood Filler	Sterling Roncraft	*Exterior wood filler.*
Tetrion All Purpose Filler	Tetrosyl	*General-purpose exterior wood and masonry filler.*

REPAIR TAPES

BRAND NAME	MANUFACTURER/SUPPLIER	DESCRIPTION
Fibatape	Neve Industrial and Technical Services	*Plaster-wall repair tape to reinforce fillings.*

PRIMERS AND SEALERS

BRAND NAME	MANUFACTURER/SUPPLIER	DESCRIPTION
Acryl 60	Thoro	*A liquid bonding agent that improves the adhesive qualities of cement, mortar and plaster.*
Alkali-Resisting Primer	Crown	*For sealing alkaline surfaces such as new plaster, cement and concrete.*
Aluminium Spirit-Based Sealer	Crown	*Guards against discoloration of paintwork by surfaces that might 'bleed'.*
Aluminium Wood Primer	Crown	*Seals creosoted wood and knotty timber.*
Aluminium Wood Primer	International Paint	*As above.*
Fungicidal Wash	Rentokil	*A fungicidal solution to kill mould growth prior to decorating.*
Sandtex Stabilising Solution	Akzo Coatings	*Stabilizing solution that binds chalky, flaking and porous surfaces.*
Sandtex White Stabilising Solution	Akzo Coatings	*As above.*
Stabiliser	Rentokil	*Stabilizing solution that binds chalky, flaking and porous surfaces.*
Stabilising Primer	Crown	*As above but available in clear and off-white.*
Universal EVA Adhesive and Bonding Agent	UniBond	*Waterproof bonding agent for exterior use.*
Universal PVA Bonding Agent	UniBond	*PVA bonding agent.*
Universal Sealer	International Paint	*General-purpose primer/sealer for porous surfaces such as plaster and concrete.*

BRAND NAME	MANUFACTURER/SUPPLIER	DESCRIPTION
PAINTS AND FINISHES		
Advance	Crown	*One-coat emulsion paint.*
Easygloss	Homebase	*Water-based gloss paint.*
Enhance Acrylic Varnish	Cuprinol	*Water-based wood varnish.*
Metalcolour	International Paint	*Galvanized-metal and aluminium paint.*
Micatex Fine Texture Masonry Paint	Permoglaze	*A fine-textured masonry paint with high durability.*
Micatex Heavy Texture Coating	Permoglaze	*As above, but with coarser texture.*
One Hour Undercoat	International Paint	*Fast-drying low-odour undercoat for interior and exterior use.*
Radiator Enamel	International Paint	*Heat-curing finish for central-heating radiators.*
Ranch Paint	International Paint	*Microporous paint that allows wood to breathe.*
Ranch Stain	International Paint	*Microporous stain that allows wood to breathe.*
Ready Mixed Textured Paint	UniBond	*Hardwearing interior/exterior textured paint.*
Sandtex Exterior Matt	Akzo Coatings	*Reinforced exterior emulsion paint.*
Sandtex Smooth	Akzo Coatings	*Exterior emulsion paint.*
Solo	Crown	*One-coat gloss paint.*
Textured Coating	Artex	*Textured wall coating.*
U-Tex	UniBond	*As above.*
WALLCOVERING ADHESIVES		
All Purpose Wallpaper Adhesive	Polycell	*Fungicidal adhesive for mixing with water.*
Heavyweight Ready Mixed Wallcovering Adhesive	Polycell	*Ready-mixed paste for hanging heavyweight wallcoverings.*
Heavyweight Wallcovering Adhesive	Polycell	*Self-mix paste for heavyweight wallcoverings.*
Lincrusta Adhesive	Crown	*Special adhesive for applying Lincrusta wallcoverings.*

BRAND NAME	MANUFACTURER/SUPPLIER	DESCRIPTION
Multi-Purpose Wallpaper Adhesive	UniBond	*Self-mix paste.*
Ready-Mixed Multi-Purpose Wallcovering Adhesive	UniBond	*Ready-mixed wallcovering adhesive.*

POLISHES

Bell Marble Polish	A. Bell & Co.	*A wax polish for marble where a tough surface is required.*

FLEXIBLE SEALANTS

Evo-Seal Out-Door Sealant	Evode	*Sealant for door and window frames.*
Evo-Seal Roof & Gutter Sealant	Evode	*Flexible sealant for leaking gutters, downpipes and flashings.*
Frame Sealants	UniBond	*Sealant for door and window frames.*
General Purpose Silicone Sealant	UniBond	*General-purpose flexible gap sealant.*
Gutter Sealant	UniBond	*Flexible sealant for leaking gutters, downpipes and flashings.*
No More Damp Sealants	Cuprinol	*Flexible caulking compounds.*
No More Gaps	Cuprinol	*Sealant for door and window frames.*
Press-In-Place Door & Window Sealant	3M Consumer Products	*Strip sealant for door and window frames.*
Press-In-Place Roof & Gutter Sealant	3M Consumer Products	*Strip sealant for roof repairs, cracked gutters and skylights.*
Press-In-Place Sealant for Wide Gaps	3M Consumer Products	*Strip sealant for door and window frames.*

WATERPROOFING TAPES

Aquaseal Flashing	Aquaseal	*Self-adhesive aluminium tape for gutter and downpipe repairs.*
Sylglas Flashing Tape	The Sylglas Co.	*Heavy-duty weatherproofing tape for repairing damaged flashings.*
Sylglas Waterproofing Tape	The Sylglas Co.	*Self-adhesive tape for gutter and downpipe repairs.*

LIQUID WATERPROOFERS

Aquaprufe	Aquaseal	*Rubberized bitumen emulsion for waterproofing floors and walls.*

CURING DAMP

BRAND NAME	MANUFACTURER/SUPPLIER	DESCRIPTION
Aquaseal 66 Exterior Water Repellent	Aquaseal	*Waterproofs and protects exterior walls.*
Aquaseal Heavy Duty Urethane	Aquaseal	*Moisture-curing polyurethane for walls and floors.*
Aquaseal 77 Interior Damp Proofing	Aquaseal	*Provides a waterproof barrier on interior walls and ceilings.*
Isoflex Clear Water Repellent	Sterling Roncraft	*Waterproofs and protects exterior walls.*
Isoflex Internal Damp Proofer	Sterling Roncraft	*Provides a waterproof barrier on interior walls and ceilings.*
Isoflex Liquid Rubber System	Sterling Roncraft	*Liquid-rubber compound for waterproofing roof coverings.*

PRESERVATIVES

Aquaseal Green Wood Preservative and Timber Protection	Aquaseal	*Liquid preservative for horticultural timbers.*
Aquaseal Wood Preservative and Timber Protection	Aquaseal	*Clear liquid preservative to eradicate dry rot and wet rot.*
Dry Rot & Wet Rot Fluid	Rentokil	*As above.*

See also Working Outdoors

ANTI-CONDENSATION PRODUCTS

Anti-Condensation Paint	International Paint	*Insulating paint.*
Condensation Absorber	DRG Sellotape Products	*A container of moisture-absorbing crystals.*
Condensation Killers	3M Consumer Products	*Absorbent crystals to cure condensation inside double-glazing units.*
Seasonal Double Glazing	DRG Sellotape Products	*Renewable double-glazing film.*

HYDRAULIC CEMENT

Waterplug	Thoro	*Quick-drying cement for patching concrete and masonry.*

WOOD HARDENER AND FILLERS

Polyfilla Advanced Formula Woodfiller	Polycell	*Flexible exterior wood filler.*

BRAND NAME	MANUFACTURER/SUPPLIER	DESCRIPTION
Ronseal Wood Hardener	Sterling Roncraft	*Strengthens and reinforces decayed wood.*
Ronseal Wood Filler	Sterling Roncraft	*Exterior woodfiller.*

DRAUGHTPROOFERS

BRAND NAME	MANUFACTURER/SUPPLIER	DESCRIPTION
Clear Liquid Draught Seal	3M Consumer Products	*Flexible sealant that is removed at the end of the cold season.*
Scotch Draught Excluders	3M Consumer Products	*Range of door and window draught excluders.*
Sellotape Draught Excluders	DRG Sellotape Products	*As above.*
Superseal Draught Excluders	Kleeneze	*As above.*

LOFT INSULANTS

BRAND NAME	MANUFACTURER/SUPPLIER	DESCRIPTION
Energy Saver Loose Lay	Rockwool	*Loose-fill granulated mineral-fibre insulant.*
Gypglas	Gyproc Insulation	*Glass-fibre insulant in rolls and batts.*
Rockwool	Rockwool	*Mineral-fibre insulant in rolls and batts.*
Supawrap	Pilkington Insulation	*Glass-fibre insulant in rolls and batts.*

RADIATOR FOIL

BRAND NAME	MANUFACTURER/SUPPLIER	DESCRIPTION
Climareflex	Delmar	*Expanded-polyurethane-backed foil to reflect heat from behind a radiator.*

INSULATED PLASTERBOARD

BRAND NAME	MANUFACTURER/SUPPLIER	DESCRIPTION
Gyproc Thermal Board	British Gypsum	*Expanded-polyurethane-backed plasterboard.*

BATH SEALANTS

BRAND NAME	MANUFACTURER/SUPPLIER	DESCRIPTION
Dow Corning Bath and Kitchen Seal	Dow Corning Hansil	*Flexible sealant for baths, basins and sinks.*
Press-In-Place Bath and Kitchen Sealant	3M Consumer Products	*Strip-sealant for baths, basins and sinks.*
Silicone Bath and Kitchen Sealant	UniBond	*Flexible sealant for baths, basins and sinks.*

BATH GLAZE

BRAND NAME	MANUFACTURER/SUPPLIER	DESCRIPTION
Newglaze	Porcelain Newglaze	*Two-part epoxy bath coating.*

INSULATION AND VENTILATION

PLUMBING AND CENTRAL HEATING

BRAND NAME	MANUFACTURER/SUPPLIER	DESCRIPTION
PLUMBING FITTINGS		
Acorn Push-Fit Plumbing Systems	Bartol	*Plastic plumbing with push-fit joints.*
Copperbend	Kopex	*Flexible copper pipe for connecting taps to pipework.*
Lead-Loc	Frazer	*Compression joint to connect a lead rising main to copper or plastic plumbing.*
Push-Fit Plumbing	Polycell	*Plastic plumbing with push-fit joints.*
Speedfix	Oracstar	*As above.*
PUMPED WC SYSTEMS		
Saniflo	Transbyn	*Shreds and pumps waste along small-bore pipes.*
Superflush	Edincare	*As above.*
DESCALERS AND INHIBITORS		
Protex	Heating World	*Central-heating descaler and corrosion inhibitor.*
EPOXY PUTTY		
Plumberfix	The Sylglas Co.	*Epoxy putty for sealing plumbing leaks.*
WATERPROOFING TAPES		
Aquaseal Flashing	Aquaseal	*Self-adhesive aluminium tape.*
Sylglas Aluminium Tape	The Sylglas Co.	*As above.*
Sylglas Flashing Tape	The Sylglas Co.	*Heavy-duty weatherproofing tape for repairing flashings.*
Sylglas Roof Repair Tape	The Sylglas Co.	*For sealing leaks in flat, pitched or corrugated roofs.*
WATERPROOFERS		
Aquaseal 88 Bituminous Mastic	Aquaseal	*For repairing cracks and joints in asphalt, asbestos, corrugated-iron and felt roofs.*
Aquaseal 66 Exterior Water Repellent	Aquaseal	*Waterproofs and protects exterior walls.*
Aquaseal 40 Heavy-Duty Waterproofer	Aquaseal	*Bituminous waterproofer for roofs.*
Isoflex Clear Water Repellent	Sterling Roncraft	*Waterproofs and protects exterior walls.*

HOUSEHOLD REPAIRS

BRAND NAME	MANUFACTURER/SUPPLIER	DESCRIPTION
Isoflex Wet Patch	Sterling Roncraft	*Liquid-rubber seal for emergency roof repairs.*

FLEXIBLE SEALANTS

General Purpose Silicone Sealant	UniBond	*Flexible caulking compound.*
No More Damp Sealants	Cuprinol	*As above.*

FILLERS

Exterior Polyfilla	Polycell	*Filler for cracked masonry, cement render and concrete.*
Multi Purpose Ready Mixed Filler	UniBond	*As above.*
Polyfilla	Polycell	*Cellulose filler for plaster and woodwork.*
Polyfilla Advanced Formula Woodfiller	Polycell	*Flexible wood filler.*
Ronseal Wood Filler	Sterling Roncraft	*Exterior wood filler.*
Tetrion All Purpose Filler	Tetrosyl	*General-purpose exterior wood and masonry filler*

FIRE CEMENTS

Belclay Fire Cement	A. Bell & Co.	*Fireproof cement to repair cracked firebacks.*
Ready Mixed Fire Cement	UniBond	*As above.*

PLASTERS

Carlite Bonding	British Gypsum	*Undercoat plaster.*
Carlite Browning	British Gypsum	*As above.*
Carlite Finish	British Gypsum	*Finishing plaster.*
Snowplast Universal	Snocem	*One-coat plaster.*
Thistle Board Finish	British Gypsum	*Plasterboard-finishing plaster.*
Thistle Universal	British Gypsum	*One-coat plaster.*

ADHESIVES

Aquaseal Firmafix	Aquaseal	*Roofing adhesive.*
Araldite	Ciba-Geigi	*Two-part epoxy adhesive.*
Universal EVA Adhesive and Bonding Agent	UniBond	*Waterproof bonding agent for exterior use.*

BRAND NAME	MANUFACTURER/SUPPLIER	DESCRIPTION
Universal PVA Adhesive and Sealer	UniBond	*PVA bonding agent.*

SEALERS

Belsealer	A. Bell & Co.	*Sealer to protect and preserve porous stone.*

● ANTI-CLIMB

Anti-Climb	E. Aldridge & Son	*Non-setting paint for downpipes to discourage burglars.*
Tor Anti-Climb Paint	Tor Coatings	*As above.*

● PRESERVATIVES

Timber Colour	Dulux	*Water-based wood preservative.*
Cedarwood Protector	Rentokil	*Red-cedar coloured preservative for exterior timber.*
Colour Fast Protector	Rentokil	*Coloured preservative that substitutes for creosote.*
Exterior Wood Preserver	Cuprinol	*General-purpose wood preservative.*
Green Preservative for Wood	Rentokil	*Preservative for horticultural timbers.*
Green Wood Preserver	Cuprinol	*As above.*
Ronseal Fencelife	Sterling Roncraft	*As above.*
5 Star Wood Treatment	Cuprinol	*Superior-grade general-purpose wood preservative.*
Supergrade Wood Preserver	Rentokil	*As above.*

CONDITIONERS

Aquaclear	Remanoid	*Pond-water conditioner.*

● ADHESIVES

Araldite	Ciba-Geigi	*Two-part epoxy-resin glue.*
Bostik Super Glue 4	Bostik	*Cyanoacrylate glue.*
Evo-Stik Resin W	Evode	*PVA woodworking glue.*
Loctite Glass Bond	Loctite UK	*Anaerobic glass adhesive.*
Loctite Super Glue 3	Loctite UK	*Cyanoacrylate glue.*

GLAZE

Plastic Coating	Rustins	*Cold-cure lacquer that is suitable as a decorative glaze for repaired china.*

BRAND NAME	MANUFACTURER/SUPPLIER	DESCRIPTION
SCREWS AND FIXINGS		
Clutch Head Wood Screw	European Industrial Services	*Security screw that, once fitted, cannot be removed.*
Chipboard Fastener	Woodfit	*Nylon insert.*
Confirmat Connector	Woodfit	*Chipboard connector.*
Hi-Lo Construction Screw	Woodfit	*Chipboard screw.*
Masterscrew	European Industrial Services	*Twin-threaded screw (slotted).*
Supascrew	European Industrial Services	*Twin-threaded screw (cross head).*
SCREW CUPS AND COVERS		
Brass screw cup	European Industrial Services	*Recessed-type screw cup.*
Plastidome	European Industrial Services	*Decorative plastic screw cover.*
Supatop	European Industrial Services	*Plastic cover for a cross-head screw.*
Surface screw cup	European Industrial Services	*Surface-mounted screw cup in brass or stainless steel.*
KNOCK-DOWN FITTINGS		
Corner brace or plate	Woodfit	*Table-frame connector.*
Panel butting connector	Woodfit	*A bolt connector for joining worktops.*
WALL FIXINGS		
Cavity Anchor Type HM	Artur Fischer UK	*Expanding-anchor cavity-wall fixing.*
Fixoplac	Artur Fischer UK	*As above.*
Frame Fixing	Artur Fischer UK	*Long nylon wall plug and plated screw for fixing door or window frames to walls.*
Gravity Toggle	Artur Fischer UK	*Gravity-operated cavity-wall fixing.*
Plasplugs	Plasplugs	*Plastic wall plugs.*
Spring Cavity Toggle	Artur Fischer UK	*Spring-operated cavity fixing.*

FIXINGS AND FITTINGS

BRAND NAME	MANUFACTURER/SUPPLIER	DESCRIPTION

● ADHESIVES

Cascamite Waterproof Wood Glue	Borden	*An exterior-grade powdered glue for mixing with water.*
Evo-Stik Resin W	Evode	*PVA woodworking glue.*
Glufilm	Art Veneer Co.	*Iron-on sheet adhesive for veneers.*
Pearl Glue	Sheppy Fertilisers	*Granular animal glue that is liquified by heating in water.*
Powerfix	Dunlop	*Water-based contact glue for veneers.*
Sheppy Tug Scotch Glue	Sheppy Fertilisers	*Liquid animal glue.*
Thixofix	Dunlop	*Solvent-based contact glue for veneers.*

PREPARATIONS AND RESTORERS

Colron Restorer and Cleaner	Sterling Roncraft	*Removes dirty and discoloured finishes from wood.*
Colron Ring Remover	Sterling Roncraft	*A mild abrasive that removes rings and blemishes left in a soft finish.*
Colron Scratch Remover	Sterling Roncraft	*Wax stick for disguising scratches in wood finishes.*
Colron Woodfiller	Sterling Roncraft	*Flexible filler for cracks, holes and chips.*
DeScratch	Anthony Green	*Wax sticks for disguising scratches in wood finishes.*
Grain Filler	Rustins	*Paste for filling open-grain timbers.*
Scratch Cover	Cuprinol	*Wax stick for disguising scratches in wood finishes.*
Shellac Sanding Sealer	Rustins	*Used instead of grain filler to prepare fine-grain woods for finishing.*
The Furniture Reviver	Anthony Green	*Cleans and revives polished surfaces.*
Wood Stopping	Rustins	*Wood filler for cracks, holes and chips.*
Woodworm Fluid	Rentokil	*Wood preservative to eradicate wood-boring insects.*

BRAND NAME	MANUFACTURER/SUPPLIER	DESCRIPTION
BLEACH		
Colron Wood Lightener	Sterling Roncraft	*Two-part bleach for wood.*
Wood Bleach	Rustins	*As above.*
WOOD STAINS		
Colron Wood Dyes	Sterling Roncraft	*Ready-mixed spirit-based stains for wood.*
Naptha Stains	John Myland	*Ready-mixed oil-based stains for wood.*
Spirit Stain	John Myland	*Spirit-based coloured stain for wood, available ready-mixed or in the form of soluble aniline powder to be dissolved in methylated spirits.*
Water Stains	John Myland	*Water-based coloured stains for wood, available ready-mixed or in the form of soluble aniline powder.*
Wood Dye	Cuprinol	*Ready-mixed spirit-based stains for wood.*
Wood Dye	Rustins	*Ready-mixed oil-based stains for wood.*
SELF-ADHESIVE VENEERS		
Microwood	Fastnet Products	*Self-adhesive wood veneers.*
FINISHES AND POLISHES		
Brown French Polish	Langlow	*Standard-grade shellac polish.*
Button Polish	Langlow	*Superior-grade shellac polish.*
Button Polish	Rustins	*As above.*
Colron Antique Oil	Sterling Roncraft	*Finishing oil for wood.*
Colron Finishing Wax	Sterling Roncraft	*Paste wax polish for wood.*
Colron Liquid Wax	Sterling Roncraft	*Liquid wax polish for wood.*
Danish Oil	Rustins	*Finishing oil for wood.*
French Polish	John Myland	*Standard-grade shellac polish.*
French Polish	Rustins	*As above.*
Gedges Brushing French Polish	John Myland	*French polish with an additive to slow the drying time to allow it to be brushed.*
Gedges Wax Polish	John Myland	*Paste wax polish for wood.*

BRAND NAME	MANUFACTURER/SUPPLIER	DESCRIPTION
Mr Jamieson's Cream Wax Polish	James Jamieson's	*Cream wax polish for wood.*
Plastic Coating	Rustins	*Cold-cure plastic lacquer.*
Pure Button Polish	John Myland	*Superior-grade shellac polish.*
Rentokil Wax Polish	Rentokil	*Insecticidal wax polish.*
White French Polish	Langlow	*Bleached shellac polish for pale woods.*
White Polish	Rustins	*As above.*

● POLISHES

Brasso	Reckitt Products	*Liquid polish for brass and copper.*
Duraglit Metal	Reckitt Products	*Polishing wadding for brass and copper.*
Duraglit Silver	Reckitt Products	*Polishing wadding for silver.*
Jewellery Care	Goddard's	*Chemical dip for cleaning precious-metal jewellery.*
Long Term Brass & Copper Polish	Goddard's	*Liquid polish for brass and copper.*
Long Term Foaming Silver Polish	Goddard's	*Mild silver polish.*
Long Term Silver Cloth	Goddard's	*Cleaning cloth impregnated with silver polish.*
Long Term Silver Polish	Goddard's	*Silver polish that slows down the effects of tarnishing.*
Silver Plating Formula	Anthony Green	*Replaces silver on worn silver-plated pieces.*
Silver Plating Polish	Anthony Green	*Silver-plate polish.*
Silversmith's Gloves	Anthony Green	*Impregnated gloves for cleaning silver.*
Silvo	Reckitt Products	*Liquid polish for silver.*
Zebrite	Reckitt Products	*Black grate polish (black lead).*

PROTECTIVE LACQUERS

Transparent Lacquer	Rustins	*Clear lacquer that protects polished metal.*

BRAND NAME	MANUFACTURER/SUPPLIER	DESCRIPTION
PAPER-REPAIR MATERIALS		
Document Cleaner	Ademco	*Open-weave bag containing powder for cleaning dirty paper.*
Document-Repair Tape	Ademco	*Self-adhesive tape for repairing torn paper.*
LEATHER DRESSINGS		
Leather Preservation Dressing	J. Hewitt & Sons	*Dressing for leather bindings.*
Renaissance Leather Reviver	Picreator Enterprises	*As above.*
SADDLE SOAP		
Belvoir Glycerine Leather and Saddle Soap	Carr & Day & Martin	*Soap for cleaning dirty leather.*
Prepared Saddle and Leather Soap	Carr & Day & Martin	*As above.*
SHAMPOO		
Dry Magic	Airwick	*Dry-powder carpet shampoo.*
1001 Troubleshooter	P.C. Products	*Spray-on carpet and upholstery shampoo.*
GREASE SOLVENTS		
Beaucare	Nicholas Laboratories	*Colourless solvent for oil and grease.*
Dabitoff	Kiwi Products	*As above.*
SPECIFIC-STAIN REMOVERS		
Stain Devils	DDD Ltd	*Range of solvents and cleaners made to remove specific stains.*

REPAIRING BOOKS AND PICTURES

REMOVING STAINS

A

Accessory
An electrical component permanently connected to a circuit – switch, socket outlet, connection unit etc.

Aggregate
Particles of sand or stone mixed with cement and water to make concrete, or added to paint to make a textured finish.

Airlock
A blockage in a pipe caused by a trapped bubble of air.

Appliance
A machine or device powered by electricity. or A functional piece of equipment connected to the plumbing – a basin, sink, bath, bidet etc.

Architrave
The moulding around a door or window.

Arris
The sharp edge at the meeting of two surfaces.

B

Back-siphonage
The siphoning of part of a plumbing system caused by the failure of mains water pressure.

Balanced flue
A ducting system which allows a heating appliance, such as a boiler, to draw fresh air from, and discharge gases to, the outside of a building.

Ballast
Naturally occurring sand-and-gravel mix used as aggregate for making concrete.

Baluster
One of a set of posts supporting a stair handrail.

Balustrade
The protective barrier alongside a staircase or landing.

Banisters
See balustrade.

Batt
A short cut length of glass-fibre or mineral-fibre insulant.

Batten
A narrow strip of wood.

Batter
The slope of the face of a wall that leans backwards or tapers from bottom to top.

Blind
To cover with sand.

Blown
To have broken away, as when a layer of cement rendering has parted from a wall.

Bore
The hollow part of a pipe or tube. or To drill a hole.

Burr
The rough raised edge left on a workpiece after cutting or filing.

Buttercoat
The top layer of cement render.

C

Came
The grooved strip of lead which holds the glass in a leaded light or a stained-glass window.

Cap-nut
The nut used to tighten a fitting onto pipework.

Casing
The timber lining of a door opening.

Catenary wire
A length of wire cable suspended horizontally between two points.

Cavity wall
A wall of two separate masonry skins with an air space between them.

Chamfer
A narrow flat surface on the edge of a piece of wood – it is normally at an angle of 45 degrees to adjacent surfaces. or To plane the angled surface.

Chase
A groove cut in masonry or plaster to accept pipework or an electrical cable. or To cut such grooves.

Circuit
A complete path through which an electric current can flow.

Concave
Curving inwards.

Conductor
A component, usually a length of wire, along which an electric current will pass.

Convex
Curving outwards.

Cornice
The continuous horizontal moulding between walls and ceiling.

Counterbore
To cut a hole which allows the head of a bolt or screw to lie below a surface. or The hole itself.

Countersink
To cut a tapered recess which allows the head of a screw to lie flush with a surface. or The tapered recess itself.

Coving
A pre-fabricated moulding used to make a cornice.

Cup
To bend as a result of shrinkage – specifically across the width of a piece of wood.

D

Dado
The lower part of an interior wall – usually defined with a moulded rail. or In the USA – a housing.

Damp-proof course
A layer of impervious material which prevents moisture rising from the ground into the walls of a building.

Damp-proof membrane
A layer of impervious material which prevents moisture rising through a concrete floor.

Datum point
The point from which measurements are taken.

DPC
See damp-proof course.

DPM
See damp-proof membrane.

Drip groove
A groove cut or moulded in the underside of a door or windowsill to prevent rainwater running back to the wall.

Drop
A strip of wallpaper cut to length ready for pasting to a wall.

E

Earth
A connection between an electrical circuit and the earth (ground). or A terminal to which the connection is made.

Eaves
The edges of a roof that project beyond the walls.

Efflorescence
A white powdery deposit caused by soluble salts migrating to the surface of a wall or ceiling.

End grain
The surface of wood exposed after cutting across the fibres.

Ergonomics
The study of the physical relationship between the human body and its surroundings.
Extension
A length of electrical flex for temporarily connecting the short permanent flex of an appliance to a wall socket. or A room or rooms added to an existing building.

F

Face edge
In woodworking, the surface planed square to the face side.
Face side
In woodworking, the flat planed surface from which other dimensions and angles are measured.
Fall
A downward slope.
Fascia board
Strip of wood which covers the ends of rafters and to which external guttering is fixed.
Feather
To wear away or smooth an edge until it is undetectable.
Fence
An adjustable guide to keep the cutting edge of a tool a set distance from the edge of a workpiece.
Flashing
A weatherproof junction between a roof and a wall or chimney, or between one roof and another.
Flaunching
A mortared slope around a chimney pot or at the top of a fireback.
Flute
A rounded concave groove.
Footing
A narrow concrete foundation for a wall.
Frass
Powdered wood produced by the activity of woodworm.
Frog
The angled depression in one face of some housebricks.
Furring battens
See furring strips.
Furring strips
Parallel strips of wood fixed to a wall or ceiling to provide a framework for attaching panels.

Fuse board
Where the main electrical service cable is connected to the house circuitry. or The accumulation of consumer unit, meter etc.

G

Galvanized
Covered with a protective coating of zinc.
Gel
A substance with a thick jelly-like consistency.
Going
The horizontal measurement between the top and bottom risers of a stair. or The depth of one tread.
Grain
The general direction of wood fibres. or The pattern produced on the surface of timber by cutting through the fibres. See also end grain and short grain.
Grommet
A ring of rubber or plastic lining a hole to protect electrical cable from chafing.
Groove
A long narrow channel cut in wood in the general direction of the grain. or To cut such channels.
Grounds
Strips of wood fixed to a wall to provide nail-fixing points for skirting boards and door casings. See also pallet.
Gullet
The notch formed between two saw teeth.

H

Hardcore
Broken bricks or stones used to form a sub-base below foundations, paving etc.
Hardwood
Timber cut from deciduous trees.
Head
The height of the surface of water above a specific point – used as a measurement of pressure; for example, a head of 2m. or The top horizontal member of a wooden frame.
Head plate
The top horizontal member of a stud partition.

Heave
An upward swelling of the ground caused by excess moisture.
Helical
Spiral shaped.
Hoggin
A fine ballast, usually with a clay content, used to form a sub-base for concrete pads or paving.
Hone
To finely sharpen a cutting edge.
Horns
Extended door or window stiles designed to protect the corners from damage while in storage.
Housing
A long narrow channel cut across the general direction of wood grain to form part of a joint.

I

Insulation
Materials used to reduce the transmission of heat or sound. or Nonconductive material surrounding electrical wires or connections to prevent the passage of electricity.

J

Jamb
The vertical side member of a door or window frame.
Joist
A horizontal wooden or metal beam used to support a structure like a floor, ceiling or wall.

K

Kerf
The groove cut by a saw.
Key
To abrade or incise a surface to provide a better grip when painting or gluing something to it.
Knurled
Impressed with a series of fine grooves designed to improve the grip.

L

Lead
A stepped section of brickwork or blockwork built at each end of a wall to act as a guide to the height of the intermediate coursing.
Lintel
A horizontal beam used to support the wall over a door or window opening.

M

Marine plywood
Exterior-grade plywood.
Mastic
Non-setting compound used to seal joints.
Microporous
Used to describe a finish which allows timber to dry out while protecting it from rainwater.
Mitre
A joint formed between two pieces of wood by cutting bevels of equal angles at the ends of each piece. *or* To cut the joint.
Mole
A tallow-soaked felt pad used to smooth a soldered lead joint.
Mono-pitch roof
A roof which slopes in one direction only.
Mortise
A rectangular recess cut in timber to receive a matching tongue or tenon.
Mouse
A small weight used to pass a line through a narrow vertical gap.
Mullion
A vertical dividing member of a window frame.
Muntin
A central vertical member of a panel door.

N

Needle
A stout wooden beam used with props to support the section of a wall above an opening prior to the installation of an RSJ or lintel.

Neutral
The section of an electrical circuit which carries the flow of current back to source.*or* A terminal to which the connection is made. *or* A colour composed mainly of black and white.
Newel
The post at the top or bottom of a staircase that supports the handrail.
Nosing
The front edge of a stair tread.

O

Outer string
See string.
Oxidize
To form a layer of metal oxide as in rusting.

P

Pallet
A wooden plug built into masonry to provide a fixing point for a door casing.
Pare
To remove fine shavings from wood with a chisel.
Pargeting
The internal render of a chimney.
Penetrating oil
A thin lubricant which will seep between corroded components.
Phase
The part of an electrical circuit which carries the flow of current to an appliance or accessory. Also known as live or line.
Pile
Raised fibres which stand out from a backing material as with a carpet.
Pilot hole
A small-diameter hole drilled prior to the insertion of a woodscrew to act as a guide for its thread.
Pinch rod
A wooden batten used to gauge the width of a door casing.
Point load
The concentration of forces on a very small area.
Primer
The first coat of a paint system to protect the workpiece and reduce absorption of subsequent coats.

Profile
The outline or contour of an object.
PTFE
Polytetrafluoroethylene – used to make tape for sealing threaded plumbing fittings.
Purlin
A horizontal beam that provides intermediate support for rafters or sheet roofing.

R

Rafter
One set of parallel sloping beams that form the main structural element of a roof.
Ratchet
A device that permits movement in one direction only by restricting the reversal of a toothed wheel or rack.
Rebate
A stepped recess along the edge of a workpiece, usually as part of a joint. *or* To cut such recesses.
Render
A thin layer of cement-based mortar applied to exterior walls to provide a protective finish. Sometimes fine stone aggregate is embedded in the mortar. *or* To apply the mortar.
Reveal
A vertical side of an opening in a wall.
Riser
The vertical part of a step.
Rising main
The pipe which supplies water under mains pressure, usually to a storage cistern in the roof.
Rolled steel joist
A steel beam usually with a cross section in the form of a letter I.
RSJ
See rolled steel joist.
Rubber
A pad of cotton wool wrapped in soft cloth used to apply stain, shellac polish etc.
Rub joint
Glued wood rubbed together and held by suction until set.

S

Sash
The openable part of a window.

Score
To scratch a line with a pointed tool. See also scribe.

Scratchcoat
The bottom layer of cement render.

Screed
A thin layer of mortar applied to give a smooth surface to concrete etc. or A shortened version of screed batten.

Screed batten
A thin strip of wood fixed to a surface to act as a guide to the thickness of an application of plaster or render.

Scribe
To copy the profile of a surface on the edge of sheet material which is to be butted against it. or To mark a line with a pointed tool. See also score.

Set
A small rectangular paving block.

Sheathing
The outer layer of insulation surrounding an electrical cable or flex.

Short circuit
The accidental rerouting of electricity to earth which increases the flow of current and blows a fuse.

Short grain
When the general direction of wood fibres lies across a narrow section of timber.

Sill
The lowest horizontal member of a stud partition. or The lowest horizontal member of a door or window frame.

Sleeper wall
A low masonry wall used as an intermediate support for ground-floor joists.

Soakaway
A pit filled with rubble or gravel into which water is drained.

Soffit
The underside of a part of a building such as the eaves, archway etc.

Softwood
Timber cut from coniferous trees.

Sole plate
Another term for a stud partition sill. or A wooden member used as a base to level a timber-framed loadbearing wall.

Spalling
Flaking of the outer face of masonry caused by expanding moisture in icy conditions.

Spandrel
The triangular infill below the outer string of a staircase.

Staff bead
The innermost strip of timber holding a sliding sash in a window frame.

Stile
A vertical side member of a door or window sash.

Stopper
A wood filler which matches the colour of the timber.

String
A board, which runs from one floor level to another, into which staircase treads and risers are jointed. The one on the open side of a staircase is an outer string, the one against the wall is a wall string.

Studs
The vertical members of a timber-framed wall.

Subsidence
A sinking of the ground caused by the shrinkage of excessively dry soil.

T

Tamp
To pack down firmly with repeated blows.

Template
A cut-out pattern to help shape something accurately.

Tenon
A projecting tongue on the end of a piece of wood which fits in a corresponding mortise.

Terminal
A connection for an electrical conductor.

Thinners
A solvent used to dilute paint or varnish.

Thixotropic
A property of some paints which have a jelly-like consistency until stirred or applied, at which point they become liquified.

Top coat
The outer layer of a paint system.

Torque
A rotational force.

Transom
A horizontal dividing member of a window frame.

Trap
A bent section of pipe below a bath, sink etc. It contains standing water to prevent the passage of gases.

Tread
The horizontal part of a step.

U

Undercoat
A layer of paint used to obliterate the colour of a primer and to build a protective body of paint prior to the application of a top coat.

W

Wall plate
A horizontal timber member placed along the top of a wall to support joists and to spread their load.

Wall string
See string.

Wall tie
A strip of metal or bent wire used to bind sections of masonry together.

Waney edge
A natural wavy edge on a plank. It might still be covered by tree bark.

Warp
To bend or twist as a result of damp or heat.

Water closet
A lavatory flushed by water.

Water hammer
A vibration in plumbing pipework produced by fluctuating water pressure.

WC
See water closet.

Weathered
Showing signs of exposure to the weather. or Sloped so as to shed rainwater.

Weep hole
A small hole at the base of a cavity wall to allow absorbed water to drain to the outside.

Workpiece
An object being shaped, produced or otherwise worked upon. Sometimes shortened to 'work'.

A

acetone 112, 141
acrylic double glazing 41
acrylic-resin lacquer 133
acrylic paints 114
adaptors 62
adhesives 110, 112
adhesive tape 111, 112, 113
adjustable spanner 144
afrormosia 130
aggregate
  storage 77
Agrément Board 40
Agrément certificate 31
airbricks 35, 38, 41, 42
airlock 46
alcohol stains 125
alterations to house 10, 11
aluminium paint 24
aluminium wood primer 19
ammonia 19, 20, 110, 127,
    132, 141
amps 56
anaerobic glue 115, 116
'ancient light' 13
angle-iron posts 97
animal glue 111, 124, 126, 127
anti-climb paint 90
ants 107
architects 13
arris rails 97
asbestos 16, 24
'asking price' 13

B

ballpoint-ink stain 141
basin wrench 147
bath
  re-enamelling 46
bathroom
  electrical socket in 62
  extractor fan in 42, 43
bats in loft 107
beam-compass cutter 144
beer stains 141
beeswax 130
belt sander 144
bending springs 144
bevel-edge chisel 144
bitumen latex emulsion 34
black-and-white prints 136
black lead 134, 141
blanket insulation 38-9
bleach 32, 110, 136
bleaching wood 125, 127
blemishes on wood 125, 126
blocked sink 48
blood stains 141
blow lamp 20
boilers 53, 54
boiler thermostats 54
bolster chisel 28, 144

bolts 89
book bindings 137
books 137-8
boundary wall
  Planning Permission 12
box spanner 144
brace 144
brace bits 145
brass 132, 133
brass polish 133
brick copings 73
bricklayer's line 145
brick paths 101
brick piers 98
bricks 73, 98
brick trowel 145
brickwork 20, 22, 34, 72-3
brown spots 136
builder's square 145
builders 10, 14
  quotations 14
Building Control Officer 10
Building Notice 10
Building-Regulations
    Approval 10
burglar alarms 91-2
butter stains 142
button polish 128
butyl pond liners 104

C

cable 59, 60, 61, 62, 66
cabinet screwdriver 145
calcium-carbide deposits 114
calcium-plumbate primer 19, 24
candle-wax stains 141
car-paint cleaner 125
carpenter's mallet 146
carpet cleaner 140
carpets 140
carpet shampoo 140, 141, 142
carpet tacks 118
carnauba wax 130
cartridge fuse 57, 58, 59
casement windows 90
cast-iron fireplaces 21, 83, 134
caustic soda 20, 127
cavity fittings 122
cavity insulation 40
cavity walls 68
ceilings 16, 17, 18, 21, 26, 27,
    32, 33, 44, 71
ceiling rose 71
cellars
  damp 34
cement 77
cement paint 25
central-heating system 52-3
ceramics 109-114
ceramic tiles 18, 28
cesspool 52
chain-link fencing 97
chairs
  repairing joints 127
chalk drawing 136

'change of use' of building 11
charcoal drawing 136
chartered surveyors 13, 14
chemical strippers 21
chewing gum 141
chimney breast
  damp 30, 31
chimney fire 94
chimney lining 81
chimney stack 30, 31
  stained 81
china
  broken 110, 112
  cracked 111
  glazing 114
  painting 114
  reinforcing repair 113
  removing rivets 111
  stains 110
china paints 114
chipboard 119
  laying as floor 76
chipboard connectors 119
chipboard screws 119
chip-pan fire 93
chipped china
  repairing 113
chipped glass 115, 116
chipped wood furniture 126
chocolate stains 142
circular saw 146
circulation pump 52, 54
cistern
  overflowing 46
claw hammer 146
clear varnish 129
clout nails 118
club hammer 146
clutch-head screw 120
cobbles 102
cockroaches 107
coffee stains 142
cold chisel 28, 147
cold-cure lacquer 113, 114, 130
cold-water tank
  lagging 43
  overflowing 47
  replacing in loft 47
collapsible anchors 122
coloured glass 116
coloured prints 136
colourfast fabrics 140
combination square 147
compression joints 47
concrete
  decorative finishes 79
  estimating quantity 77
  laying 78
  laying vinyl on 79
  mixing 77
  repairing 19, 80
  storage of ingredients 77
concrete floor
  damp 34
concrete paving
  breaking up 103
  laying 101, 102

pond edging 104
concrete posts 97
condensation 32, 39, 40, 41, 72
Conservation-Area Consent 11
conservation areas 11, 12
conservatory
  Planning Permission 12
  repairing leaks 82
consumer unit 57, 58
contact glues 124
convector radiators 53
cooker hoods 43
cooking-fat stains 142
cooking utensils 133
copal varnish 21, 138
copings 73
coping saw 147
copper 132, 133
copper pipework 47
copper polish 133
coral 133
cork 38
corner-plate fitting 121
corner roller 147
cornices
  replacing 71
corrosion
  on brass 133
  on pewter 134
corrugated plastic sheet 119
countersunk screw 120
cracked china 111
cracks
  in concrete 19, 80
  in rendering 80
cranked spanner 147
crayons 141
crazy paving 101
cream wax polish 130
creosote 97
crosscut saw 147
cross-head screw 120
cross-head screwdriver 147
cross-peen hammer 148
crowbar 148
cupboard doors 128
cupboards 122, 130
cutting-in brush 148
cyanoacrylate glue 111, 116

D

darkened wood 127
damar varnish 138
damp 10, 17, 29-36
damp patches 30, 31, 33
damp-proof course 17, 30, 31
decorating 11, 15-28
decorative paint effects 26
dehumidifier 32, 33
demolition
  Building-Regulations
  Approval 11
dents in wood 125
diamond-tipped drill bits 113
discoloured wood 127

discoloured varnish 138
disc sander 148
dishwasher
  installing 51
distemper 18, 27
distilled water 138
document cleaner 136
document-repair tape 137
documents 137
dog kennel 108
door bolts 89
door chain 90
door frame 119
door locks 88
doors
  catching 86
  curing damp 33, 34
  jamming 86
  maintenance 35
  removing from hinges 85
  sealing draughts 38
  setting hinges 84
  stripping 11, 20
  trimming 84
door viewer 90
doorway
  blocking off 85
double glazing 41, 43-4, 53, 91
double insulated 56, 61
double-pole switch 65
double socket 62
dovetail saw 148
drainage, garden 99
drainage, pond 106
drain auger 148
drain rods 148
drain pipes 17, 30
draughts 38
drawers 130
  sticking 128
drawing-ink stains 141
drill bits 28, 113
drilling
  ceramic tiles 28
  china 113
  glass 28
drinking glasses 114-15
driveway
  Planning Permission 12
  recommended width 101
dry leather 138
dry rot 35, 42
dual screws 89
duplex-head nails 118
dust in varnish 130
dusting brush 149

E

earthenware 111
electricians 55
electrician's screwdriver 149
electrical appliances and
    fittings 61, 63
  overheating 56
electrical circuits 57, 65

electrical plugs 58, 62
electrical sockets 59, 62, 63
electrical wiring
  colour-coding 59-60
  in insulation 39
electricity 55-66
  turning off supply 57
electronic mains tester 149
encaustic tiles 27
engineer's pliers 149
epoxy glue 111, 112
estimates 14
exfoliated vermiculite 38
expanded polystyrene 32, 33,
    38, 40, 43
extensions
  brickwork 73
  employing an architect 13
  Planning Permission 12
exterior decorating 11, 22, 25
exterior-grade emulsion 25
extractor fans 42-3

F

fabrics 140
false ceiling
  installing 44
fanlights 90
feed and expansion tank 52
felt-tip pen stains 141
fence posts 97
fences 96-7
fibre wall plugs 121
files 149
filling knife 149
finishing sander 150
fireback 83
fire blankets 93
fire extinguisher 93
fireplace
  sealing off 41, 84
  ventilation 84
fire resistance 10
fires 43, 93-4
fire surrounds 19, 21-2
firmer chisel 149
fish 103, 106
fixings and fittings 117-22
flashing 30
  repairing leaks 82
flashing tape 30
flat paintbrush 150
flat roof 40, 81, 82
flex 60-61
flexible pond liners 103, 104
flour-and-water paste 138
floorboards 28, 75, 76, 130
floorboard saw 150
floor tiles
  cleaning 27
flush-mounted sockets 63
foam drum sander 150
foaming silver polish 130, 134
footings 78
force pump 150

foundations 78, 96
fountain-pen ink stains 141
foxing 136
frame cramp 150
frenchman 150
French polish 110, 125, 128, 129, 130
French polishing 129
frozen pipes 47
frozen pond 106
fruit-juice stains 142
fungal growth 136
fungicide 17, 27, 32, 137
furniture 123-30
fused connection unit 63
fused spurs 64
fuses 57, 58

G

galvanized nails 118
galvanized window frames 24
garden drainage 99
garden lighting 65
garden-pool pump
   running flex 65-6
garden rake 150
garden shed
   laying concrete base 79
garden tap
   installing 49
garden terracing 99
garden walls 73, 78
gas alarms 93
gas fire 83
gas-fired boiler 54
gas torch 20
gate posts 98
gates 98
G-cramp 128, 151
gents saw 151
gilding china 113
gimp pins 119
glass 91, 109, 114, 115, 139
glass cutter 151
glass-fibre blankets 38, 43
glaze for china 114
glue
   anaerobic glue 115
   animal glue 110
   cyanoacrylate glue 111
   epoxy glue 111
   PVA woodworking glue 111, 124
   stains 110, 124
gluing
   china 111
   glass 115
   upholstery trimmings 119
   woodwork 124
gold jewellery 133
gouges 151
graining 26
grass stains 140
grate polish 134, 141
gravel garden 102

gravity toggles 122
grease stains 137, 142
greenhouse
   using preservative in 36
grooved posts 97
guttering 17, 18, 30

H

hacking knife 151
hacksaw 151
hand-coloured prints 136
hand drill 151
hand-printed wallpaper 27
hairline cracks 80
hardstanding
   Planning Permission 12
hard water 49, 114
hawk 151
heat-exchanging ventilator 43
heave 80, 96
hinge bolt 89
hole saw 151
holes in prints 137
hook scraper 152
hot-air stripper 20, 152
hot-water cylinder 38, 50
hot-water pipes
   draining 50
hot-water supply 53
household repairs 67-8
hydraulic cement 34
hydrochloric acid 110, 114
hydrogen peroxide 110

I

identification
   of property 92-3
industrial alcohol 128
industrial paints 23
infestation 107
ink stains 125, 141
inlay 133
insect holes 137
insecticide 107, 108
insulating paint 32, 33
insulating tape 61
insulation 37-44
interior alterations 11
internal damp proofer 34
ivy 97

J

jack plane 152
jade 133
jewellery
   cleaning 133
jigsaw 152
jointer 152
jointer plane 152
joints, furniture
   repairing 127

joists
   locating 69
joist brace 152
junior hacksaw 152

K

kettle 152
kitchen cupboards
   updating 126
kitchen worktops
   joining 121

L

lacquer 113, 114, 133
lacquering metal 133-34
lagging 38, 43
laminated glass 91
latch locks 88
lath-and-plaster walls
   removing 68
lawns 102
lead
   in paint 23
leather 137-8
leather dressing 138
lighting
   security 92
light switches 64
limescale 49, 110, 114
Lincrusta 26
lining paper 27, 32
linseed oil 128
liquid-rubber compound 30
liquid sander 20
listed buildings 11, 12
Listed-Building Consent 11
loadbearing walls 66
local-authority consent 10-13
local-authority grants 38
locks 88-90
loft
   bats in 107
   conversion 11
   damp in 32
   insulation 38, 43
log path 102
long-term silver polish 132, 134
loose-fill insulation 38, 39
loose pages in book 137
louvre windows 90

M

make-up stains 141
marble
   cleaning 19, 83
   protecting 83
   stripping 22
marbling 26
marginal shelves (pond) 104
marking gauge 153
marking knife 153

marquetry 127
masking tape 25
mastic guns 153
mastic varnish 138
mattock 153
metal
   stripping 21
metal flashing 82
metallic powders 113
metal polish 116, 125, 132-34
metalware 131-34
mice 107
microporous paints 23, 24
mineral-fibre blankets 38, 39
mineral wool 38
miniature circuit breakers
      (MCBs) 57-8, 59
mitre cramp 150
moisture-absorbent crystals 31
moisture-curing polyurethane
      34
monitored burglar alarm 92
mortar 34, 74
mortise chisel 153
mortised posts 97
mortise lock 88
mortise sash lock 88
mortise security bolt 89
mould 17, 27, 32
mouldings 21, 70
mouse traps 107
mud stains 140
musty smell 31, 35

N

nails 118, 119
nail-varnish remover 141
natural stone 102, 106
   pond edging 104
nibblers 153
nicotine stains
   on ceiling 17
night-latch lock 88
noggings 68
non-fused spurs 64
non-reflective glass 138

O

oak 130
official approval 9-14
oil and grease solvent 141
oil heater
   causing condensation 32
oil paintings 138
oil stains 142
oily woods 130
old prints 136, 137
opals 133
open-ended spanner 153
open-grain woods 130
outdoors 95-108
outdoor-lighting kits 65
oval nails 118

overdoors 70
overflows 46, 47
overflow safety valve 49

P

padsaw 154
paint 16-17, 19-26, 32, 114
painting 11
   ceramic tiles 18
   new plaster 17
   radiators 25
   timber/wood 18
paintings 138
paint pads 154
paint rollers 154-5
paint scraper 25, 155, 164
paint shield 25, 255
paint strippers 20, 21, 22
paintwork
   flaking 22
   preparation 20
panel connector 121
panel pins 118
panel saw 155
paper 137
paperhanger's brush 155
paperhanger's scissors 155
paraffin 134
pargeting 81
partitions 68
partition walls 122
party walls 68
passive burglar alarm 91
pastel drawing 136
paste brush 155
paste polishes 130
pasting table 155
paths 99, 102
patina on pewter 134
patios 79, 99, 100
paving slabs 99, 101
payments 14
pearls 133
pencil drawing 136
penetrating damp 30, 34, 35,
      40
perimeter burglar alarm 91
personal-attack button 92
pests 107-8, 124, 125
pets 140
pewter 134
piano
   painting 130
pickaxe 155
picture glass 138
pictures 138
picture varnishes 138
pine 130
pin hammer 156
pipe roller 156
pipes 17
   draining 50
   installing 50
   lagging 38
   plastic 47

repairing holes 46
   thawing frozen 47
Planning Permission 10, 11, 12
planting (pond) 104, 105
planting crates 104
plaster
   application 70
   holes in 18
   over tiles 70
   painting new 17
   storage of 70
   types of 69
   wallpapering new 17
plasterboard
   as insulation 39, 40
   cracks in 16
   fixing 118
   holes in 18, 19
   for dry lining walls 69
   for soundproofing 44
plasterboard nails 118
plasterer's rule 156
plasterer's trowel 156
plastic-laminated cupboards
      126
plastic posts 97
plastic wall plugs 121
plastics
   double glazing 41
plated nails 119
plier wrench 156
plug adaptors 62
plug-cutting tools 120
plugging chisel 156
plugs, electrical 58
plumbing 45-54
   noisy 48
plumb line 156
pointing 33, 72
   weatherstruck 72
pointing trowel 156
polish
   metal 116
   wax 124, 129
polishing wadding 132
polybutylene pipes 47
polycarbonate
   double glazing 41
polyester film
   double glazing 41
polyethylene pond liners 104
polyethylene sheeting
   as insulant 39, 40
polystyrene
   double glazing 41
polyurethane varnish 21, 129,
      130
pond edgings 104
pond heater 106
pond liners 103
pond plants 104, 105
ponds 103-6
post-hole auger 156
pottery 111, 113
poultice strippers 21, 22
power drill 157-8
power-drill bits 158

power plane 158
profile gauge 159
prints 136-7
protective multiple earthing (PME) 65
pump-action screwdriver 159
putty knife 159
push-fit connectors 47
PVA woodworking glue 111, 124, 128, 137
PVC pond liners 104

Q

quotations, builders' 14

R

radial circuit 59, 63
radiator brush 159
radiator enamel 25
radiator roller 159
radiators
 'bleeding' 54
 efficiency 53
 faults 52
 insulating 38
 painting 25
 removing 52
 siting 53
rafters
 insulating 39
raised-head screw 120
ratchet screwdriver 159
rats 107
ready-mixed concrete 78
'ready-mix' mortar 74
recirculation cooker hoods 43
re-enamelling bath 46
regilding china 113
reglazing china 114
regrinding glass 114
reflective glass 138
reinforced-concrete posts 97
reinforcing china repairs 113
reinforcing pins 113
rendering
 cracks in 80
residual-current circuit breaker (RCCB) 64
restraint bar 90
retaining walls (garden) 99
retouching china 114
reviving polish 128
rewiring
 testing 56
rigid pond liners 103
rim-latch lock 88
ring circuit 59, 63
ring main 59
ring spanner 159
ripsaw 159
rising damp 30, 31, 35
rivets 111
rockery 106

rock-fibre blankets 38
rolled steel joists (RSJs) 69
roller tray 160
roof covering 81
roof linings
 patching holes in 81
roomstat 53, 54
rot
 dry 35
 wet 34, 35
round-pin sockets 62
rust 18, 19

S

saddle soap 137
salt 132, 133, 141
sand
 blasting 21-2
 storage 77
sash cramp 160
sash stops 89
sash-weight-cord knot 84
sash-window locks 89
sash windows
 draughtproofing 38
 stuck 85
 ventilation 89
satellite dish
 Planning Permission 12
saw file 28, 160
scorch marks 57
scraper 20
scratches in wood 125, 126
screw cup 120
screwdriver 118, 120
screw gauges 120
screw inserts 119
screws 119-20
sealant
 bath 46
 strip 33, 46
 window frames 33
seam roller 160
second-hand bricks 73
secondary double glazing 41
security 87-94
security chain 90
security lighting 92
security screw 120
self-adhesive veneers 126
septic tank 52
serrated trowel 160
shavehook 20, 160
sheet-metal cutter 160
'shell' chips in china 113
shellac 18, 110, 128, 129, 130
shoe-polish stains 142
shovel 160
shower
 electric-powered 65
 runs cold 48
 water pressure 47
shower surround 28
shuttering 118
shuttering nails 118

silencer tube 47
silicon-carbide paper 113, 129, 130
silicone-rubber sealant 30, 46
silicones 130
silver and silverware 132, 133
silver-plating formula 133
silver-plating polish 132-3
silver polish 130, 132
silversmith's gloves 132
single socket 62
sink
 unblocking 48
sink plunger 48, 160
size 27
skirting boards
 draughty 38
sledgehammer 161
slip-joint pliers 161
sloping site (pond) 105
smell of paint 24
smoke detectors 93
smoke pellets 108
smoke stains
 on ceiling 17
smoothing plane 161
smoothing roller 161
sockets, electrical 59
 installing in kitchen 63
soft mallet 161
soldering irons 125, 161
soot stains 140
soundproofing 43, 44
spade 161
spalling 72-3
spear-point glass drill 161
spillage 140
spirit level 161
split wood 128
spokeshave 162
spring toggles 122
spur cable 63, 64
squeegee 162
stained varnish 129
stains 81, 83, 139-42
 on ceilings 17
 on china 110
 on glass 114
 on walls 17
stain remover 125, 128, 141, 142
stairs
 squeaking 75
staple gun 162
staples 111
steam generator 127
steaming out dents 125
steam wallpaper stripper 162
steps
 constructing 103
stepping stones 102
stilson wrench 162
stippling 26
stone 101, 102
straightedge 162
strap wrench 162
stripped-pine furniture 130

stripping 20, 21
structural alterations 11
structural survey 13
subsidence 80, 96
sugar soap 18, 20, 28
sun-bleached wood 130
sunken nail heads 118
supplementary bonding 64
surface-mounted bolt 89
surface-mounted sockets 63
Surform files 163
survey 13
surveyors 13, 14
syphonic toilet 48

T

table fixing 121
table legs
   levelling 128
tacks 118
talcum powder 113
tank cutter 163
tape measure 163
taps
   draining 50
   installing in garden 49
tar deposits 81
tar stains 142
tarnishing 132
tea stains 142
teak 130
tenon saw 163
textured coatings
   removing 16
textured paint 16
textured-paint remover 16, 21, 22
thermostats 53
thermostatic shower unit 48
thermostatic valve 52
tile cutter 163
tile-cutting jigs 163
tiles
   ceramic 18, 28
   floor 27
   plastering over 70
   waterproof sealing 46
tiling 28
timber preservative 35, 36, 97, 108
tinsnips 163
titanium dioxide 111
toilet
   draining cistern 50
   installing 48
   unblocking 48
toilet cistern
   noisy 47
   overflowing 46
tools 144-65
torn paper 137
trees
   felling 12-13, 96
   planting 96
   storm-blown 102

trickle ventilation 42
triple glazing 44
triple sockets 62
try square 163
tube bender 164
tube cutter 164
turpentine 130
turquoises 133
TV aerial
   Planning Permission 12
twin-threaded screws 120

U

undercoat 22, 23
universal saw 164
upholstery 140, 141
upholstery braid
   fixing 119
upholstery shampoo 141, 142
upholstery tacks 118
urine 140

V

vapour barrier 72
varnish 20
   cold-cure lacquer 114, 130
   copal 21
   picture 138
   polyurethane 21, 129, 130
veneers 21, 124, 126, 127
ventilation 10, 37-44, 89
   blocked-off fireplace 31
   in loft 32-3, 35
   under floors 35
vinyl floorcovering 79
vinyl gloves 164
vinyl wallpaper 26, 27
volts 56

W

wallbrush 164
wallpaper 16, 17, 18, 26-7
wallpaper paste 27, 137
wallpaper scraper 164
wallpaper stripper 16
wall plugs 121
wall-repair tape 16
walls
   cavity 68
   cracks in 80
   curing damp 30, 33, 34
   decorative paint effects 26
   efflorescence 17
   footings 78
   lath-and-plaster 68
   loadbearing 68
   mould on 17
   party 68
   Planning Permission 12
   soundproofing 43
   stripping 21

wall studs
   locating 69
washing machine
   installing 51
wasps 108
waste-disposal unit
   wiring 64
water conditioners 106
water filters 49
water hammer 48
water level 165
water pressure 47, 48
waterproofing liquid 34
waterpump pliers 161
water softener 49
water stains 125
watts 56
wax crayons 124
wax sticks 126
wax polish 124, 129, 130, 133
waxed paper 138
WC
   draining cistern 50
   installing 48
   unblocking 48
WC auger 165
weak joints 127
weather bar 33
weatherboard 33
weather resistance 10, 24, 25
weatherstruck pointing 72
web cramp 165
wet-and-dry paper 24, 115
wet rot 34, 35
wheelbarrow 165
white rings on furniture 125
white-ring remover 125, 128
wickerwork 125
window locks 98, 90
windows 11
   damp near 31, 33
   double glazed 41
   draughtproofing 38
   maintenance 35
   painting 20, 24
   security 89, 90
   ventilation 89
wire brushes 165
wired glass 91
wire strippers 165
wiring insulation 59
Wiring Regulations 56, 64
wood and woodwork 123-30
   nails 118
   painting 20, 22-3
   protecting 124-5
   sealing 18, 19
   stripping 21, 125, 127
   sun-bleached 130
   treating rotted 35
wood bleach 125, 127
woodboring insects 124
wood filler 35, 124
wood hardener 35
wood preservative 35, 36, 97, 108, 124, 125
woodscrews 119

wood stains 24, 124, 125, 129
wood varnish 114
wood veneers 124, 126, 127
woodworking adhesive 124
woodworking (animal) glue 110, 124
woodworm 124, 125
wooden gates 98
wooden float 165
wooden floor
  stripped 130
wrought-iron gates 98

Z

zinc-phosphate primer 19
zone control (heating) 54

COLLINS

OTHER BESTSELLING COLLINS TITLES BY JACKSON & DAY

COLLINS COMPLETE DIY MANUAL

". . . packed with quality advice
backed by 3,000 crisp
illustrations . . ."
Daily Mail

". . . for a thorough understanding
of all areas of house maintenance
and improvement, its detailed
description is unbeatable."
Traditional Homes

COLLINS COMPLETE WOODWORKING MANUAL

". . . bursting with ideas."
Practical Householder

". . . a fine book."
Traditional Woodworking

"I am always suspicious when a
publication is described as
'complete' but in this case it is a fair
description. It is really bang up to
date, and attractively produced. It
will become a friend to lean on
when practical advice is required."
Woodworking International